D0073057

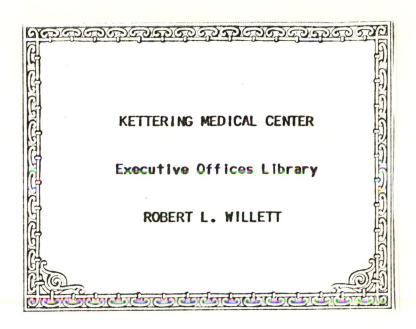

KETTERING MEDICAL CENTER

Executive Offices Library

ROBERT L. WILLETT

Hellenistic Culture and Society

General Editors: Anthony W. Bulloch, Erich S. Gruen, A. A. Long, and Andrew F. Stewart

Hellenistic Philosophy
of Mind

Hellenistic Philosophy
of Mind

Julia Annas

UNIVERSITY OF CALIFORNIA PRESS

BERKELEY   LOS ANGELES   OXFORD

University of California Press
Berkeley and Los Angeles, California

University of California Press, Ltd.
Oxford, England

Library of Congress Cataloging-in-Publication Data
Annas, Julia.
    Hellenistic philosophy of mind / Julia Annas.
        p.   cm. — (Hellenistic culture and society)
    Includes bibliographical references and index.
    ISBN 0-520-07554-4 (hard.) — ISBN 0-520-07659-1 (pbk.)
    1. Philosophy of mind—History.   2. Philosophy, Ancient.
3. Stoics. 4. Epicurus. I. Title. II. Series.
B187.M55A56   1991
128'.2'0938—dc20   91-10694
                                                        CIP

Printed in the United States of America

9 8 7 6 5 4 3 2 1

The paper used in this publication meets the minimum
requirements of American National Standard for Information
Sciences—Permanence of Paper for Printed Library Materials,
ANSI Z39.48-1984. ⊗

Contents

Preface

I began the project of writing this book in 1983, and it has been through a number of different versions. It was originally intended as part of a larger collaborative work on Hellenistic philosophy as a whole; but the larger work lagged while my chapter kept on growing and (I hope) improving, until finally it seemed more appropriate to let it expand to a more appropriate length as an independent publication. Since 1983 I have worked periodically on the book as well as on other research, and I have been able to work in more depth on some topics relevant to the book, such as Epicurean emotions, Stoic epistemology, and Epicurus' difficult views on agency. The book has improved from this, and also from the critical distance one can achieve when returning to familiar material after an interval. My aim has remained the same; I hope to provide a clear introduction to a fascinating subject, one that will help to make the subject accessible to readers with differing backgrounds, philosophical and classical.

There is no area of ancient philosophy which is officially called "philosophy of mind"; but as practicing philosophers all know, the official demarcations of one's subject matter may not answer to the ways the subject develops, and I hope that readers will agree that when we look at the texts, what we find is in fact philosophy of mind. The contributions of the Stoics and Epicureans have long suffered neglect and sometimes contempt, partly from lack of sympathy with their fundamental principles and partly from misconceptions as to what the

Stoics and Epicureans were trying to do. I have tried to be both sympathetic and critical, but my principal aim is to present a clear view of the Stoic and Epicurean theories, their major advantages and some problems they face.

I spent the academic year 1983/84 at the Center for Hellenic Studies in Washington, D. C., as a junior fellow, doing research for this book. I am very grateful to Bernard Knox, then the director, and to everyone at the Center for making that such an enjoyable year. The Center is an ideal place for research, and like many junior fellows, I only wish I could return again. Several people read and commented on the first complete draft of the book. I am especially grateful to Myles Burnyeat, Jonathan Barnes, Tony Long, Martha Nussbaum, Brad Inwood, Christopher Gill, and Malcolm Schofield. Others who have helped me with portions of the book are David Sedley, Simon Laursen, Gisela Striker, and Stephen Everson. I have benefited from discussion of papers relevant to parts of the book at the Duke University Conference on Tradition and Innovation in Epicureanism in the spring of 1989 and the Fifth International Symposium Hellenisticum in Syam, France, in August 1989. In the spring of 1989 I gave a seminar at the University of Arizona based on material from the book. I learned much from the graduates taking the seminar, especially from Stephen Laurence and from Victor Caston (visiting that semester from the University of Texas at Austin). Subsequently my colleague Rob Cummins read the whole manuscript and made valuable comments, many of which forced me to be more critical of crucial arguments or to make the progress of the argument clearer for readers who are not specialists in ancient philosophy. In my final rewriting I have been helped by detailed comments from Tony Long and from a referee for the University of California Press. With all this generous help I am especially sorry for mistakes and confusions that remain, for which I alone am of course responsible.

I have been aided in two bouts of work on the book by having study leave from the Philosophy Department at the University of Arizona, and I am very grateful for this, as well as for the stimulating atmosphere and beautiful surroundings I enjoyed at Tucson. I am also grateful to Jonathan Barnes for joint seminars on Hellenistic philosophy which we held in Oxford and for continuing to inspire and stimulate my interest in Hellenistic philosophy by his own work. I am very grateful to Michele Svatos for preparing the Index Locorum and for enormous assistance with the General Index.

The book is dedicated to my husband, David, who has been supportive and helpful intellectually and in every other way through the various stages of the book's progress (including periods when there was no progress), and to our daughter, Laura, who has been a source of joy for all eight years of her life, and seven of the book's.

Introduction

Modern philosophy of mind, like most areas of philosophy, harks back from time to time to predecessors in the ancient world. Usually the predecessor singled out is Aristotle, the great founder of the subject. Aristotle's *De anima* and *Parva naturalia* are the first works to study psychological phenomena seriously in a philosophical way. Rooting "study of the soul" firmly in biology, Aristotle's works are the ancestors not only of philosophy of mind, as that is studied in philosophy departments, but also of systematic psychology, the more purely scientific study of psychological and mental phenomena. And Aristotle's approach is still of interest to modern philosophers, as is witnessed by the huge amount of research devoted in the last two decades to understanding Aristotle's theory of the soul and classifying it as physicalist, dualist, or functionalist.[1]

Aristotle's successors, the philosophers of the Hellenistic or post-Aristotelian period, have been comparatively neglected. This is a pity, because the theories are sophisticated and interesting. It is also somewhat surprising, since even from the perspective of modern interest the Hellenistic theories have a great deal more in common with modern concerns than Aristotle's does. Furthermore, Hellenistic accounts of partic-

1. For a selection of recent work and reference to the vast secondary literature, see Nussbaum and Rorty (1991).

ular phenomena, such as perceiving, are often of great interest in their own right. Thus, both on grounds of their intrinsic interest and from the viewpoint of modern concerns, it seems reasonable to expand our picture of ancient philosophy of mind to include Aristotle's great successors.

Hellenistic philosophy of mind has been generally neglected in the history of recent scholarship because Hellenistic philosophy generally has been undervalued, an imbalance that is now being corrected. In the recent past, however, this period of philosophy of mind was thought especially worthy of neglect. It was dismissed as crude, as a mere throwback to earlier ideas,[2] and even as a type of theory which was patently inadequate, but whose faults were overlooked in the haste to get to what was really supposed to matter, namely, the ethical conclusions.[3]

Why was Hellenistic philosophy of mind held to be crude? The main reason is that all the major theories are physicalist; they hold that the mind is (with refinements we shall examine) something physical. And until surprisingly recently the philosophical background of scholars interpreting Hellenistic philosophy was one in which the dominant theory was dualism. Hence we frequently find scholars dismissing Hellenistic theories as inadequate in principle on the grounds that they merely study the material conditions for mental activity to be possible,

---

2. Hellenistic theories often criticize, and make use of, pre-Socratic ideas; but so does Aristotle, who is not usually dismissed as a mere throwback. The relative importance attached by Stoics and Epicureans to their intellectual forebears is still uncertain and controversial.

3. Cf. Jaeger (1913, 56): "In der krasser Materialität der Seele erblicken sie [die Stoiker] wie die Atomisten den festen Anker, mit dem das politisch wurzellose Individuum, der *apolis* des Hellenismus sein vereinzeltes Dasein im Gesetzesfrieden des ehrwürdigsten aller Staat gründete, dem *kosmos* der sich wandelnden und umformenden Urstoffe." This general claim, that Hellenistic philosophy is a rush to ethical certainty motivated by the unbearable *anomie* of the postclassical period, is now thoroughly discredited. Further, the more important ethics is to a philosopher, the more important it is to have a *firm* basis for it, rather than a faulty one.

and omit mental activity itself.[4] More recently interpreters have tended to have an intellectual background in which it is physicalism that is dominant and dualism that is not taken seriously. And this makes it easier for us to understand the Hellenistic theories, for in that period also physicalism was seen as the norm.

The terms "physicalism" and "materialism" have been used for many different kinds of theory. The theories that we shall examine in detail, those of the Stoics and Epicureans, are theories of a kind which I shall call physicalist. "Physicalism" here covers theories which claim that everything that exists is physical. "Physical" here in turn means "falls under the laws of physics." Something is physical if and only if it can be described and explained using only the concepts and methods of physics. So much is true of ancient and modern theories. Ancient versions of physicalism will differ from modern ones to the extent that ancient physics differs from modern—that is, considerably. In its ancient form, physicalism is the theory that everything that exists, including the soul, falls under *phusikē*, enquiry into the constituents and structure of the universe. On this definition, Aristotle is a physicalist, although he defines the soul as the form of the body, because Aristotelian physics everywhere studies form as well as matter.[5] The ancient notion of *phusikē* was broader than our notion of physics, and there was nothing in the ancient world corresponding to the modern thesis that physics is paradigmatic for the other sciences, or that they can be reduced to it in some unified way. Correspondingly, ancient versions of physicalism are less strong and methodologically less restricted than modern ones.

Ancient physicalism is a weak notion, but not a contentless one. Some philosophers did deny it. To deny physicalism, in

4. As late as Sandbach (1975, 84) we find the following: "To explain in material terms the *psychē* and its functions was an impossible undertaking, but one which had to be attempted."

5. Cf. *DA* 403a24–b16. (The difficult doctrine of separable *nous* may provide a limited exception to this.) Thus the ancients, with their very broad account of *phusikē*, tended to find the difference between Aristotle's and later theories less striking than we do.

the ancient world, is to deny that the soul falls under scientific study, to claim that the soul is not part of the natural world and operates in ways that cannot be understood by studying that world. This position is often called dualism,[6] since it implies that there are two radically different kinds of thing in the universe, the physical things and the psychological or mental things, which are different in kind and do not fall under the same kind of enquiry.

In antiquity there are no defenders of dualism except Plato and the Platonic schools, who are very much the exception. Plato himself in several dialogues and particularly the *Phaedo* claims that souls are "separate" from bodies and in every way a completely different kind of entity. He not only accepts, but emphasizes, the fact that on his view the relationship of soul and body is deeply problematic. Plato believes that it is deeply mysterious and that we do not understand it. Platonic dualism was marginal and uninfluential during the Hellenistic period. It was revived in the Middle Platonist schools but even then was far from dominant.[7] Later it was to have a spectacular revival in the time of the Neoplatonists, and through the Platonic schools it was to have a startling effect on Christianity, turning it from a metaphysically neutral religion into a religion apparently committed to a dualistic view of the soul, a view which has had lasting influence for many centuries.[8] But in the Hellenistic period dualism was not widely viewed as a philosophically serious position. Physicalism was taken for granted as the norm, and not taken to require special argument.

Ancient physicalism, it is clear, is extremely weak. It is quite distinct from reductivism, the thesis that items of one kind (in

6. But I have avoided using "monism" for the theory opposed to dualism, mainly because it has been used in discussions of the Stoics for a quite distinct thesis.

7. For Middle Platonists on the soul, and their effect on the Neoplatonists, see Deuse (1983).

8. It was not until the twentieth century that theologians recovered the early, metaphysically neutral position.

this case, souls) can be "reduced" to items of another kind (in this case, bodies). Modern forms of reductivism often rely on bridging laws to "reduce" one science to another, and unsurprisingly this is absent in the ancient world, where science did not make the modern kind of appeal to laws. Still, we can see a recognizable impulse toward reductivism in some ancient philosophers, notably some of the pre-Socratics. Democritus distinguishes between the qualities that we can experience, and what there is "in truth," namely, atoms and void. Anaxagoras claims that everyday talk of change is misleading and does not answer to anything; what really goes on, at a level far below perception, is quite different. One of the authors in the Hippocratic medical corpus gives a reductive account of various psychological phenomena in terms of the influences of climate.[9] These authors are not merely physicalists; they add the claim that our prephilosophical talk of souls, for instance, does not answer to anything real; souls are just atoms and void, for example. Because these authors do not specify any particular mechanism for reduction, their position remains somewhat indeterminate; it is not clear, for example, whether what is in mind is reductivism proper (there are Xs, but they can be reduced to Ys) or eliminativism (there are really no Xs, only Ys).

The impulse toward reductivism nascent in some pre-Socratics, and so much stronger and more sophisticated in modern theories, is virtually absent from Hellenistic philosophy of mind; it appears only marginally in some members of Aristotle's school. Indeed, we actually find Epicurus arguing *against* Democritean reductivism.[10] Hellenistic physicalism is nonreductive; it is a generally accepted position that we humans are part of the natural world, and investigated by the normal processes of enquiry into that world. Facts about humans, whether their bodies or their souls, come under *phu-*

9. Democritus frag. B125 Diels-Kranz (hereafter DK) (cf. frag. A49); Anaxagoras frag. B17 DK; the author of *Airs, Waters, Places*.
10. See part 3, chapter 6, section a.

sikē, natural science. But natural science is not assumed to lead us to deny or to reinterpret familiar facts about ourselves, or to try to reduce them to other kinds of fact.

If physicalism is as weak a position as this, is there anything distinctive about the Hellenistic theories which justifies us if we see them as nearer to modern physicalism than Aristotle is? So far we have merely marked off Platonic dualists from everybody else and noticed a few pre-Socratic reductivists. Are there any general differences of kind between Aristotle and his successors in their studies of the soul? Intuitively it has always been felt that, whether it has been seen as a good or a bad thing, Aristotle's successors are physicalists in some stronger sense than Aristotle is. But if they are not reductivists, and physicalism is a general, shared assumption, wherein does the difference lie?

While it would be a mistake to exaggerate the differences, there are some general points that can be laid out in an introductory way. Firstly, there is a sense in which the Hellenistic theories are more science-driven than Aristotle's is. This should not be misconstrued as claiming that Aristotle's theory is independent of his science. On the contrary, it is firmly located in his biological works. It is, however, part of Aristotle's own scientific work and outlook; it fits with his biology and metaphysics because all of them involve applications of his own metaphysical conceptions, such as form and actuality, matter and passivity, and so on. The *De anima* fits into Aristotle's overall philosophical project; it is not cut to fit the science in particular. By contrast, there is in the Hellenistic period, in which there have been general scientific and medical advances, a generally available scientific paradigm for the study of human psychology. And although Stoic and Epicurean accounts of the soul are clearly intended to fit well with other parts of Stoic and Epicurean philosophy, they are also just as clearly intended to fit the general scientific paradigm. This point is much more important for the Stoics than it is for Epicurus, who is generally inclined to give more weight to common sense than to science; but he too feels that he must take account to some extent of the commonly accepted scientific assumptions about humans. The Hellenistic period was a golden age for medical, scientific, and technological discoveries, and it was a more self-consciously "scientific" era than the preceding one; as in all such eras, philosophy tended to be more concessive toward science than it had been. This is why this book begins with a study of the scientific and medical background before moving on to the major theories themselves.

Secondly, Aristotle's physicalism includes the metaphysical notion of form, which is different in kind from the matter whose form it is. Aristotle takes himself to have advanced on the crude thinking of the pre-Socratics, who tried to explain the functioning of living beings in terms merely of the physical constituents. By contrast, Aristotle thinks that he needs to appeal to form adequately to explain the idea of function, which is crucial for living beings. Thus he criticizes Democritus for saying that vision is the mirroring of the thing seen by part of the eye; if that is all it is, he says, why do mirrors and other reflective surfaces not see?[11] To explain seeing we need to appeal not only to what the eye is made of but to the way the eye functions; and nothing short of Aristotelian form, different in kind from matter, will do this. The Hellenistic theories all reject this kind of move; they explain the functioning of the eyes, ears, and so on in terms of the physical structure of the relevant parts of the body and in terms of physical processes that are common to the workings of differently functioning parts.

It is this more than anything else which has led to their being considered naive throwbacks who had learned nothing from Aristotle's criticism of Democritus. But this is premature; for the Hellenistic theories, wrong and naive though they appear to us, have made great advances over the pre-Aristotelian theories. The Hellenistic thinkers offer explanations not in

11. *Sens.* 438a5–13. Cf. *GA* 5. 8 for similar criticism of Democritean explanations.

terms of mirroring but in terms of highly theoretical entities, defined by sophisticated theories which embody recent scientific advances. They are thus justified in thinking that their theories and explanations appeal to far greater complexity of structure than those of the pre-Socratics did. And it is because of this that the Hellenistic thinkers think that they do not need to appeal to metaphysical notions like that of Aristotelian form. Thus their theories are metaphysically far more economical than the Aristotelian kind; they appeal to an underlying complexity of structure to explain the functioning of living things, not because they are unaware of the kind of appeal to form that Aristotle makes, but because they think that scientific explanation will in fact do the job. It is not clear, of course, that they are right here. And the contemporary force and power of their theories is very easy for us to miss, because we cannot take their theoretical terms (pneumatic tension, atoms and void) seriously from the scientific point of view. Still, the idea that the complexity of the underlying structure alone will explain the functional organization of living things, without appeal to principles like form, is one that is taken very seriously in modern philosophy of mind; even if it is wrong, it is certainly not naive. Scholars are often pained and baffled by the lack of Hellenistic reponse to what we see as Aristotle's powerful arguments about form and function. Often the problem is solved by the assumption that Aristotle's school treatises were not generally available until Andronicus' edition in the first century B.C. But it is just as likely that these ideas drew no reaction because they were seen as outdated, and thus needing no response.[12]

Finally, and most strikingly, Aristotle's account of the *psuchē* or soul is clearly marked by his focus on finding what distin-

12. Bignone (1936) argues that Epicurean philosophy was formed without knowledge of Aristotle's school treatises; Sandbach (1985) argues a similar case for the Stoics. It is hasty, however, to infer lack of knowledge from lack of response. It would be premature, for example, to argue that modern philosophers who do not feel the need to argue against Descartes have no knowledge of his works.

guishes *empsucha*, living things. For Aristotle the soul is the principle of life, and this drives many of his concerns; he is interested not just in the general principles of functional organization for living things, but in aspects of living such as breathing and sleeping. His long account of perception focuses on the causal mechanisms of perceiving rather than on its phenomenology or content. The Hellenistic theories, on the other hand, while thinking of the soul as the principle of life, do not primarily focus on this; they are more interested in what we call the mind or mental phenomena. Their accounts of perceiving, thinking, and so on are weak where Aristotle's are strong, namely, in giving accounts of the different mechanisms of the senses and other organs and in examining their workings in biological detail. They are, however, strong where Aristotle is weak, namely, in giving an account of the content of mental activity and the ways in which this is related to our abilities to think, to use concepts, and to engage in language use. Although the Hellenistic theories' interest in the mental is in some ways different from the kind of interest that we tend to find standard, since they are uninterested in questions of privileged access or the kind of certainty which mental events can provide, we shall see that the major theories focus quite strongly on the mind, as well as on the principle of life. Sometimes scholars are reluctant to call Aristotle's theory a theory of the mind, since for him the *psuchē* or soul is so clearly the principle of life and not to be identified with what we think of as the mind. While the point is terminological, it is perhaps worth saying that if we want to restrict the term "philosophy of mind" to theories which focus strongly on what we think of as the mind and the mental, then the Hellenistic theories are the first systematic philosophies of mind.[13]

13. I say "systematic" since it would be foolish to deny that there is any concern with the mental prior to the Stoics and Epicureans. The pre-Socratic fragments are hard to evaluate, but Plato's concern with the soul is sometimes a concern with the mind (though he does not sharply distinguish this from concern with the principle of life nor from concern for the whole personality).

In many ways these points bring the Hellenistic theories closer to modern concerns than Aristotle's kind of theory is. But I am not of course claiming that this is the only reason for taking them seriously. I hope that this book will convince the reader that these theories are philosophically interesting in their own right, and that they deserve more serious study than they have received until recently. I hope that this book will help us to achieve pictures, rather than caricatures, of theories which are well worth the effort of depicting.

The Hellenistic age conventionally extends from the death of Alexander the Great in 323 B.C. to the battle of Actium in 30 B.C. Philosophically, this is an age in which the established schools, those of Plato and Aristotle, continue, but in changed or reduced form, and major new philosophical movements arise. Further, from the philosophical point of view, 30 B.C. is not the end of anything. By the first century B.C. the major new schools had been established, and apart from the rise of Middle Platonism and the renewal of sceptical schools the philosophical scene remained essentially unchanged until the dramatic rise of Neoplatonism. I shall give a brief and selective account of the philosophical background, focused on understanding our main concern, the philosophy of mind of the Stoics and Epicureans.

a) The School of Plato

Plato died in 347 B.C. His own works continued to be read in the Hellenistic period, and his arguments about the "separate" nature of the soul in the *Phaedo* were studied and criticized.[14] But his successors in the Academy, during the period generally called the Old Academy, seem to have been interested in the soul only in the context of a systematic and mathematized metaphysics. Thus Speusippus called the soul "the form of the all-extended," and Xenocrates called it a "self-moving number."[15] Doubtless we would have a better idea of what these

14. See chapter 1, section c on Strato.
15. Speusippus frags. 96–100 Isnardi Parente; frags. 54–55 Tarán.

formulae meant if we had fuller and more sympathetic accounts of their context. However, it is worth noting that Aristotle, who had access to such a context, found the "self-moving number" formula absurd; he pours scorn on it in the *De anima*, whether fairly or not we cannot tell.[16] Xenocrates' successors, Polemon and Crates, seem to have concentrated on ethics, and the Academy was then turned by its next head, Arcesilaus, to a repudiation of dogma and a sceptical stance toward the doctrines of all schools, especially the Stoics. The sceptical or New Academy continued until the first century B.C.; its weakening form of scepticism provoked a breakaway movement which adopted a more extreme scepticism and revived the legend of Pyrrho the sceptic, and after the sack of Athens in 87 B.C. the Academy as an institution died out.[17] In the next century Plutarch and others produced what is called Middle Platonism, a systematic set of doctrines based on Plato's dialogues. None of these movements contributed anything positive to philosophy of mind in this period.

b) The School of Aristotle

Aristotle's own philosophy of mind did not found a strong tradition in his own school. The story will be told more fully (in chapter 1, section c), since it is part of the story of the scientific background to the Hellenistic theories. Aristotle's successors Theophrastus and Strato continued scientific research; but the school thereafter concentrated more on ethics and, perhaps because of the destruction of its research facil-

---

See Tarán ad loc.: "The probability is that Speusippus himself put forward the definition of soul as *idea tou pantei diastatou* as an interpretation of Plato's meaning in the *Timaeus*." The Old Academy seems to have taught a systematic metaphysics and argued that it lay behind Plato's dialogues. See Xenocrates frags. 165–212 Isnardi Parente.

16. *DA* 408b32–409a30. As often, Aristotle regards Xenocrates' theory as the worst and most absurd of those on offer.

17. See Glucker (1978) for the history of the late Academy.

ities in wars, was in a fairly run-down condition during the Hellenistic period. The heads of the school after Strato were nobodies, and the Lyceum finally petered out as an institution after the sack of Athens, like the Academy.[18] The first century B.C., however, saw the first scholarly edition of Aristotle's school treatises, and the beginning of what has continued ever since, scholarly text-based exegesis of Aristotle. Alexander of Aphrodisias, a commentator of the second century A.D., is the most notable exponent of this and is often invaluable as a source for the Hellenistic theories which he combats from an Aristotelian point of view.

Thus in the period after Aristotle the philosophies of Plato and of Aristotle were not nearly as dominant as we might infer from our own view of their relative importance. Indeed, many of the new schools drew their inspiration from Socrates rather than from Plato. Among these were the Cynics, who rejected conventions, and the Cyrenaics, who held that our final end is pleasure. The only schools which contributed to philosophy of mind, and which we shall look at in depth, were the Stoics and Epicureans.

c) The Stoics

Stoicism was founded by Zeno of Citium (b. 334), who came to Athens and taught in the Stoa Poikilē or Painted Porch. Zeno seems to have laid the foundations of most of Stoic theory, though it is often hard to distinguish his contributions from later ones. While Zeno was initially influenced by the unconventional Cynics, he founded a definitively philosophical school, in which pupils were trained to argue, and he developed a systematic theory with distinctively Stoic logic, physics, and ethics. His pupils Ariston, Herillus, and Cleanthes developed different emphases in Stoicism. Cleanthes was the official head of the school, and his successor Chrysippus (c. 280–207 B.C.) was in effect the second founder of the Stoa. Chrysippus

18. See Lynch (1972).

had a systematic and powerful mind and wrote voluminous-
ly; thereafter "official" Stoic views were given their form by
him. His successors, notably Diogenes of Babylon and Antipater of Tarsus, made contributions of their own but within
the lines of orthodoxy. However, two later figures, Panaetius
(c. 185–109 B.C.) and Posidonius (c. 135–50 B.C.), were seen
as differing significantly in their approach and are often
called Middle Stoics. For our purposes this matters only with
regard to Posidonius' theory of the emotions, which is indeed distinct from the standard Stoic view, and in interesting
ways.

d) The Epicureans

Epicurus (341–270 B.C.) founded a new school of philosophy
in his famous Garden at Athens and was a prolific writer on
many aspects of his systematic philosophy. We have some of
his more popular works, which have come down in the man-
uscripts of the later biographer Diogenes Laertius, and we also
possess large numbers of fragments of school treatises and
lectures, from the Epicurean library of papyrus rolls found at
Herculaneum. Epicurus' school was famous, or notorious, in
antiquity for its fidelity to the thought of its founder, and
throughout the Hellenistic period we find no outstandingly
original Epicurean thinkers. We do have, however, two sources from the first century B.C. who help greatly to fill out our
knowledge of Epicurean philosophy of mind: the Roman poet
Lucretius, who wrote a six-book poem on topics in Epicureanism, and the fragmentary papyrus rolls of Philodemus, an
Epicurean philosopher, from the Herculaneum library.

As already made clear, the Hellenistic age was one which
was aware of great scientific advances. Science became di-
vorced from philosophy and developed on its own, creating a
situation where philosophers had to take account of an independent scientific tradition. I shall not here make a general

survey of Hellenistic science and medicine,[19] but in the next chapter I will sketch the scientific and medical background necessary for us to make proper sense of the Stoic and Epicurean theories. If we simply begin, for example, with the Stoic claim that the soul is *pneuma* and that *pneuma* is "breath," we may not only be baffled but conclude, incorrectly, that the theory is some kind of philosophers' fantasy. It would in fact be intelligible to its first audience as a theory with a respectable scientific background; so it is to this that we must first turn.

19. For this see Lloyd (1973), and for useful collections of papers see Giannantoni and Vegetti (1984) and Barnes, Brunschwig, Burnyeat, and Schofield (1982).

Part One

——

The Background

1

The Medical and
Scientific Background

a) **Aristotle**

Among the greatest of Aristotle's achievements is the development of an extensive and impressive biology. But as well as producing a distinctive biological corpus of his own, Aristotle began the development of what was to be the main concept of the very different biology and medical theory of the Hellenistic age. What is most striking about Hellenistic medical theory, by contrast with Aristotle's work, is the prominence it gives to the notion of *pneuma*, which originally means "breath." But the start of the spectacular rise of *pneuma* to theoretical heights in fact can be found in Aristotle himself.

Why would breath be important to a biologist, apart of course from the investigation of the process of breathing itself? The answer seems more obvious if we recall that for Aristotle the soul or *psuchē* is primarily the principle of life and thus is what makes the difference between a living and a nonliving thing. What is it that makes a living body be *alive?* Trivially, the presence of soul. It is soul which makes the body function as a living body. However, can we say anything more precise than this—can we locate the workings of the soul in any one particular process more than any other? Conspicuously, a corpse ceases to breathe and becomes cold; and from an early date body heat or breath or both were regarded as candidates for the particular vehicle of the soul's functioning. It is not surprising, therefore, that Aristotle inclines to the view that either heat or breath is the immediate bodily vehicle of the soul. The idea is perhaps unsophisticated, but obvious enough.

For Aristotle there is not much to choose between heat and *pneuma* as the soul's immediate vehicle, and indeed he makes no systematic attempt to give *pneuma* a specific role in psychology. Thus there is no developed *"pneuma* theory" in the biological works, and it is easily missed.[1] In the main it is heat which Aristotle regards as most directly necessary for the presence of soul.[2] But in a few passages, scattered in the corpus, Aristotle says unmistakably that it is *pneuma*, not heat, which is required for the soul's functions of movement, reproduction, and sensation. Giving this role to *pneuma* is not in opposition to giving it to heat; for we find that there can be "soul heat" in the *pneuma.*[3] However, heat does not figure in the way *pneuma* produces animal motion or sensation,[4] and the standard function of breathing in Aristotle's psychology is a cooling one. So we can infer that Aristotle has not thought through the roles of *pneuma* and of heat in a large overall theory.[5]

1. *Pneuma* is ordinary Greek for "wind" as well as for "breath," and there had been philosophical theories, like those of Diogenes of Apollonia, and medical theories, like those of Philistion and the Sicilian medical school, in which air, wind, and breath figured prominently, as well as some puzzling later treatises in the Hippocratic corpus which made use of *pneuma* (on these see Harris 1973, chap. 2).
2. Cf. *DA* 416a9–18; *Juv.* 470a19–20, 474b10–12. At *PA* 652b7–17 Aristotle says, "Some people propose that a living thing's soul is fire or some such power, but this is a crude proposal. Doubtless it is better to say that it comes about in such a body. The cause of this is that the hot is the most serviceable body for the soul's functions." Because of this role of heat he talks of "vital heat" (*thermotēs zōtikē*) at *GA* 739b20–26 and "soul heat" (*thermotēs psuchikē*) at 739a9–12.
3. *GA* 762a21 (cf. 736b29–737a1).
4. Animal motion: *MA* 10; sensation: *GA* 744a3, cf. 736b29–737a1.
5. *Somn.* 456a6–11.

For Aristotle, *pneuma* is not a special substance; it is just warm air.[6] The *pneuma* important in living things differs from ordinary warm air in being "connate," *sumphuton,* a functioning part of animal metabolism, and as such acquires no new or surprising properties.[7] Nonetheless, "connate *pneuma*" acquires a more and more extended role. In *De motu animalium* 10 it brings about movement without itself being altered; there are no constraints on its pushing and pulling, since it is heavy relative to what is naturally light, and vice versa; it gives animals their strength. It seems, in the odd and possibly corrupt passages at *De generatione animalium* 744a3 and 781a21, to play a role in all sensation. It also has a crucial role in reproduction: it differentiates the parts in the embryo at 741b37–39 and seems to be the vehicle for transmitting the soul in the strange passage at 736b30–737a1, where the *pneuma* is said to contain some substance important for all soul functioning and akin to the "fifth element" making up the stars.

Some have been tempted to systematize Aristotle's scattered remarks into a reconstruction making *pneuma* central to his psychology; but this is a mistake, given the scattered and unsystematic nature of the evidence.[8] It would also be wrong to think, as some have, that *pneuma* is meant to operate in a way which imports something "divine" into an otherwise biological account. These passages together suggest that *pneuma* is more than just an ordinary item in the Aristotelian world. But we should be chary of making Aristotelian biology flagrantly break the laws of Aristotelian physics.[9] It is more plausible to

6. *GA* 736a1–2.

7. *Somn.* 456a11–13; *Juv.* 475a8–14; *PA* 659b13–18, 669a1–2.

8. This is done by Peck (1942, 1953). Aristotle does make the astounding claim at *GA* 789b8–12 that nature uses *pneuma* like a tool in most things; but this is not borne out by his writings.

9. Solmsen (1968c) regards *GA* 736b30 as revealing Aristotle's finally "satisfactory" answer to the question of "how the soul functions come to be present in the foetus," because at last we see that "something divine . . . is found operating in the biological phenomena." It is strange that an unmotivated dualist breach in a physicalist system should seem the only satisfactory part of it.

hold that *pneuma* is just an ordinary physical substance—warm air—and that Aristotle's more startling claims about it come from the thought that it will acquire new and perhaps surprising properties when functioning in a unified and self-maintaining living being.[10] Aristotle has no overall coherent view of the biological role of *pneuma;* perhaps he would have developed one if he had lived longer. However, we find in Aristotle an example of the way *pneuma* can leave its intuitive base and become a theoretical entity, indeed one which can expand to fill the needs of theory.

The passages about *pneuma* in Aristotle are not integrated into his own psychology. It was left to the Stoics to develop the idea that all the functions of a living thing can be explained by the workings of a single substance operating in differentiated ways, and to identify this with *pneuma.* And it was left to the Hellenistic doctors to connect *pneuma* with a centralized system like the heart or the nerves. But Aristotle had taken the first step in making *pneuma* a theoretical entity that could be thought to do work in biology.

b) Hellenistic Medical Theory

In the Hellenistic period there were significant advances in medical discoveries, and medical theories enjoyed great prestige.[11] Much research was done in the new scientific center of Alexandria, rather than in established philosophical centers like Athens. As a result of these discoveries we find emerging a new scientific paradigm of human functioning, one which

10. With Balme (1972, 160–64) and Nussbaum (1978, essay 3 and notes to *MA* 10).
11. See Harris (1973) (who quotes and translates otherwise inaccessible texts); Phillips (1973); Lloyd (1973); Solmsen (1986c); von Staden (1989). The following summary is drastically selective, picking out only what is relevant to understanding Stoic and Epicurean theories; and I am keenly aware of the amateur and limited nature of my own understanding of the subject. Suitable caution on the use of medical texts which even now are insufficiently researched is urged by Hahm (1977, 180 n. 60).

affected the philosophers' understanding of what they needed to give an account of. The Stoics were more influenced by current medical research than the Epicureans, but even the latter show unmistakable signs of awareness of contemporary medicine. Epicurus' general idea of the human soul and how it functions, and of the appropriate methods of explaining it, is far closer to the Stoics' than to Aristotle's.[12]

Praxagoras of Cos (fl. c. 300 B.C.)[13] improved knowledge of the vascular system; he had a theory of the pulse and distinguished arteries from veins. However, he made the influential mistake of concluding that only the veins contain blood. The arteries (which in a corpse would be found empty)[14] he took to be a system of hollow channels originating in the heart and ramifying through the body, ending in tiny channels called *neura* (a word at this time covering both tendons and nerves). In a living animal the arterial system, like the venal system, would be pumping something out; unequipped with theory or observation making it plausible that this could be blood, Praxagoras took it to be *pneuma*. We have seen how by this time *pneuma* could be thought of as having an expanded theoretical role. This assumption made possible further explanations: the pulsing of the arteries, for example, was taken to be due to bubbles arising in the veins and entering the arteries through the heart.

12. I shall not discuss in detail the second-century doctor Asclepiades of Bithynia, who had a curious theory that matter was particulate and that in particular all disease was due to blockage of the flow of corpuscles in the body's interstices or "pores." This theory has often, from Galen onward, been associated with Epicurean atomism. The recent study by Vallance (1990) argues that Asclepiades' *anarmoi onkoi* are weak, breakable corpuscles and that the theory relies on their shattering and reforming, making them completely unlike Epicurean atoms. Vallance finds Asclepiades' intellectual filiations within the medical, rather than the philosophical, tradition.

13. See Steckerl (1958); Solmsen (1968c). Steckerl argues against Jaeger that Praxagoras was not a follower of Diocles of Carystus.

14. Greek beliefs forbade dissection of human bodies, a prohibition later violated by Herophilus and Erasistratus. Greek doctors' knowledge of human anatomy would primarily be from wounds.

Praxagoras' picture, however crude and confused, was significant in at least two ways. Firstly, it is like what we find in Aristotle in that *pneuma* in a living thing is ascribed many significant properties, but in a way which is entirely consistent with physicalism. *Pneuma* is not a bizarre substance which just happens to exist in nature; it is just a familiar substance, but one which is taken to explain various functionings in a living being and which is therefore taken to have properties which make it adequate for the job.[15]

Secondly, what we might call Praxagoras' arterial-neural system (arteries not being clearly distinguished from nerves) originates in the heart; we have a picture, however erroneous, of a system which does some of the jobs of what we call the nervous system, and with a central organ directing it. The heart pumps out blood through the veins to nourish the body, and *pneuma* through the arteries to make it sensitive and reactive. We have what is lacking in Aristotle—a centralized mechanism which explains why the body is a sensitive and reactive whole. And *pneuma* plays an important role in this.[16]

Herophilus of Chalcedon (fl. c. 270 B.C.) and Erasistratus of Ceos (fl. c. 260 B.C.) made spectacular discoveries about the vascular and nervous systems.[17] Working in the new research institute at Alexandria under the protection of the Ptolemies, they were able to ignore the hitherto impregnable Greek taboo

15. Praxagoras seems to have identified the soul with the *pneuma* in the heart, but we lack any background to this which would clarify his motivation, and in particular which would show if this were reductivist in intent.

16. Aristotle does to some extent centralize the workings of the senses and sense-related faculties such as memory and dreaming in the heart, but this is built up only gradually in the *Parva naturalia* and is neither discussed in the more theoretical *De anima* nor brought into any relation to the *pneuma* theory. (See, however, Nussbaum 1978, essay 3.)

17. See Harris (1973, chap. 4); Solmsen (1968c); von Staden (1989). Verbeke (1945) claims that Erasistratus held different theories at different times, maintaining late in life that nerves were solid rather than hollow (see Galen *PHP* 602 Kühn [hereafter K], 440 de Lacy); but this is uncertain.

against dissecting human corpses. Having steeled themselves to violate tradition in cutting open the dead, they went on to cut open the living. Celsus tells us that "Herophilus and Erasistratus did what was by far the best thing in cutting open alive criminals they received from the kings out of prisons" to observe their internal workings.[18] (Histories of medicine are generally silent about the moral crime performed to make a scientific discovery.) At dreadful price, the nervous system was discovered; Erasistratus corrected Praxagoras' confused picture by showing that the nervous system is quite distinct from both venal and arterial systems and is centered in the brain. But Erasistratus took over from Praxagoras his most influential mistake, namely, the view that the heart distributes blood through the veins to nourish the body, and *pneuma* through the arteries to energize and sensitize it.[19]

One can see that the earlier model seemed compelling, even in the face of new discoveries, and that theoretical economy would suggest that the newly discovered brain-centered system should be explained as far as possible on the model of the supposedly understood vascular system. On the other hand, there are obvious empirical problems; blood flows immediately from a cut artery, for example, and the *ad hoc* explanations given for this are extremely uncompelling.[20] Still, the theory had continuing power, which could not be countered

18. *Med.* 23. Celsus adds the comment that it is "not cruel" to torture a guilty few for the benefit of greater numbers of future beneficiaries. This is, as far as I know, the only example of pure consequentialist reasoning in the ancient world. It is common enough, in ancient as in modern ethics, to think that consequences matter, but it is otherwise unknown in ancient ethics to argue that consequences *determine* what is right and wrong. It is especially striking in this case because of the horrendous nature of what the doctors did.

19. On Herophilus' view see Harris (1973, 180ff.) and the magisterial study by von Staden (1989). Herophilus held that the arteries contain both blood and *pneuma*, but we do not know how he thought them to be related.

20. Both the Anonymous Londiniensis and Galen (e.g., *An in arteriis*) are particularly scathing about Erasistratus' explanation of this (the cut allows *pneuma* to escape, and blood is sucked into the void from the veins). See also Viano (1984).

until knowledge of the whole area was fundamentally improved, for example, by discovery of the circulation of the blood.[21] The theory that the arteries contain *pneuma* is a classic example of a theory which survived continual exposure to what should have been a deadly counterexample, until a better alternative theory was available.

The idea that the nervous system works by something like hot air sounds so immediately ludicrous to us that it is worth making the point that what counts as an illuminating model for physical or psychological processes, rather than as a misleading or comic one, may well depend on factors external to the development of science. Thus in the Victorian period, when recent advances in technology were illustrated for most people by the steam engine, steam propulsion sounded perfectly natural as a model for psychological activity. This sounds peculiar to us, but that is because to us steam propulsion is no longer an advanced model of technology. Our current models for the mind are based on computers, and these will doubtless sound as bizarre to our successors as the model of steam propulsion does to us. In the Hellenistic period the appeal of *pneuma* to explain human functionings derived not from technological developments as such, but from the prestige of advancements in empirical medicine, such as those deriving from the discovery of the nervous system.

Theoretical economy led to the connection of the nervous system with *pneuma*; but it led at once to what seemed like undesirable duplication: why do we need *two* systems to distribute *pneuma*? Erasistratus found the obvious solution: heart and brain distribute different kinds of *pneuma*. This makes the best overall sense of the new discoveries without radical theoretical departures. Air breathed in goes to the lungs and thence

21. See Lonie (1964); and Harris (1973, 216): "Blood was just nature's material for replenishments, the idea that it should wander about returning to its source would have been utterly meaningless." Blood was universally thought to be the body's nourishment, not the vehicle of nourishment, and to be distributed by the heart like water from an irrigation pump. Until this belief was overthrown there was little to suggest that arteries and veins might form a single system.

to the heart, whence it is distributed as vital (*zōtikon*) *pneuma;* some of this goes to the brain, where it is transformed into psychic (*psuchikon*) *pneuma*. The former accounts for lower functions like metabolizing; the latter for higher, psychological functions.[22] Thus *pneuma* turns out to be an even more resourceful theoretical entity than Aristotle had envisioned; to explain different types of human functioning we postulate different types of *pneuma*. This theoretical flexibility is not yet a weakness, but it is clear that there are few empirical constraints on explanatory appeal to *pneuma*. It is a dangerously handy theoretical tool.

This was the broad scientific picture of the functioning of living beings that developed during the Hellenistic age and became available to educated common sense. The Stoics, in particular, adopted the idea that *pneuma* is a single, but highly differentiable, vehicle whose workings can explain a wide variety of human functioning. They kept, however, Praxagoras' original confused picture of one *pneuma* system, rather than two, located in the heart, and thus they failed to make use of the most up-to-date and, we can see, more correct theory, which gave the brain something like its proper role. Their reasons for this, as we shall see, were not scientific. However, one of the most important features of the Stoic theory was its adoption of the model of a centralized system. The Stoics are in debt to contemporary science not just in making soul *pneuma* but in making its association with the body take the form suggested by the discoveries of the Hellenistic doctors: it is what makes the living body function, by driving a centralized system that is linked to all parts of the body.

It is easy for us to find the Stoic view of the soul as a heart-centered *pneuma* system absurd, but if we look at it in this

22. Galen tells us that Erasistratus "does not simply assume the matter in question . . . but supports with no few arguments his assertion that psychic (*psychikon*) *pneuma* starts from the head, and vital (*zōtikon*) *pneuma* from the heart" (*PHP* 281K, 164 de Lacy). Unfortunately, Galen fails to tell us what these arguments were. On the different kinds of *pneuma* cf. Galen *Usu resp.* 502K; *PHP* 185K, 78 de Lacy; *Puls.* 760K; [Galen] *Intro.* 697K.

way, we are in danger of missing the point that it draws on the most sophisticated scientific model available. Given Hellenistic medical discoveries (imperfectly understood as they were) and the development of *pneuma* as the most adequate theoretical entity available to account for different human functionings in a unified way, the Stoics were drawing on the best available account of the mind; for although they had many wrong beliefs about it, they grasped the fundamental idea: the soul is located in the workings of a centralized system which accounts for the body's functioning. Given a more correct and acceptable scientific account, they would have located the soul in the workings of the nervous system.

c) Aristotle's Legacy

Aristotle left a school devoted to research in an Aristotelian spirit, not to the preservation of Aristotelian doctrines. Much later, in the second century A.D., we find Alexander of Aphrodisias developing a psychology explicitly designed to be faithful to Aristotle; but his immediate successors in the Hellenistic age go their own ways, and his ideas of the soul are taken up unevenly and with no very impressive results.

Both Theophrastus and Meno, his immediate pupils, did keep up-to-date with the increasing importance of *pneuma* in contemporary medical theory.[23] Indeed Meno in his history of medicine reads *pneuma* remorselessly back into earlier theories.[24] We also find Aristotle's own ambivalence about the

23. Theophrastus reports that some doctors thought *pneuma* to be the source of vital heat and of movement (frag. 11 Wimmer); cf. also *On Fire* 76, where fire is said to be the most "pneumatic" of the elements. In general Theophrastus seems to have limited himself to criticizing previous thinkers (cf. Stratton 1917) including Aristotle (see the appendix to Hicks 1907).

24. The copious references to Aristotle in the medical papyrus written by Anonymous Londiniensis are generally ascribed to Meno's *Iatrika*. *Pneuma* is prominent in his account of Philolaus (col. 18.8–49) and, strikingly, of Hippocrates (5.35–7.39), to whom he ascribes

roles of heat and *pneuma* reproduced in Diocles of Carystus, who was established by Werner Jaeger as a younger contemporary of Aristotle.[25] For Diocles, the body's own heat contributes to the formation of the four humors; but *pneuma*, warm air we breathe in, functions extensively in the body, being centered in the heart and distributed from it as "psychic" *pneuma*.[26] It seems to be identified with the "soul power" which is said to "carry" the body and provide its ability to move.[27] Diocles did not distinguish arteries from veins and thought of both blood and *pneuma* as distributed in a single system from the central heart.[28] *Pneuma* thus energizes the body from a central source (in a way reminiscent of that described in *De motu animalium* 10) and has taken over sensation and thought.

A dismal little work known as *On Pneuma* has come down to us in the Aristotelian corpus, though it was clearly written in the later Lyceum, since the author knows of Erasistratus' discoveries. Assuming that we have "connate *pneuma*," it raises questions in an indecisive way about *pneuma*'s relation to perception and movement and its location in the arteries or tendons. *On Pneuma* is a depressing work, showing clearly that medicine and psychology in the Lyceum were aware of, but

an aetiology of diseases in terms of air blasts (*phusai*) which depend on the nature of the *pneuma* in us. Even the author of the papyrus takes Meno to task for characterizing Hippocrates as a primitive *pneuma* theorist; in the Hippocratic corpus only the *Peri phuseōn* gives any handle for such an interpretation, but it does not tally with Meno's account and anyway may be a late addition to the corpus. Meno is clearly desperate to give current *pneuma* theory a respectable ancestry; as Diels (1893, 433) points out, "er war überzeugt, ein grosser Schulstifter wie Hippokrates müsse sich über seine Principien im Zusammenhang geäussert haben, und diese Principien müssten im Einklang stehen mit dem herrschenden Ansichten der Mediciner."

25. See Wellman (1901), who, however, accepts the earlier dating for Diocles controverted by Jaeger (1938a, 1938b, 1940). Edelstein (1967) finds Jaeger's redating too late.

26. Frags. 44, 59 Wellman.

27. Frags. 42, 17 Wellman.

28. Frag. 14 Wellman.

not abreast of, the work in the shiny new research center at Alexandria.[29]

Only Strato of Lampsacus has a philosophically interesting and developed *pneuma* theory of the soul, remarkably similar to the Stoics'. Unfortunately, we know of it only piecemeal and often through Stoic-influenced sources.[30] *Pneuma* is, for Strato, either identical with the soul or its immediate vehicle enlivening the body. It is annoying that we do not know his precise position on as fundamental a point as this; perhaps he identified soul and *pneuma* using Stoic-type arguments, or perhaps he retained an Aristotelian view of the soul as the body's form, with *pneuma* as its immediate vehicle.[31] Strato seems to have retained Aristotle's view that the *pneuma* relevant to life was "connate" to the body.[32] However, his *pneuma* plays a larger role than Aristotle's; it is spread throughout the body but has a "ruling part" or centralized organ in the head.[33]

Strato's most interesting view about the soul was that it is strictly a unity: no part of it is "separable," like Aristotle's separable thinking, and thought and perception are not mutually independent; they are both processes (*kinēseis*) of the same kind, and, further, "perceiving without thinking is completely impossible," since even if our senses are in working order we do not take anything in unless thinking is also present.[34] Strato supports this with the alleged fact that if our attention wanders while reading, we cease to perceive the letters. Presumably, he is thinking of reading aloud, as was

29. See Jaeger (1913, sect. 3), whose dismissive verdict is confirmed by Solmsen (1968c) and does not depend on Jaeger's controversial claim that chapter 9 is a Stoic addition.

30. Cf. Plutarch (frag. 111 Wehrli), who uses the Stoic *hēgemonikon* in describing Strato's view. See Wehrli (1950); Movia (1968, pt. 2); Gottschalk (1965).

31. Tertullian represents the soul-body relation for Strato as analogous to breath in a flute (frag. 108), but he at once adds Aenesidemus and Heraclitus as holding the same idea, and it is hazardous to press the passage.

32. Frag. 129.

33. Frags. 108–9 and 119–21.

34. Frag. 112.

standard in the ancient world, and the phenomenon he has
in mind is that of finding oneself, through inattention, reading
out something which is not in the book before one. It is still
controversial how one should describe this. Strato clearly rejects the view that something has become scrambled in one's
thinking between the perceptual input and one's verbal out-
put. He favors the solution that the perceptual input itself must
have been faulty in some way.

In a highly interesting passage from Plutarch the following,
which was to be an important theme for the Stoics, is ascribed
to Strato:

> Not only our desires but also our griefs, not only our
> fears and envies and *Schadenfreuden* but also our hurts
> and pleasures and pains and in general all sensation comes
> about in the soul;[35] it is not in the foot that we feel hurt
> when we stub it, nor in the head when we bang it, nor
> in the finger when we cut it. For everything else lacks
> sensation except the governing part (*hēgemonikon*);[36] the
> blow is quickly relayed to this, and its sensation we call
> pain. When noise sounds in our ears we suppose it to be
> outside us, adding to the sensation the distance from its
> origin to the governing part (*hēgemonikon*). Similarly,
> we suppose the hurt from a wound to be not where it
> had sensation, but where it had its origin, taking the soul
> to be drawn toward the place where suffering occurred.
> (*Utrum anim. an corp.*; frag. 111 Wehrli)

The soul is affected as a whole and is rational as a whole;[37]
and its vehicle is the physical substance *pneuma*. It all sounds

35. "Sensation" is *aisthēsis;* this can often be translated "perception," but the wide range of phenomena that Strato refers to would
not naturally all be thought of as perceptions.

36. This is a technical Stoic term and may have been read back
into Strato's theory later. The *hēgemonikon* is what centralizes and
unifies the soul's functioning; mental events like pain are registered
in it rather than in the part of the soul where the damage occurred
(e.g., the foot). Even if Strato did not use the Stoic term, he seems
to have had something very similar in mind.

37. Cf. Sext. Emp. *Math.* 7. 350, where Strato is said to have said
that the *dianoia* is identified with the senses.

so Stoic that it is a pity that we know so little of Strato on the soul. We possess extensively only his critical remarks; Olympiodorus in his commentary on Plato's *Phaedo* preserves many of Strato's criticisms of the arguments for the soul's immortality.[38]

Strato, "the natural scientist," is the only one of Aristotle's successors in the Lyceum who studied the soul for its own sake. Among other members and associates of the Lyceum we find merely incidental and often frankly weird views about the soul. Two contemporaries of Theophrastus, Aristoxenus and Dicaearchus, became notorious for their claim that the soul is a "harmony" or attunement of the body. Aristoxenus was a musical theorist and probably did not write specifically on the soul, while from Dicaearchus we have some statements but no arguments.[39] But we can produce some plausible background, since Plutarch tells us that Dicaearchus was a constant opponent of Plato,[40] and it seems that, like Strato, he was opposing the *Phaedo*'s arguments for the soul's immortality.

In the *Phaedo* the theory is put forward that the soul is an "attunement" of bodily items; Socrates sees that denying the soul existence as a substance distinct from the body undermines any belief in the soul's immortality, thus the theory is refuted. The theory is propounded by Pythagoreans; and Aristoxenus and Dicaearchus, who had Pythagorean interests, surely saw themselves as producing a new improved version of the view. Aristotle still finds it necessary to refute at some length the theory that the soul is an "attunement."[41] However, there are many unsolved puzzles here. We do not know why

38. Frags. 118, 122–27. There is an English translation of some of them in an appendix to Hackforth (1955).

39. For Aristoxenus see Wehrli (1945, frags. 118–21). Wehrli (84–85) thinks that Aristoxenus may not have written on the soul, and that he is coupled with Dicaearchus because of his views on "harmony" and because of their shared background and interests. On Dicaearchus see Wehrli (1944, frags. 5–12); Gottschalk (1971); Movia (1968, pt. 2).

40. Frag. 5.

41. *DA* 407b27–408a28.

the *Phaedo*'s arguments retained such fascination for generations of Lyceum scholars, nor why that theory is associated with Pythagoreanism when it seems in straight conflict with the Pythagorean view that souls outlive bodies and transmigrate between them. Lastly, and most frustratingly, we do not really know what the attunement theory *is*. In the *Phaedo* it shifts around among a variety of positions; it is never clear whether individual souls can share the same attunement or not.[42] Aristotle also argues against a number of alternatives. One would expect Dicaearchus by this point to show some sophistication and precision in argument. But all the indications are that he had a merely crude and aggressively stated view: there is no such thing as the soul, and our intuitive distinction between living and lifeless things answers to nothing real.[43] Unless our sources misrepresent a more nuanced view, Dicaearchus was merely trying to attack Plato by claiming that the soul was "nothing but" an attunement of elements, and so not immortal; we have no trace of a wider interest in the soul.[44]

We find a totally different attitude in Heracleides of Pontus (c. 390–310 B.C.) and Clearchus of Soli (fl. c. 250 B.C.).[45]

42. Further, when the theory is introduced, it is physical states (hot, cold, dry, wet, etc.) that are "attuned" (*Phd.* 86b–c); but Socrates later argues (94b–e) against the view that it is items like hunger and pleasure that are attuned.
43. See esp. frags. 7 and 8. Revealingly, we tend to get the same short slogan over and over again: "nihil omnino animum esse," "*mē einai tēn psuchēn*," and so on. We are told that Dicaearchus discussed the soul in his three-book "Corinthian" dialogues (frag. 7) and denied its immortality in the three-book "Lesbian" dialogues (frag. 9). Either our sources are defective or not much of these dialogues was devoted to the soul. This is a pity, since Dicaearchus' tone suggests that his motivation at least was eliminativist rather than reductivist, and it would have been interesting to have a clear example of eliminativist thinking about the soul in the ancient world.
44. See frags. 11, 12, 12a. In frag. 7 we do find the claim that the soul is "equally spread" throughout the body, but Wehrli considers this a Stoicizing reinterpretation.
45. For Clearchus see Wehrli (1948); for Heracleides, Wehrli (1953); Gottschalk (1980); Movia (1968, pt. 2).

Heracleides belonged as much to the Academy as to the Lyceum, and Clearchus admired Plato and wrote an encomium on him.[46] Both of them were interested in parapsychology and out-of-the-body experiences. Clearchus told the story of Cleonymus, who after being laid out for dead recovered after three days with stories of the Beyond, later recognizing on earth someone he had met There.[47] According to Proclus, Clearchus convinced Aristotle that the soul is "separate" from the body and can enter and leave it by getting him to be present at a séance when a boy's soul was "drawn out of him" with a wand, leaving him impervious to pain, and then "put back."[48] Heracleides wrote popular works in which similar stories figure. It all sounds very Edwardian.[49]

Because of these stories, and their association with Platonic, as well as Aristotelian, thinking, both Clearchus and Heracleides have been regarded as maverick dualists in a physicalist age. But while we are very ill informed about Clearchus, Heracleides was no dualist; he regarded the soul as composed of a physical substance, light.[50] Nor do we need to suppose that either was a dualist; they show no interest in dualist arguments, and their concerns do not demand it. Every age which, like the Hellenistic and Victorian ages, sees great advances in science and technology and in which science has prestige will tend to have its camp following of pseudoscience. When the mind and soul are discussed in terms taken from science and medicine, the reaction takes the form of parapsychology with messages from the Beyond, gamma rays, and so on. In a scientific age ideas which are really imaginative and spiritual may emerge in a pseudoscientific form which

46. Frag. 2.
47. Frag. 8.
48. Frag. 7.
49. In one work Empedocles is said to have resurrected a woman who had been in a coma. Heracleides was also keen on the wisdom of the East: he wrote about Zoroaster and about the legendary northern shaman Abaris.
50. When not in a physical body it occupies a less gross, ethereal body in the Milky Way (frags. 97, 98c; Gottschalk 1980).

renders them ludicrous rather than profound. We do best to see Clearchus and Heraclcides as interested in the spiritual aspect of the soul, rather than as contributors to philosophy of mind. It is unfortunate that they lived in an age in which their ideas had to be expressed in unsuitable forms.

From later generations in the Lyceum we get nothing but fitful spurts of information. Ariston of Ceos revived (perhaps against the Stoics?) a sharp distinction between the rational and nonrational soul.[51] Critolaus identified the soul with *aether*, the fifth element.[52] But we have no idea what these isolated bits of doctrine meant in their contexts. The Lyceum never had an orthodox "line" on the soul, and, apart from Strato, Aristotle's followers did not produce any original or striking ideas about it. Their interests lay elsewhere, and the initiative given to philosophy of mind by Aristotle's *De anima* passed from his own school to the new schools of the Hellenistic period.

51. See Wehrli (1952). But the relevant fragment (= Porph. *De an. fac.* apud Stob. *Ecl.* 1. 49.24, p. 347.21 Wachsmuth) is not there, as Wehrli assigns it to the Stoic Ariston of Chios. Von Arnim is of the same opinion, so the fragment appears as *SVF* 1. 377. The two Aristons were frequently confused even in antiquity, and the provenance of this fragment is especially difficult because it lacks context in either. I agree that it should belong to the Peripatetic, with Movia (1968, 150–55) and Ioppolo (1980, 272–78).

52. Wehrli (1959, frags. 16–18); Movia (1968, pt. 2). It is not even certain whether this applies to the whole soul or only to *nous*, the thinking part.

Part Two

The Stoics

2

The Soul and the Mind

a) Physicalism

The Stoics are unmistakably physicalists; they claim that soul is body, a physical thing, and by a physical thing they uncompromisingly mean a three-dimensional solid object.[1] Soul is *pneuma*, which, as we have seen, by this date is not merely commonsensical breath, but a theoretically more powerful entity. The Stoics made extensive use of *pneuma* in their general physics;[2] in identifying soul with *pneuma* they were conforming, as we have seen, to the general shift in scientific

1. *To trichei diastaton meta antitupias* (SVF 2. 381; cf. D. L. 7. 135). See Hahm (1977, chap. 1), who argues that for the Stoics body can be defined as what is capable of acting or of being acted upon. But this is hardly equivalent to the more commonsense definition and would, if taken as basic, trivialize the arguments to show that soul is body, which rely on the principle that only bodies can act or be acted on. Probably the Stoics regarded the principle about action as true of body, but not definitive of it. But they do not seem to have made this unambiguously clear; Sextus frequently makes trouble for them by playing the two principles of three-dimensional solidity and action off each other. See also Long and Sedley (1987, 45, with commentary on p. 273).

2. See Long and Sedley (1987, 47, with commentary for passages on the use of *pneuma* in Stoic physics).

paradigm on this topic since Aristotle. We shall return to the question of what identification with *pneuma* comes to; for the moment we shall concentrate on Stoic grounds for identifying soul with a physical item in the first place.

One might think that in principle the Stoics do not need to argue for physicalism about the soul, for they think that everything that exists is physical anyway. However, this does not in fact settle the matter; for while they do hold that everything that *exists* is physical, they hold that there are things which do not exist. Their highest genus is the *ti* or "something," which covers not only things that exist, the physical things, but also things that "subsist," which are not physical. These are time, place, the void, and *lekta*, items to which we shall return because they play an important role in the Stoic account of mental activity. The general physicalism of the Stoics therefore does not settle the matter. In any case, we would expect the Stoics to offer some arguments directed to the physicality of the soul in particular, since they claim that their theories are supported by our "common conceptions," or the consensus of our intuitions. So, when they make a claim which on its own is counterintuitive, as they frequently do, we expect to find some effort on their part to show that the claim in question coheres with or is supported by a reasonable number of our other intuitions.[3] And, judging from the number of arguments that we find for the physicality of the soul, the claim that soul is body was thought to need support, given the way that it runs up against some at least of our intuitions.

We have a number of ancient Stoic arguments on this point;[4] most of them turn out to be problematic, but one at least gives

3. Often we do not find this, because of the state of our sources. On "common conceptions" see Todd (1973). The Stoics' claim about intuitive support was found unconvincing by some in antiquity: Plutarch wrote an entire book defending the thesis that the Stoics appealed on various matters to mutually contradictory intuitions.
4. For the most interesting extended ancient discussions see Tert. *De anim.* 5 (= *SVF* 1. 137, 518; 2. 773, 791); Alexander *De an. mant.* 113–18 Bruns, esp. 117.

us some insight into the Stoics' motivation, and the others can be understood in the light of it. Diogenes Laertius reports that according to the Stoics "the soul is a [nature] which can perceive. This is the *pneuma* connate to us; therefore it is a body."[5] This, of course, only shows the soul to be body if *pneuma* is body; and this would be convincing to a Stoic, who already accepted this, but would not seem to have much impact on uncommitted common sense. An obvious retort would be that if the soul really is *pneuma*, then *pneuma* cannot be a physical entity.

Tertullian reports an argument of Zeno's:

1. What leaves the animal when it dies is body.
2. The animal dies when connate *pneuma* leaves it.
   Therefore, from (1) and (2),
3. Connate *pneuma* is body.
4. Soul is connate *pneuma*.
   Therefore, from (3) and (4),
5. Soul is body.[6]

"Connate" here means only that the *pneuma* is something we are born with, part of our physical nature as human beings. This argument seems not only to share the fault of the previous one but to augment it; no one inclined to reject the conclusion would accept the first premise, and the argument seems doomed to convince only the converted. Probably we should take seriously the suggestion that many of Zeno's "arguments" were never meant to be ways of convincing non-Stoics, but played the different role of encapsulating Stoic beliefs in memorable and striking form. On this view, they played a pedagogical role; they clarified the Stoic position and made it easier to learn, but are not to be considered as "arguments for physicalism" in any ordinary sense.[7]

5. D. L. 7. 156 (= *SVF* 2. 774).
6. *De anim.* 5 (= *SVF* 1. 137).
7. On this see Schofield (1983). Zeno's "arguments" would on this view play somewhat the same role as Epicurus' *Kuriai doxai*. Alexander (*De an.* 18. 27 Bruns [= *SVF* 2. 793]) reports another

Cleanthes offers an interesting but baffling argument:

1. Children are like their parents not only in body but also in soul (i.e., they resemble them in character, not just in looks).
2. Likeness and unlikeness are properties of body, not of nonbodily things.
   Therefore
3. The soul is body.[8]

Once again we have a problem over the acceptability of one of the premises, in this case, (2). Why would anyone not already convinced of the truth of physicalism accept this? If Cleanthes had any arguments for (2), we do not know of them.[9]

The same problem afflicts an argument of Chrysippus':

1. Death is the separation of soul from body.
2. Nothing nonbodily is separated from body, for nothing nonbodily touches body.
3. The soul both touches and is separated from body.
   Therefore
4. The soul is body.[10]

Here the first premise is just prethcorctical common sense; but the second imports a definition of separation as the opposite of "touching."[11] Even if we allow Chrysippus that only bodies can touch,[12] we do not have to grant that only things

---

Stoic "argument" of this type: that of which the parts are body is body; the soul has a part, perceiving, which is body; therefore it is a body.

8. *SVF* 1. 518 (= Tert. *De anim.* 5; Nemesius *De nat. hom.* 32).

9. And Alexander, criticizing this argument at *De an.* 117 Bruns, appears not to know of any either.

10. *SVF* 2. 790 (= Tert. *De anim.* 5; Nemesius *De nat. hom.* 2, 46, 791).

11. See Hahm (1977, 15–16). Compare Pl. *Prm.* 149a4–5; Arist. *Ph.* 226b21–23.

12. The Stoics appear to have no direct defense of this; both Tertullian and Seneca (*Ep.* 106. 3–80) refer to Lucretius for the *Epicurean* belief that only body can touch or be touched (Lucr. 1. 304; cf. 3. 166). One could, however, allow the Stoics that explicit

which touch can be separated. Alexander simply denies the argument; there are perfectly good uses of "separate," he claims, in which things are separated which are not bodies, and do not touch one another.[13]

Although this argument is scarcely satisfactory, it does point to something important: the Stoics are pressing the point that it is hard to make sense of the interaction of physical things with nonphysical things. Touch is a kind of interaction; the Stoics' most successful argument, to which we now turn, can be seen as a more general version of this point.

Another of Cleanthes' arguments is, by contrast with all the others, cogent and interesting (unfortunately, we do not know by comparison with the others how prominent it was for the Stoics):

1. Nothing nonbodily suffers together with (*sumpaschei,* is affected together with) body, nor body with the non-bodily; only body with body.
2. But the soul suffers with the body (e.g., when it is ill or cut) and also the body with the soul (when we are ashamed the body goes red, pale when afraid, and so on).
   Therefore
3. The soul is body.[14]

This can be readily simplified to the following:

1. Only bodies interact.
2. Soul and body interact.
   Therefore
3. Soul is body.

If any commonsense belief is well entrenched, it is that soul and body interact. Embarrassment leads to blushing, a cut

---

defense is not needed, since common sense accepts that physical things cannot touch nonphysical things.

13. *De an. mant.* 117.

14. This argument is found in the same two sources as Cleanthes' first (*SVF* 1. 518).

leads to pain. On its own this is not decisive support for any
theory of the soul; for it is as compatible with dualism as with
any form of physicalism: soul and body might be different
kinds of thing and interact in a *sui generis* way. The Stoics,
however, hold another belief which underpins this argument.
They think that the interaction of soul and body must be
straightforward *causal* interaction. And whatever analysis of
causation we give, it must surely be uniform for souls and
bodies. It would be unacceptably *ad hoc* to have one kind of
causation for bodies and another for souls; it would amount
in effect to accepting that soul-body interaction was just a
mystery. Given this background belief about causation, the
argument is straightforward. Whatever the appearances, souls,
which interact with bodies, must themselves be bodies, for
only bodies can causally act and be acted upon.[15]

Aristotle points to interaction of soul and body but concludes not that soul is body, but that it is the body's nonbodily
form.[16] The Stoics do not entertain this possibility seriously;
and they do so not because they are dogmatically committed
to physicalism, but because they take soul-body interaction
seriously and are also thinking of interaction as causal interaction. Whereas Aristotle associates cause (*aitia*) with explanation and, as is well known, claims that there are four irre-
ducibly different kinds of explanation, only one of which we
think of as causal explanation, the Stoics (and indeed post-
Aristotelian philosophers more generally) think that the core
notion of a cause is what moves something or gets something
done—a conception obviously much closer to the modern
one.[17] Thus the Stoics are able to move directly and econom-

15. Cf. Sext. Emp. *Math.* 8. 263 (= *SVF* 2. 363) and Cic. *Varro*
39 (= *SVF* 1. 90) for the thesis that only bodies can act or be acted
on. Our sources do not relate this clearly to the thesis that there
must be a uniform analysis of causality for bodies and for souls,
but the line of thought I suggest is both very obvious and clearly
preferable to the thesis that the Stoics just dogmatically contradicted Plato and Aristotle on this point without any argument.
16. *DA* 403a16–b19.
17. See Frede (1980).

ically from common sense, and their views on causation, to their conclusion about the physical nature of the soul.

All of these arguments have two important features. One is that they are a priori, like most modern arguments for physicalism.[18] They do not rely on the established success of any science; they emerge from reflection on the view of the soul available to common sense, together with considerations about causality. Though simple, they are powerful and hard to refute. Secondly, they are not reductive. Soul is a kind of body, but nothing follows just from this as to our giving up or modifying any of our other beliefs about the soul. Our commonsense view of our inner life has not yet been affected in any way.

b) Soul in the World

Stoic physics is strikingly unmodern in that their natural world is alive; for the Stoics cosmology is cosmobiology. "Chrysippus in the first book of his *Providence*, Apollodorus in his *Physics*, and Posidonius say that the world is a living being, rational, animate, and intelligent."[19] Thus our souls are not the only things in the universe that can be called soul, for "soul penetrates through the whole universe, and we by sharing in it as a part are ensouled."[20] The reasoning behind this is simply an employment of what was later to be called the principle that the cause is greater than the effect: we cannot understand how

18. See Davidson (1980) for a classic statement of the difference between this kind of argument from the nature of causation and arguments current earlier in this century that are more empirical and essentially constitute a claim that the success of science in other fields compels us to interpret its results in the case of the human mind in physicalistic ways. These earlier arguments are much weaker. Further, there is no ancient analogue to them because of the comparatively primitive empirical results of ancient science.

19. D. L. 7. 142–43. See Hahm (1977, chap. 5).

20. Cleanthes apud Hermias *In gent. phil.* 14 (Diels, *Dox. Graec.* 654 [= *SVF* 1. 495]).

rational living things can be produced in a universe the materials of which lack these properties to any degree.[21]

This might seem to cast a different light on the conclusions of the last section. Soul is a physical body, and so it is part of the natural world. But the natural world turns out itself to be something which is alive. So nothing seems to have been achieved by the previous arguments; we seem indeed to have gone round in a depressingly small circle.

In fact no real methodological difference is made to Stoic philosophy of mind by the thesis that the natural world is itself a kind of living thing. It is true that that thesis removes most of the motivation for reductivism. The Stoics are not in the position of modern theorists who claim that all mental events are physical events and thereby reduce the nature of the mental to that of the physical, removing the notion of the mental from our everyday picture of the world. Rather, they place the human soul in a scientific and metaphysical picture of the universe in which there is continuity between humans and the rest of nature. We are not ensouled beings in an otherwise soulless universe; the nature of the soul and mind, that is, is not just in itself problematic for the Stoic worldview. Apart from this, however, the larger picture of the cosmos as a living thing has strikingly little effect on the way that the Stoics explain the nature of the human soul. The human soul is not different in kind from the world soul in that both are *pneuma;* but we shall see, in our account of the functioning of the human soul, that the human soul is very specific in a number of ways which do not carry over to the world soul.[22]

Further, while the Stoics prided themselves on the general and holistic character of their philosophical theory, it is also true that various parts of it are developed in comparative in-

21. Cf. Pl. *Leg.* 892b, the first statement of this claim. See Nagel (1979b) for an interesting discussion of this kind of view, which he calls panpsychism.
22. It makes no sense, for example, to think of the world soul employing *lekta* or making assents—at least not in the kind of way characteristic of humans doing these things.

dependence from one another. The detail of Stoic logic or ethics, for example, cannot be derived from general Stoic metaphysical principles. Similarly with philosophy of mind; although it is embedded in a general account of the universe, none of its central defining theses are derivable from (or even uniquely appropriate to) the general principles.

The world soul is, however, relevant to one question about the human soul. Soul is body, but what kind of body? From Chrysippus onward the evidence is overwhelming that the soul is *pneuma*, and there is some evidence that this was also the view of Zeno and the early Stoics.[23] But there is a minor stream of evidence that for the early Stoics the soul was fire, namely, hot matter.[24] Of course these views can be reconciled; *pneuma* is originally just warm air, and saying that soul is fire or heat may merely be a crude way of saying that *pneuma* functions by way of the heat in it.[25] But the split in the evidence looks serious if we take into account not only Zeno's and Cleanthes' scrappy fragments on the human soul, but their more extensive discussions of the world soul; Cleanthes distinctly identifies its essential working with heat and locates its "ruling part" in the sun. And human souls can hardly be made of different stuff from the world soul.

We seem to have one of the few cases where there is a change of doctrine in the early Stoa, and there is much to be said for the solution suggested by several scholars: Zeno and

23. D. L. 7. 157 (= *SVF* 1. 135); cf. *SVF* 1. 136–38 for Zeno's view that the soul is *pneuma enthermon*; *SVF* 1. 521 for Cleanthes.

24. Alexander (*De an. mant.* 115–16 Bruns) says that for the Stoics soul is *pneuma* or fire; Cicero says three times that for Zeno the nature of both mind and senses was fire (*SVF* 1. 134 = *Varro* 39, *Fin.* 4. 12, *Tusc.* 1. 19). Cleanthes' account of the world soul makes its essence fire or heat, if we follow Solmsen's convincing claim (1968d) that the whole section of Stoic cosmology in Cic. *Nat. d.* 2. 23–32 should be assigned to Cleanthes. See also Hahm (1977, chap. 5).

25. Ambivalence about the roles of *pneuma* and heat goes back to Aristotle; and we have one (admittedly late and compressed) report that "Zeno said that heating (*thermasia*) and *pneuma* were the same thing" (*SVF* 1. 127).

Cleanthes probably thought the human soul to be *pneuma*, but
gave a crucial role to the heat it in, locating the world soul in
the functioning of cosmic heat.[26] Chrysippus, however, established *pneuma* as what both human souls and the world soul
are.

This minor point is interesting for two reasons. One is that
it shows the influence of medical science. We have seen in
part 1 that the notion of *pneuma* was significantly developed
by medical writers in the Hellenistic period. Chrysippus threw
overboard the earlier, more picturesque theory in favor of one
that took over an important feature from the current scientific
paradigm in the relevant area. In other words, he was making
his predecessors' theories more scientifically up-to-date. The
other point is that the resulting theory is very economical and
powerful. If we make the effort to distance ourselves from our
own scientific knowledge, we can appreciate its simplicity,
combined with its taking its starting point from current medical science. *Pneuma* functions everywhere in the world; it is
the single theoretical item that explains the functioning of
stones and plants as well as of humans. The differences in the
way it works in, for example, animate and inanimate things
are explained in terms of difference of "tension" (*tonos*) of
the *pneuma*.[27] Thus we have a single substance, *pneuma*, and
a single mechanism, tension, to explain a wide variety of phe-

26. Solmsen (1968d); Hahm (1977, chap. 5); Lapidge (1973,
1978). See also Todd (1978). Cleanthes may have taken this thought
farthest. The idea may well be influenced by Heraclitus, some of
whose views were taken up by the Stoa.
27. Lapidge (1973) complains that this change threatens Stoic
physics with incoherence, for originally Zeno distinguished between
the principles (*archai*)—creative fire and passive matter—and the
elements (*stoicheia*)—earth, air, water, and ordinary fire. Cosmic
pneuma, however, takes on the role of the *archē* creative fire, while
being composed only of the elements air and ordinary fire. (This is,
as Lapidge points out, essentially the same criticism as Alexander's
at *De mixt.* 224 [= *SVF* 2. 310].) However, *pneuma* plays the role
of *archē* not just because of its composition from *stoicheia*, but
because of its degree of *tonos*. Further, we get a more unified and
economical theory, which dispenses with the arbitrary difference
between creative and ordinary fire. See also Todd (1978).

nomena in a coherent way. We have a scientifically unified picture of the world, with no gap of principle between mental and physical.

c) The Soul-Body Relation

How are the two kinds of physical substance, body and soul, related? They are a case of total blending or mixture (*krasis di' holōn*). We find this idea running through Stoic accounts from Zeno to Hierocles (second century A.D.).[28] Hierocles emphasizes that soul is not in body like a substance in a container;[29] their relation is more intimate and thorough than that. However, total blending is not explanatory of the soul-body relation in particular; indeed the Stoics used that relation as a "clear witness" of what total blending is, assuming that we have a clear intuitive idea of the soul-body relation as a peculiarly intimate one, an idea which we can then extend to other cases.[30]

In Stoic physics, there are three ways in which stuffs can be related.[31] One is juxtaposition, of which an example is a mixture of beans and grains of wheat. However practically impossible it might be to sort out the different kinds (compare the heroine's task in fairy tales), they do not blend; the stuffs retain their own properties because they do not form a new stuff. Another is fusion, as in cooking. The eggs, flour, and other ingredients form a new stuff with new properties; they do not retain their own properties and are not recoverable from the new stuff. The third is total blending. Two stuffs are blended through and through so that there is no part of the blended mixture which does not consist of both; yet each of

28. For Zeno see *SVF* 1. 145; Hierocles, col. 4.1–53. See Long and Sedley (1987, 48) for Stoic texts on mixture.
29. Which was the Epicurean view; see p. 147, below.
30. Alexander *De mixt.* 217.32ff. (= *SVF* 2. 473).
31. Our main source is Alexander *De mixt.* 4ff. See Todd (1976) for translation and discussion. See also D. L. 7. 151; Plut. *De comm. not.* 1078b–e; White (1986); and Sorabji (1988).

the original stuffs retains its own properties and is in principle recoverable from the blending.[32] Examples apart from the soul-body relation are heat and iron "blending" to produce hot iron, and water and wine blending to form watery wine.

The theory is obviously designed to correct Aristotle, who denies that two stuffs can form a new stuff without losing their original properties, claiming that one cannot blend a drop of wine with a large amount of water, for the wine will lose its own properties.[33] Chrysippus claims in obvious opposition that a drop of wine can blend with the whole ocean.[34] This notorious example brings to the fore the point that the Stoic theory of total blending appears paradoxical when applied to very unequal quantities. If a drop of wine totally blends with the ocean, then there is no part of the wine-and-ocean that is not constituted of wine and of ocean, each retaining its own properties and in principle recoverable. But this means that the drop of wine will have to pervade the entire ocean. Then, however, the wine and the ocean will have to occupy the same space as each other and as the wine-and-ocean blend; and how can this be when they have very unequal quantities?

The Stoics add to their problems here by making the extraordinary claim that this theory can be established from our intuitions about mixtures.[35] Ancient opponents, who attack the theory on many fronts, certainly show that this is wrong and even perhaps that the theory is *un*intuitive. But it is not in fact paradoxical. Because the Stoics have a continuum theory of matter, they do not have a problem with dividing small quantities; there is a subdivision of the drop of wine for every sub-

32. Stob. *Ecl.* 1. 155.5–11 (= *SVF.* 2. 471) gives the example of dipping an oiled sponge into a blend of water and wine to take up the water. Sorabji (1988) confirms that this works.

33. *Gen. corr.* 328a26–8. Aristotle thus denies an alternative between juxtaposition and fusion.

34. D. L. 7. 151; Plut. *De comm. not.* 1078e. Sandbach (1985) argues that the Stoic theory is not designed to oppose Aristotle, but he is effectively countered by Sorabji (1988) and by Long and Sedley (1987, 2: 288).

35. On this aspect of the theory see Todd (1973).

division of the ocean. Further, paradox is removed if we distinguish, as a recent scholar does,[36] between quantity as volume, the amount of space occupied, and quantity as mass, which remains invariant through changes in volume. Thus a small mass of wine, when blended with the ocean, will take up a much larger volume, namely, the volume occupied by wine-and-ocean. But since mass is distinct from volume, there is no problem with the small quantity (mass) of the wine and the large quantity (volume) of the wine-and-ocean.

Total blending is found in many types of case. Is the soul-body relation reasonably to be thought of as a case of it? Is it, further, an intuitively forceful "witness"—a strikingly good case—of this relationship? If we remember that intuitively the soul is what makes a living thing be alive in the way appropriate to that kind of thing, then certainly this presupposes that the item in question has no part which is just soul or just body. So it seems that body and soul cannot be simply juxtaposed.[37] But could not soul and body be fused? Why should we prefer total blending as an explanation? The point of insisting on total blending rather than fusion in other cases is to accommodate the claim that the two items retain their actual properties. But we have no idea of what the *distinct* properties of soul are; we encounter ensouled bodies and soulless bodies (after death) but never souls other than in an embodied state. So we have no empirical reason to demand an analogue,

36. White (1986) (and cf. Sharvy 1983). White argues effectively against Todd (1973, 1976), who accepts that total blending of unequal quantities is paradoxical, and argues that the Stoics did not accept it for empirical stuffs, only for the relation of *pneuma* to the passive elements. See also Sorabji (1988).

37. Hierocles has an interesting, but very puzzling, argument (cols. 3.56–4.53). He establishes as premises the points (1) that soul and body are physical, (2) that they are totally blended, and (3) that the soul is a perceptive power; and he concludes that perception in an animal is *self*-perception. (On this see p. 59 below). He uses as an intermediate step the point that since soul holds body together in "tension," their interaction will be or involve *tonikē kinēsis*; but unfortunately the text of the papyrus is very fragmentary at this point.

in the case of soul and body, for cases like wine and water, where the actual distinct properties are clear.[38] Total blending accommodates the point that body and soul have the same relation throughout the extent of the ensouled body, while being unlike in quantity (it being assumed that soul is a finer kind of body than body). But fusion would cope with this point just as well. At most, therefore, the Stoics can say that their account is compatible with common sense and "folk psychology"; it is hardly established by it.

In any case the intuitive level of talking about soul and body is not basic. For soul is *pneuma;* and *pneuma* functions everywhere in the world, but not in the same way; rather it works at different levels of "tension." To understand how the soul works we must look further at these levels.

(d) The Scale of Beings

In the world around us we see items that are nothing more than collections of other separable things, such as armies, flocks, choruses; they are not unified single items. Ships, houses, and the like, whose parts have been put together in a way to stop them separating, are better examples of unified items, but they are still clearly composite; we have one item only because different items have been put together in a more-or-less temporary way. But there is an obvious difference between all of these and things that are "unified" (*henōmena*) or "grown together" (*sumphuē*), because they have an internal principle of unity making them into single items.[39] This is roughly the distinction which Aristotle marks as holding between things which do not, and things which do, have a nature. In Stoic philosophy these are things which are held together

38. Still less, of course, can we demand separation in principle, as with the oiled sponge separating wine and water. Death separates soul and body, but we need a reversible process to give us an analogue to wine and water or other familiar empirical cases.

39. Sext. Emp. *Math.* 9. 78 (= *SVF* 2. 1013); Plut. *Praec. coni.* 34 (= *SVF* 2. 366).

by *pneuma*. They form a hierarchy as the *pneuma* has different degrees of tension, which result in ever more unified functioning. There is a *scala naturae* or scale of things from the less- to the more-unified in functioning, from flocks of sheep at the bottom to living things at the top.[40]

The lowest form of unified functioning is *hexis* (state), found in things like stones which do no more than cohere; in them, unity of functioning comes to no more than holding together. Plants, which grow and reproduce, are held together and made cohesive in their functioning by *phusis* or nature. Animals, which perceive and act, cohere as they do because of *psuchē*, soul, and rational animals (humans and gods) because of *nous*, intelligence. It is obvious that what increases in degree of unification is not the thing itself but its functioning. Thus increase in tension of the *pneuma* is associated not with greater physical cohesiveness and stability, but with increase in the diversity and flexibility of behavior and response, for increase in these respects demands a greater degree of unification as a functioning being. Animals, for example, grow and reproduce, like plants, but they do these things in more complex and flexible ways, perceiving and reacting to the world in ways not available to plants.[41] Rational animals do all these things, but in ways that they are aware of and can articulate in language; and because they can articulate to themselves what they are doing, they are aware of alternatives in ways that animals are not, and can choose between those alternatives. This striking increase in complexity and flexibility is possible because rational beings are in turn more unified as functioning beings

40. For the Stoic *scala naturae* see Philo *Leg. all.* 2. 22–23, *Quod deus* 35–48 (= *SVF* 2. 458), *De aet. mund.* 75; Clem. *Strom.* 2. 487 (= *SVF* 2. 714); [Galen] *Intro.* 697 and 726 (= *SVF* 2. 716); D. L. 7. 138–39 (= *SVF* 2. 634); Plut. *De virt. mor.* 451b (= *SVF* 2. 460); Galen *Ad Iul.* 260K (= *SVF* 2. 718); Cic. *Nat.d.* 2. 33–34, 81–82, 122, *Off.* 2. 11; Origen *De princ.* 3. 1.2–3 (= *SVF* 2. 988); Sen. *Ep.* 102. 5–6 (= *SVF* 3. 160). See Inwood (1985, chap. 2); Long (1982).

41. Hence soul is defined by perception and impulse; cf. Hierocles, col. 4.22–27: "Only nature will be left, instead of soul, if deprived of impulse and perception."

than animals are. It is with rational beings that we find the notion of a unified self, something prominent and crucial in Stoic philosophy of mind.

The Stoic hierarchy recalls Aristotle's hierarchy of kinds of soul; as in Aristotle, higher levels affect and can transform the workings of the lower.[42] The fetus in the womb, in Hierocles' extensive account, has only *phusis*, nature[43]—it is what we would call a human vegetable. Only at birth does it acquire soul, and become not only alive but alive in the way appropriate to a human being. Its now being able to perceive and react transforms its life into the life of something which is more than a plant.

The hierarchy is frequently characterized in terms of the different kinds of movement appropriate to each level, in a way which focuses our attention on what I have called complexity and flexibility. This comes out most explicitly in a passage of Origen:

> Of moving things, some have in themselves the cause of movement, while others are moved only from without. Thus things that are carried are moved only from without, like logs and stones and everything which is matter held together only by state (*hexis*). . . . Living things and plants and, in a word, what is held together by nature (*phusis*) and soul (*psuchē*) have in themselves the cause of moving. . . . Of things with the cause of moving in themselves, some are said to move from (*ek*) themselves, some by (*apo*) themselves; from themselves in the case of things without soul, by themselves in the case of things with soul. Things with soul move by themselves when an ap-

42. But cf. Philo *Leg. all.* 2. 22ff. (= *SVF* 2. 458), which suggests a more "additive" account: we exhibit *hexis* insofar as we contain parts like bones, *phusis* insofar as we contain plantlike parts like hair and nails, and *psuchē* insofar as we perceive and act. Most of the evidence would suggest that our *hexis* is displayed in our having a cohesive bodily structure, and *phusis* in our entire metabolic functioning. On the different levels of soul see the valuable article by Long (1982).

43. Col. 1.1–30.

pearance (*phantasia*) occurs and calls forth an impulse (*hormē*). Now in some animals when appearances occur and call forth impulse it is their nature which deals with appearances (*phusis phantastikē*) in an orderly way and moves the impulse, as when in the spider there is an appearance of web spinning and impulse follows to spin a web; it is its nature which deals with appearances that calls it forth to this in an orderly way, and nothing else in the animal other than this nature dealing with appearances has been convinced. . . . But a rational animal (*logikon zōion*) has reason as well as the nature dealing with appearances, reason which judges the appearances and nullifies some while accepting others, so as to lead the animal in accordance with them. (*De princ.* 3. 1.2–3 [= *SVF* 2. 988])[44]

This passage makes clear that the higher forms of *pneuma* tension are explaining ever more complex and flexible forms of behavior. A plant which grows, blooms, and produces seed is "moving" and changing according to its nature; it is not just being moved by something else, like a stone. A spider spinning its web is acting in ways vastly more complex than the plant; it is receptive to information coming in from its environment, and responds to it. It is sensitive to "appearances" and can cope with and respond to them. Still, there is something mechanical and instinctive about its behavior when compared to that of rational beings who can articulate options to themselves and choose between them, and whose actions are thus not laid down by patterns of instinct, because they can make use of "reason."

Soul, then, is not just *pneuma*, but a specific level of *pneuma*, with the degree of tension required for it to function as *pneuma psuchikon*, the *pneuma* of a soul, unifying a body and enabling it to perceive and act in certain ways. The body with which the soul interacts is not inert matter; it is a body

44. See also *De orat.* 6. 1 (= *SVF* 2. 989). See Inwood (1985, chap. 2), who discusses the relation of these passages to a divergent account in Simplicius (*Comm. in Arist. cat.* 306 [= *SVF* 2. 499]).

already held together and enabled to function in vegetative ways by *pneuma* in the form of *phusis* or nature. So the soul interacts with an already living body, a body functioning in the way appropriate to plants, which are alive. And the living body in turn is unified by nature-*pneuma* holding together, and enabling to function appropriately, an item that is already cohesive, held together by state- or *hexis-pneuma*. We do not get to anything not unified by *pneuma* till we get to the decaying corpse (and even then, as the Stoics remarked, the bones are pretty solid).

This schema has some mildly surprising results. According to the Stoics, growth and what we would call the metabolic functionings are not due to soul, but to nature. In keeping with this they say that plants have nature, but no soul, and that embryos before birth, when they acquire soul, are alive in a merely plantlike way. One striking result of this is that metabolic functioning in a living person is ascribed to the body, not to the soul. Thus not all the characteristic ways a living person functions are due to her soul. Soul is not, as it is in Aristotle, what marks the living from the nonliving. There are some living things (plants) that do not have soul; and not all the functions of living things which are ensouled are due to their soul.

Soul is, rather, what animals and humans share; it is what makes them more than vegetables. It is their perceptive and reactive functions which are due to soul, and, in the case of rational beings, their rational mode of perceiving and reacting. However, the Stoics often use "soul" another way; Sextus says that some Stoics claimed that "soul" had two distinct uses. One of these applies to soul as what animates the whole compound. The other applies to soul as *hēgemonikon* or "governing part." We shall see, in the next section, that it is not too misleading to think of this as the mind, and in this use the Stoics were thinking of the distinctively mental side of human functioning. Sextus adds that this use, for the mind, is what we think of when we use certain phrases which contrast soul and body.[45] Certainly in the later Roman Stoics like Se-

45. Sext. Emp. *Math.* 7. 234. Long (1982) is interesting on the

neca and Marcus Aurelius we find very free use of terminology which draws a sharp, almost Platonic contrast between the mere body and the all-important mind or rational soul.[46] When body and soul are sharply contrasted in this way, it may seem that these writers are lapsing into dualism, or at least dualist ways of talking. This does not follow, for the contrast of body and soul in these passages is ethically motivated, not the outcome of dissatisfaction with physicalism. Nonetheless, it brings out a striking feature of the Stoics' use of "soul."

The Stoics are certainly revising common sense when they narrow the use of "soul" to the mind instead of applying it, as Aristotle does, simply to the whole range of life functions. They are also creating a problem for their own theory. The soul that is totally blended with body is soul in the sense of what unifies the living body as a body of a perceptive and reactive kind. But soul in the narrower sense of the *hēgemonikon* is not this. Rather, as we shall see, the *hēgemonikon* is located in part of the body. And it provides a mechanism which explains why the whole body functions as it does, as a whole body. For both these reasons, it cannot be identified with soul where that refers to what is totally blended in every part of the body; it must be soul in a different sense.

We can appreciate that this problem is quite acute if we recall Cleanthes' argument for the physicality of the soul. That relied on the causal interaction of soul and body. We can now see that in that argument "body" must refer to the total blend of soul and body, while "soul" refers to the *hēgemonikon*. For

---

two uses of "soul" and the kind of contrast that is made when the soul is thought of as the mind.

46. Seneca uses very violent metaphors: the body is a clog on or prison of the soul (e.g., *Ep.* 65. 16, 25ff.); the soul longs to escape (e.g., *Ep.* 78. 10 and 79. 11–12); the separation of soul from body is a birth from a foul and stinking womb (*Ep.* 102. 27–28). Marcus is not consistent; sometimes he talks as though we should identify with the pure reason in us, which is distinct from both body and soul (cf. 3. 16: body/soul/*nous* and 12. 3: body/*pneuma*/*nous*). But sometimes *hēgemonikon* replaces *nous* (2. 2); sometimes soul includes thinking. See Bonhoeffer (1890, 30–37); Pohlenz (1970, 1: 342–44 and 2: 168).

soul in the sense of what is totally blended with the body cannot possibly be what causally interacts with body; the notion
of total blending rules that out. So it is not simply that the
Stoics have their own technical notion of soul (what is totally
blended with the body) and also fall into an intuitive way of
speaking from time to time, which contrasts soul with body.
For the purposes of their own arguments they *need* a notion
of soul which contrasts with that of body, and thus are forced
into using "soul" in two ways, one for the mind and one for
what is totally blended with the living body to produce what
we intuitively call "body."

It might be objected that there is no real problem here,
since no important Stoic arguments rest on using the notion
of "soul" ambivalently. However, the problem underlines the
magnitude of the step the Stoics took when they moved from
using "soul" not just for what distinguishes the functioning of
perceptive and reactive beings, but also for what distinguishes
the things with minds from the rest of nature. It is a bigger
step than they were perhaps fully aware of.

e) Soul and Self

We have seen that the unity of functioning is important for
the Stoics in the case of both the animal and the human soul.
Indeed theirs is the first philosophy of mind which stresses
what we would call the unity of the self.[47] As well as its role
in their accounts of perceiving and other psychological phenomena, Stoic concern with the self emerges in an explicit
discussion of a topic relevant to the Stoics' moral philosophy;
for they hold that moral development takes off from a natural
basis in all of us, which they hold to be a concern with the
self based on knowledge of the self. According to Chrysippus
the first object of affinity or familiarization that a human has—

47. See Long (1991) for an account that stresses this and links
it with the Stoics' account of appearances in perceiving and thinking.

that is, the first thing which it has direct motivation to pursue—is its own constitution and the self-knowledge it has of it.[48] Cicero repeats the point: as soon as we are born we seek what is familiar to us, and this presupposes that we care for our own constitution, which in turn presupposes that we have a sense or perception of ourselves.[49]

From birth on, then, we have self-perception. What exactly is it, however, that we confidently ascribe to newborns? We have a fairly extensive account of self-perception from Hierocles' *Elements of Ethics,* containing several arguments to show that we have it continuously from birth. We can hope, then, that by looking at the arguments, and the rest of Hierocles' account, we can glean more accurate information about what self-perception is.[50]

The first argument appeals to animals' and humans' behavior.[51] We just know that our eyes are for seeing and our legs for walking; we do not have to experiment and find out facts like these by trial and error. Indeed, the idea that I might have to find out, by trying and failing to see with my ears, that I see with my eyes is ludicrous. And this shows that there are some things that we know about ourselves just by being ourselves; an animal perceives itself as being the kind of animal it is, functioning the way it does. Some animals' behavior patterns are bizarre, and Hierocles gives us many examples, appealing to "well-known facts" such as the "facts" that some

48. D. L. 7. 85 (= *SVF* 3. 178). *Suneidēsis* ([self]-knowledge) has been suspected; Cicero and Seneca talk of *sensus sui*, Hierocles of self-*perception*. See, however, Cancrini (1970), who corrects Zucker (1928): *suneidenai* is used by both Aristotle and Xenophon of animals, and its original meaning is just that of what one alone or best knows oneself. It seems best, then, not to tamper with the text. This will then be the second surviving use of the noun, the first being Democritus frag. B297 DK.

49. *Fin.* 3. 16 (= *SVF* 3. 182); cf. Sen. *Ep.* 121.

50. See Inwood (1984), who discusses Hierocles' extensive use of examples and the point that Hierocles is unusual in laying so much stress on perception, at the expense of the soul's other defining characteristic, impulse (col. 1.31–37).

51. Cols. 1.51–3.52.

snakes spit their venom without having to bite their victim and that beavers, when being pursued by hunters who want to kill them for the oil in their testicles, will castrate themselves in order to survive. The point of appealing to unusual, rather than commonplace, behavior is to underline the point that however exotic the response, the animal never has to learn it; it already knows how to behave like the kind of animal it is. Hierocles goes on to argue, again from the best explanation of behavior, that self-perception is continuous through life and that it starts from birth.[52] Apart from animals, his prime examples are the ways humans behave in characteristic and goal-directed ways during sleep (cols. 4.53–5.30).[53]

He has three more technical arguments to show that all perception is what he calls self-perception. One is that perceiving an object, however minimally, involves perception of oneself;[54] tasting something sweet, for example, involves awareness that "I am sweetened." All perceiving has a subject as well as an object; mentioning only the object leaves out part of what perceiving is. Thus all perceiving presupposes self-perception. This is a highly interesting point; Kant was later to produce a far more elaborate argument for this conclusion.

The second argument is more battling: all "dominant powers" (*hēgemonikai dunameis*) apply first to themselves.[55] The *hexis* of a stone has to make itself cohesive to make the stone cohesive; the *phusis* of a plant has to make itself grow before it makes the plant grow; the soul which makes an animal perceive objects must first make itself perceptive of itself. The argument seems obviously fallacious; and in any case it is the animal, not its soul, which is supposed to perceive itself.

52. Cols. 3.54–56, 5.35–52.
53. Cols. 4.53–5.30.
54. Cols. 5.60–6.10. He uses terms like "we are whitened," "we are sweetened," which must recall the Cyrenaic account of perception, which makes it minimally interpretative. See Glidden (1974) and McKirahan (1992).
55. Col. 6.10–22.

The third argument, unfortunately fragmentary in part, goes as follows: soul and body are both bodies and interact throughout, being totally blended.[56] Soul is a perceptive power; thus there is a constant two-way "grasp" of soul by body and body by soul. However, it is hard to see how this can amount to an animal's perceiving itself. It would seem to amount to the claim that we are always aware of every part of our body and our soul—a claim either strikingly false or very unclear.

Although his more technical arguments fail to establish it, Hierocles' use of examples and the explanation he offers for them do much to establish his conclusion, that perception, in both animals and humans, presupposes self-perception, and that perceiving beings are capable of self-perception continuously and from birth. What exactly does Hierocles mean, in modern terms? Clearly not consciousness, if that is taken to be or involve an experience or awareness of oneself. That seems ruled out by his range of examples, which focus on animals rather than on human experience. He seems to mean that an animal has, prior to experience (coded into it, as we might say), a conception of itself, understood as a conception of being a kind of animal, plus a reflexive capacity to grasp that *it* is that kind of animal. Only in humans, however, is this articulated in thought.

If this is right, then to understand a snake's peculiar behavior when it is, say, spitting poison, we have to say that something is going on in it which we have to represent as something like "I'm a spitting snake, so I'll spit the poison; I don't need to bite." However, the *snake* is not thinking this: it just acts because of the way its nature is formed. Only humans can articulate such thoughts; so we are not attributing self-awareness to the snake. We are reminded of Chrysippus' reaction to the behavior of a dog which sniffs its prey

56. Cols. 3.56–4.53. Unfortunately, the text is defective where Hierocles is discussing the *tonikē kinēsis* whereby soul-*pneuma* unifies the living body and makes it perceptive.

down two roads and then sets off, without sniffing, down the only other available road. Chrysippus claimed that what was going on in the dog must have the form of "Either p or q or r; but not p and not q, therefore r"; for only so can we explain the remarkable fact that the dog goes off down the third road without needing to sniff, having worked out that the third road is the only possible route. However, Chrysippus was adamant that the dog was not thinking "Either p or q" and so on. Rather, something was going on in the dog, and driving its behavior, which in a human would be something which the human could think.[57] Similarly, the point that animals have unified selves (or, as we might better put it, are unified selves) does not imply that they are like rational humans in being aware of being unified selves.

This line of thought about self-perception is an interesting one. It seems open to the obvious objection that sufficiently complex and characteristic *plant* behavior seems to demand self-perception to explain it. It is clear that the Stoics would not have accepted the consequence that something is going on in a plant which we have to represent as "I'm a rose, so I'll bloom now" or the like; but it is not clear how they would have met the objection. The absurdity of having a rose think that it is a rose is irrelevant, since the Stoics do not hold that a snake or a beaver is thinking that it is a snake or a beaver. Are there any differences of principle between plants and animals to which the Stoics could appeal to give them independent support for rejecting the extension of self-perception to plants? Perhaps it could be held that plant behavior, while often extremely complex and sensitive to different conditions, falls short of the kind of complexity that requires self-perception to explain it. Plants cannot *learn*, for example; their entire behavioral repertoire is programmed into them. If something like this could supply a plausible line of demarcation, the Stoics would be left with a viable

57. For the example see Sext. Emp. *Pyr.* 1. 69, and for discussion of it and Philo's response in *On Animals* see Annas and Barnes (1985, 46–48).

claim. Of course some animals—social insects, for example—seem more like plants in this respect than like other kinds of animals. But if so, this would be grounds for denying them self-perception.

f) Parts and Faculties of the Soul

We have seen that for the Stoics there is a sense in which soul is what is totally blended with the body; but there is also another sense in which it can be contrasted with the body, a sense in which it refers to the mechanism which is causally responsible for the functionings of a human being. In this sense the soul is localized; it is a centralized system which is responsible for the differentiated functioning of the senses—and, the Stoics add, voice and reproduction, taking these to be distinct functions. Hence the soul itself is said to have eight parts: the five senses (sight, hearing, touch, taste, smell), voice, reproduction, and the *hēgemonikon* or "governing part."[58] We have an extensive passage from Chrysippus that supports this:

> The soul is *pneuma* connate with us, extending as a continuum through the whole body as long as the free-flowing breath of life is present in the body. Now of the parts of the soul that have been assigned to the several parts [of the body], that of them which extends to the trachea is the voice; that to the eyes, sight; that to the ears, hearing; that to the nostrils, smell; that to the tongue, taste; that to the entire flesh, touch; and that which extends to the testicles, possessing another such *logos*, is seminal. That part where all these meet is in the heart, being the governing part (*hēgemonikon*) of the soul. This being so, there is agreement about all other parts, but about the governing part of the soul there is disagreement, some placing it in one region, others in another. . . . Thus the place seems to elude us,

58. See, for example, D. L. 7. 110 (= *SVF* 2. 828). Panaetius

since we have neither a clear perception [of it], as we had with the others, nor sure signs from which this matter might be inferred; otherwise disagreements among physicians and philosophers would not have grown so great. (Galen *PHP* 287–89K, 170 de Lacy)[59]

The parts do not differ in composition; the soul is all just *pneuma*. They differ in location; each extends (*diēkein*) through a different part of the body. They also differ in function; since the tongue can both taste and touch, we infer that both touch- and taste-*pneuma* extend through it. But the Stoics make little of distinctness of function as opposed to distinctness of location.

The *hēgemonikon* centralizes the senses and other functions, like an octopus whose tentacles are the extensions of *pneuma* to the senses, or a spider sitting in the middle of its web, sensitive to every change in it.[60] What happens in the sense organs is "transmitted" (*diadidonai*) to the *hēgemonikon* and recorded there; the Stoics "intend this, that the movement aroused in a member by a contact from without be transmitted to the seat of the soul's rule, so that the animal may perceive it."[61] Thus they come to say that the sense organs are affected, or even that the pain is there, but that the *perception* of the pain happens in the *hēgemonikon*.[62]

Although we have seen that the Stoics rejected the most recent and correct account of the matter, we can clearly see the influence of a model quite unavailable to Aristotle, that of the nervous system. When a sense organ is disturbed, the part of the soul appropriate to that organ transmits the message (visual for the eyes, olfactory for the nose, and so forth) to the soul's centralizing organ. Once we accept *pneuma* as

---

rejected voice and reproduction as separate parts (frag. 86), reducing the soul's eight parts to six.

59. Trans. de Lacy.

60. Aët. *Plac.* 4. 21 (= *SVF* 2. 836); Calcidius *Ad Tim.* 220 (= *SVF* 2. 879).

61. Galen *PHP* 247K, 134 de Lacy; trans. de Lacy.

62. Aët. *Plac.* 4. 23.1 (= *SVF* 2. 834); Plotinus *Enn.* 4. 7. 7 (= *SVF* 2. 858).

the transmitting mechanism and the heart, rather than the brain, as the center, the model is easy to transpose into modern terms.

The influence of the model is profound, as can be seen in at least three ways. Firstly, we have seen that when the Stoics distinguish two senses of "soul," they tend to take the second, more restricted one to refer not to the entire mechanism of the eight-part soul, but just to the *hēgemonikon*. Clearly, they tend to think that the soul *is*, properly speaking, the *hēgemonikon;* and we can see why they think this, since it is there that what happens in the rest of the soul is registered. The rest of the soul, its remaining parts, comes to look like extra links in a causal chain beginning with the body. Plutarch complains that the Stoics cram all the events of our psychological life into the tiny space of the *hēgemonikon;* this has some analogies with modern objections to taking all our mental life to occur in the brain.

Secondly, Stoic philosophy of mind is deeply influenced by the thought that the soul is a communication mechanism. If the *hēgemonikon* receives input from all the other parts, registers, unifies, and makes sense of it, then it will at once seem obvious that what it receives are messages, that it transmits information, that it operates in a language common to all the senses, and so on. This thought does not remain at the level of metaphor. The Stoics' detailed accounts of perception and action are explained in terms of the reception and interpretation of articulable content. Content is dominant in Stoic philosophy of mind, and one reason for this is that their basic model of the mind is one which encourages them to focus on the content of experience rather than on its phenomenological qualities. This is perhaps the most distinctive and original feature of Stoic philosophy of mind; its distance in this respect from Aristotle can to some extent be explained by the differences between their underlying models.

Thirdly, the Stoics stress the unity of the soul far more than Aristotle does; again we can see an underlying model which facilitates and encourages this. Beings capable of per-

ceiving and reacting are unified selves; and there are many
ways in which the accounts of perceiving and acting rely on
there being a unified self which does the perceiving and
acting. Animals as well as humans are selves;[63] an animal's
hēgemonikon, however, will unify its psychological events in
a merely automatic and instinctual way. Because humans are
rational, everything in a human *hēgemonikon* will be organized and interpreted in a rational way. For the Stoics the
hallmark of rationality is the ability to use language, and
hence we find that the human *hēgemonikon* functions
throughout in terms of a kind of language; human, but not
animal, experience is seen in terms of communication and
content. Hence there is a division of kind between animal
and human inner life. And hence the Stoics denied to animals not only reasoning but emotions and even desires;
since animals cannot articulate and interpret in language the
content of their experience, they have only quasi forms of
what in humans are desires, emotions, and so on.

Given these points, the *hēgemonikon* can be thought of,
not too misleadingly, as the mind, and the Stoic theory of
the soul as a theory of our mental life. As such a theory, it
is strikingly un-Cartesian; the Stoics show no interest in the
kinds of concern which led Descartes to his conclusions
about the mind. The contents of the *hēgemonikon* are not
taken to be accessible to introspection by privileged inner
view; nor are they epistemologically basic, nor in any interesting sense private. But the *hēgemonikon* is very like a non-
Cartesian mind: it centralizes, unifies, and interprets what
goes on in the rest of the soul. Even the intellectual associ-
ations of mind as opposed to soul attach to the *hēgemonikon*;
in careless accounts it is sometimes referred to as the *dianoia*, a standard word for "thought."

63. Cf. Arius Didymus *Epit. phys.* frag. 39 Diels (= *SVF* 2. 821):
every soul has a kind of *hēgemonikon* in it, which is life, perception,
and impulse.

As well as parts, the soul has faculties or powers (*duna-meis*). The Stoics define a *dunamis* as what brings about many events and controls the subordinate activities.[64] A *dunamis* of the soul will be a power or disposition to produce mental events. Some scholars have thought that the Stoics cannot really have thought that the soul contained permanently differentiated powers; for they think that only physical particulars exist, and hence it is thought that they would have had difficulties over the existence of dispositional powers.[65] This has led to the ascription to them of the strange view that there are no lasting differentiations in the soul; rather they are left, on this account, with a soul which is uniform and changes with every mental event without ever acquiring long-term differentiations. But we have no good reason to land them with this view. Since they are physicalists, they can simply take reference to dispositional powers to be in effect reference to the underlying differentiated structures, since that is what these powers in fact are.

Zeno and Chrysippus, we are told, put the soul's powers together like qualities in a subject, positing the soul as a substance existing before the powers.[66] In other words, some of the soul's powers belong to it the way qualities belong to a subject. Thus some Stoic powers or faculties can be distinguished by the fact that they belong to different subjects. Thus the powers of sight-*pneuma* will differ from those of hearing-*pneuma*, since the latter is a different subject, being

64. Simpl. *Comm. in Arist. cat.* 224 (= *SVF* 3. 203). See Inwood (1985, chap. 2).

65. Bonhoeffer (1890, 94–112) has a sensible discussion that has unaccountably been ignored until recently. Inwood (1985, chap. 2) gives the best modern account and discusses the controversy between Pohlenz (1965a esp.) and Philippson (1937), together with Voelke's (1965, 1973) revival of Pohlenz's view.

66. Iambl. *De an.* apud Stob. *Ecl.* 1. 367–69 Wachsmuth (relevant parts of which = *SVF* 2. 826 and 831). Iamblichus may be importing Aristotelian ideas in talking of subject and qualities, but his account is still valuable.

a physically distinct stretch of *pneuma*. This will serve to distinguish dispositional powers whose subjects can be distinguished, for example, by different location. However, other powers have the same underlying subject and differ only in their "individual quality" (*idiotēs poiotētos*); and this, of course, will be true of the important case of the *hēgemonikon*, "for, just as the apple has in the same body its sweetness and its scent, so the *hēgemonikon* has put together in the same [body] appearance (*phantasia*), assent (*sunkatathesis*), impulse (*hormē*), and reason (*logos*)."[67] We hear elsewhere of the "rational state" (*hexis logikē*) and the "impulse state" (*hexis hormetikē*).[68] The functioning of the mind, or *hēgemonikon*, can thus be classified as the manifestation of four different powers. Appearance is manifested in our reception of information through the senses (what we receive is itself called appearance). Assent is manifested in our interpretation of the information we receive. Impulse is manifested in our acting on it. Reason is manifested in the fact that humans do all these things in a rational way, one that is articulable in language.

Why, in that case, is it distinguished here as a power separate from the other three? Perhaps the point is that although we all have it, we need to develop it into a mature disposition. Although rationality underlies and informs all our mental life, it is still a disposition which is developed from experience and from what we learn to do with experience. It

67. Iambl. *De an.* apud Stob. *Ecl.* 1. 367–69. The apple as an example of one object with several qualities turns up in disconcertingly many philosophical schools. It is common in the Aristotelian commentators, deriving apparently from Alexander *De an.* 31. 4–5. But Sextus ascribes it to Pythagoreans (*Math.* 7. 103), and the sceptics used it; it found its way into Aenesidemus' Third Mode, and so turns up in Sextus (*Pyr.* 1. 94–97) and in a very confused form in D. L. 9. 81. Macrobius (*Sat.* 7. 14.20–30) discusses it in the context of Academic scepticism. Why the apple became a standard example, and what its use here would suggest, we cannot say.

68. Simpl. *Comm. in Arist. cat.* 102 (= *SVF* 3. 238); cf. Philo *Leg. all.* 3. 210 (= *SVF* 3. 512); Arius Didymus apud Stob. *Ecl.* 2. 87.11.

does not automatically accompany the exercise of the other powers in the way in which it ought to do. This points to an interesting difference between reason and the other powers: reason is a power that we can *improve*. Further, our only way of improving the other powers is by improving our reason.[69]

Both ancient and modern critics have accused the Stoics of "rationalism" about the soul; they have been supposed to have too simple a view of the soul, one in which the soul is wholly rational. It is true that reason is important in the Stoic soul; but its role should not be misunderstood. The soul's composition is simple; it is just *pneuma*. But this does not prevent it from having eight parts, including the centralizing *hēgemonikon;* and this functions in four distinct ways which each manifest a different power of the soul, of which reason is only one.[70] We shall find the Stoics saying, particularly in connection with the emotions, that the soul contains no element that can oppose reason. What they mean is not in any opposition to any of the above, and it is not the thesis that reason is a particularly strong and bullying element in the soul which represses any opposition. Rather, reason is not separable; it is involved in every activity of a human soul. Since rationality is manifested in language use, this thesis that the entire soul is rational, that is, that every mental event is rational, takes the form of a thesis that every mental event involves some analogue to the use of language.[71] We shall see this in detail in the following chapter.

That reason is involved in every mental event is, for the Stoics, among other things a truth about the workings of *pneuma*. Reason is *pneuma* at a higher degree of tension

69. Chrysippus in *On Reason* defined reason as "a collection of concepts and preconceptions (*ennoiai* and *prolēpseis*)" (Galen *PHP* 445K, 304 de Lacy [= *SVF* 2. 841]). That is, it has to be built up as an ever more solid and coherent grasp of experience.

70. Cf. Chrysippus in Galen *PHP* 445K, 306 de Lacy (= *SVF* 2. 841).

71. Of course problems remain as to how this lines up with our intuitive understanding of "rational"; see pp. 105–6.

than the rest of soul-*pneuma;* consistently with the rest of
the physical theory, this will make the soul physically more
cohesive. Thus not only will the soul be more cohesive than
the physical body, the rational soul will be more cohesive
than nonrational soul-*pneuma.* And since what is more cohesive is less easily destructible, we can understand why it
became orthodox Stoic doctrine that the soul will survive
the person's death, the more rationally developed souls lasting longest.[72] Cleanthes believed that all souls will survive
death; Chrysippus, only those of the wise.[73] This seems to be
a disagreement over the necessary degree of pneumatic tension. This thesis is clearly a minor and somewhat bizarre by-
product of the physical theory and has no ethical repercus-
sions. Souls last longer than bodies, but they are not immortal. And what survives is not the individual personality; death
is the end of me, and though something survives, it is not
continuous with me and will not be rewarded or punished
for what I have done.[74] Chrysippus is even said to have
taught that postmortem souls were spherical.[75] Partly no
doubt this is because since Plato circular motion had been
thought the most appropriate for reason; but a role is also
probably played by the fact that I cannot seriously think that
my mental life will be continuous with processes in a pneumatic balloon, which is what my soul will be after my death.

We have seen that much of the Stoic theory of the soul is
influenced by contemporary medicine, particularly the dis-

72. See Hoven (1971) for the evidence; also Bonhoeffer (1890,
54–67). Sextus (*Math.* 9. 71–74) retails a fanciful Stoic belief, of
uncertain date, that after death souls will collect in the region
nearest to the moon, presumably the appropriate place for items
with just their degree of pneumatic tension.
73. D. L. 7. 157 (= *SVF* 2. 811).
74. See Hoven (1971, 76–78): there is one passage which does
explicitly ascribe teaching about afterlife rewards and punishments
to Zeno—Lactant. *Div. inst.* 7. 7.113 (= *SVF* 1. 147). But the rest of
the evidence is so heavily against this that it is best to suppose
either that Lactantius is flatly mistaken or that Zeno was really
allegorizing popular beliefs.
75. Schol. in *Iliad.* 23. 65 (= *SVF* 2. 815).

covery of the nervous system. The Stoics made, however, one rather large concession to folk psychology. They did not follow Erasistratus in locating the *hēgemonikon* in the brain. Instead we find that Chrysippus wrote at length defending the view that the *hēgemonikon* is located in the heart, reverting to the earlier and cruder view which is found in Praxagoras.[76] Like Galen, who criticizes Chrysippus extensively, we may be puzzled by this rejection of science in favor of arguments from intuition, etymology, and even poetry.[77]

However, Chrysippus' problem is clear enough. Folk psychology and ordinary talk about the soul places emotions and feelings clearly in the heart; when affected by fear or other emotions, that seems to be where we feel things happening. To maintain that fear, for example, was really being felt in the brain would sound odd; we do not feel afraid in the head. But the Stoic view of the soul, as we have seen, makes every mental event involve a rational, articulable element, something transmitted to the *hēgemonikon* and interpreted there. If the *hēgemonikon* is in the head, this would suggest that, in ancient terms, the soul could be divided; fear could be felt in one location, but the information instigating the fear would be registered somewhere else. This would threaten the Stoics' whole view of the soul, in which every

76. Galen *PHP* 185K, 78 de Lacy.
77. The arguments are uniformly unimpressive to those no longer sharing the same commonsense views: when we say *"egō"* ("I") the long last syllable inclines us to nod down toward the chest (*PHP* 215K, 104ff. de Lacy); articulate speech, and therefore reasoning, comes up from the heart, not down from the head (*PHP* 279K, 162 de Lacy); the poets' words suggest that emotions and feelings are in the heart (*PHP* 314K, 194 de Lacy; cf. 293K, 174 de Lacy); etymology suggests it (*PHP* 328–29K, 206 de Lacy); the myth of Athena can be accommodated to it (*PHP* 348K, 222 de Lacy). The main appeal is to intuition and received consensus (cf. *PHP* 310K, 192 de Lacy). (The extensive quotations from Chrysippus are collected by von Arnim as *SVF* 2. 879–911.) Zeno had certainly thought that all the soul's activities are in the heart (*PHP* 294K, 176 de Lacy), but piety to the forebear cannot wholly explain this point; on other issues Chrysippus was ready enough to bring the theory scientifically up-to-date.

mental event involves the registering of information. Hence Chrysippus has no real choice; though from the passage above it is clear that he was uncertain and not very happy on this point, he had to follow folk psychology and interpret the doctors' discoveries to suit; the brain clearly plays a role, but it has to be a subordinate one.[78]

It can certainly be argued that Chrysippus should not have been so impressed by the emotions in this regard. The Stoics hold, after all, that the pain I feel in my foot is not really in my foot, but in the *hēgemonikon*, although it is certainly obvious to common sense that if I feel it anywhere, it has to be in my foot. Why not give a similar account of the fact that fear, elation, and so on are felt in the heart? We could feel fear and other emotions in the heart, and yet it could be true that what is felt in the heart is just the experience which is registered in the *hēgemonikon*. If the Stoics had been prepared to give an account of the emotions uniform with their account of pain, they could have argued that the *hēgemonikon* was in the head, even though fear is felt in the heart. It is not clear why Chrysippus found common sense so much more compelling where the emotions are concerned.[79]

However, we should not be too ready to follow ancient critics in regarding Chrysippus' move as merely retrograde science. Rather, he is interpreting limited scientific discoveries in the light of a philosophical theory about the soul and making the assumption, generally unquestioned, that common sense forms a constraint against extensive revisions of our views about what the soul is.

78. *PHP* 254–55K, 140 de Lacy. However, later we find Diogenes of Babylon trying to combat some Stoics who did think that the *hēgemonikon* was in the head (Philodemus *On Piety* 15 [= *SVF* 3. s.v. Diogenes 33]). We do not know how they proposed to deal with the problems this raises for Stoic theory.
79. I owe this point to Rob Cummins.

3

Perceiving and Thinking

a) Perceiving

Perception and impulse define soul, which marks off animals and humans from plants. The Stoics have extensive accounts of both the way we perceive, and the way we react to, the world around us. A perception is, as we would expect, a physical event. But it is one which crucially involves thought and language; the Stoic theory, though in some ways undeveloped, is the most interesting ancient account of perception, and the one which most systematically explores the aspect of perception that we call content.[1]

"Perception (*aisthēsis*) is said by the Stoics to be (1) the *pneuma* extending (*diēkon*) to the senses (*aisthēseis*), (2) the apprehension through them, (3) the makeup of the sense organs, in which some people are defective."[2] Thus "perception"

---

1. Though it does not fit into any ancient philosophical niche (which is perhaps the reason for its comparative lack of development), the evidence for it is unhandily divided between "physics" and "logic" (Diogenes Laertius' account of the physical process turns up under both "physics" and "logic" [7. 52, 55, and 157] and the account of content comes elsewhere under "logic"). For the relevant texts, see Long and Sedley (1987, 33, 34, 39, 40, 41).

2. D. L. 7. 52.

is used of the entire physical process, including the bodily parts involved. The workings of the senses have a uniform explanation in terms of *pneuma:* the way in which "body affects body" in the case of the soul has to be by pneumatic tension. Hence there can be little to say about the differences between the senses, except that pneumatic tension takes a phenomenologically different form. Sometimes complications are required—with the distance senses, for example, since *pneuma*, being body, has to function by contact. With hearing, the *pneuma* in the ears makes contact with the disturbance in the air caused by the sounding object. But sight is harder, for it is counterintuitive to suppose that objects disturb the air just by being seen. The solution is that the seeing-*pneuma* in the eye makes an object visible by "tensing" the air-*pneuma* into a kind of illuminated cone with the object at base and eye at apex; the tension of this air is experienced as sight.[3] The problem with this kind of solution is not just that it is wildly wrong; all ancient theories are far off the mark, at least where seeing is concerned. The problem is rather that we see how fatally easy it is to adapt *pneuma* to theoretical need, when there is little or no empirical constraint on explaining diverse phenomena by diverse workings of *pneuma*.

A perception is more than a physical event—it is experienced by the perceiver as something with *content*. When discussing perception from this point of view, rather than just giving the physical *pneuma* story, the Stoics separate the two stages of appearance (*phantasia*) and assent (*sunkatathesis*). These are themselves, of course, both physical events. An appearance is the way something appears to someone. The notion is not limited to perceptual appearances, but the Stoics in fact think that all appearances are appearances to our senses, even though this does not limit them to providing information solely about what is available to the senses. When an object strikes a perceiver in some way—visually, tactually, or whatever—the perceiver receives an appearance. The result

3. See Ingenkamp (1971); Hahm (1978).

is an "imprint" (*tupōsis*) in the soul. "Imprint" is a metaphor from stamping a seal, and the early Stoics understood this in different ways:

> Cleanthes understood the imprint in terms of recess and projection, just like the imprint of seals on wax, but Chrysippus thought such a thing absurd; for firstly, he says, when the mind is presented with (*phantasioumenēs*) a triangular and a square thing on one occasion, then the same body will at one and the same time have round it triangular and square shapes simultaneously—or even circular—which is absurd. Also when several appearances come about in us simultaneously the soul will contain far too many shapes, which is even worse. So he himself supposed that "imprint" was used by Zeno in place of "alteration," so that the definition is like this: "An appearance is an alteration of the soul"; so we no longer get the absurdity of the same body's receiving far too many alterations at one and the same time when many appearances come together in us; for just as the air receives countlessly many different blows together when many people are talking at once, and immediately sustains many alterations, so the *hēgemonikon* will undergo something analogous to this when it receives various presentations (*poikilōs phantasioumenon*). (Sext. Emp. *Math.* 7. 228–31 [= *SVF* 2. 56])

Appearances are representations; perception is a process whereby things are represented to the agent in various phenomenologically different modes. The Stoics stress this aspect of perception far more than does Aristotle, who also lays much less emphasis than they do on the functional unity of the agent to whom things are represented by the various senses.[4] The emphasis of the theory seems to change with Chrysippus, judg-

4. In some passages of the *Parva naturalia* Aristotle seems to be talking about perceiving in a way that makes it representative, but this aspect is absent from his standard account of normal perceiving in the *De anima*. As has frequently been noticed, the *Parva naturalia* lays much more stress on the unity of the perceiving agent than the *De anima* does.

ing from the above passage. Zeno and Cleanthes appear to have understood the representative nature of appearances in a way that has perenially been found tempting: an appearance to a perceiver of a round thing, say, is itself in some way round in form. Chrysippus saw that this can lead to absurdities, and produced a theory in which the mind is affected by appearances, but in a way which involves the reception and articulation of information in linguistic form, rather than involving images or anything similar in structure to the thing represented.

How radical is Chrysippus' change to the earlier theory? It is easy to think of Zeno and Cleanthes producing a classically bad kind of theory, one which purports to explain how the agent perceives, say, a round thing by getting something round—the representation—into the perceiver. In a crude form, this kind of account clearly makes no progress, since the round item inside the perceiver still requires interpretation and understanding as much as the round item outside the perceiver. However, it is uncertain just what Zeno and Cleanthes thought was the relation between representation and the perceiver's response,[5] and possibly they had something more sophisticated in mind. It may have been that they thought of the imprint as something conveying the form or structure of the thing perceived, and producing perception by way of that structure. We have no idea of the detail that they would have required to spell out this idea in any plausible kind of way, but it is not in principle a bad idea to think that a representation functions by being in some way like in structure to what it represents. This is in no way incompatible with the idea that the information conveyed could be spelled out in linguistic form. And so Chrysippus may well have complicated, rather than replaced, his predecessors' theory. At any rate from Chrysippus onward what was found most striking about the theory was the extent to which it analyzed perception in terms of the

5. And Sextus, our source here, has no motivation to make any version of the theory sound plausible. In this paragraph I am indebted to Rob Cummins.

reception of content and its articulation in linguistic form. But this does not exclude the thought that a perceptual appearance represents its object in a way which is like it in form. Indeed, some such approach offers a good chance of doing justice to the kinds of phenomenological difference that there are between the senses.

Assent is an event in the soul also, in which the soul reacts rather than just being affected. About this we have only metaphor from Zeno. He would hold out his hand and compare the outstretched hand to appearance; closing the fingers a little he compared to assent.[6]

But as well as being physical events, appearance and assent involve what I have called content, which the Stoics explain in terms of reason: "Of appearances, some are rational (*logikai*) and some nonrational (*alogoi*): rational are those of rational animals, nonrational, of animals that are nonrational. The rational ones are thoughts (*noēseis*), the nonrational ones have no name."[7] In humans, rational animals, reason is involved in every mental event; this is explained in the case of perception by saying that our appearances, the way things strike us perceptually, are actually thoughts. Perceiving is thinking, not the reception of raw data. Perceiving and thinking are not separate faculties; for humans there is no way of taking in information about the world that does not involve thinking.

This is further explicated by the association of rationality and thinking with the use of language. An appearance is rational, or is a thought, because it in some way contains or realizes content which can be articulated in language: "The appearance leads the way, and then thinking, which can express itself in language (*eklaletikē*), puts forward in language what the effect produced by the appearance is."[8] We can express this by saying that for humans their appearances have

6. Cic. *Varro* 145 (= *SVF* 1. 66). See Arthur (1983). Assent is a weak state, stronger ones being apprehension and knowledge; on these further stages see Frede (1984); Annas (1990).
7. D. L. 7. 51 (= *SVF* 2. 61).
8. D. L. 7. 49 (= *SVF* 2. 52).

content, which can be articulated in language. We could call this content propositional content, since it is expressed in a proposition or "sayable," a *lekton*.

"A *lekton* subsists in a way corresponding to a rational appearance, and a rational appearance is one where one can establish in language the object of the appearance."[9] A sayable or *lektor* is what is expressed or meant in an utterance; it is "what is said" when someone uses language, in a broad use of "saying" which covers not only statements but prayers, commands, wishes, and more. (Strictly, this is a complete *lekton*; there are also incomplete *lekta* corresponding to parts of utterances, notably predicates, which will be considered in the chapter on action. In this section, *lekton* is used for a complete *lekton*.)[10] A *lekton* is incorporeal and thus is not to be identified with any thoughts or with any of what goes on in one's head when one says something. It is in some ways tempting to identify *lekta* with meanings and to take complete *lekta* to be propositions, where propositions are thought of as the meanings of sentences.[11] However, *lekta* have some properties which propositions, taken as the meanings of sentences, do not usually have. They are tensed; they can change their truth value, and they can "perish" or go out of existence. Thus they are not to be identified with what is meant by a sentence where that is thought of as being timelessly true. On the other hand, they cannot be identified with what is meant on a particular occasion; otherwise they could not change their truth value.[12] In this context what is most important about *lekta* is that they are what is conveyed in language, and are not to be identified either with the language itself or with the thing or state of affairs referred to:

9. Sext. Emp. *Math.* 8. 70 (= *SVF* 2. 187).
10. See Long and Sedley (1987, 33) for passages on *lekta*.
11. Another reason for thinking of them as propositions is that *lekta* expressed in statements that have a truth value are said to be the truth bearers, another role for which propositions have been cast.
12. On this aspect of *lekta* see particularly Frede (1974, 2. A).

The thing signifying is the utterance, "Dion," for example; the thing signified [the *lekton*] is the actual thing shown by it, which we grasp as it subsists for our thought, and which foreigners do not understand although they hear the utterance; the referent is the external object, for example, Dion himself. (Sext. Emp. *Math.* 8. 12 [= *SVF* 2. 166])

Lekta are conveyed in language; in our minds they are conveyed in a language of thought.

Perception in humans involves *lekta*, since it involves receiving an appearance which is a rational appearance, one containing propositional content, and also involves assent to the *lekton* expressing the content of that appearance. Perception, in other words, may be an experience with a certain kind of phenomenological feel, but more importantly it is reception of and commitment to information about what is perceived. In perception, only one kind of *lekton* is involved, namely, statements or *axiōmata;* for perception involves assent to something's being the case, not to a wish or a prayer or an imperative that it be the case.[13] And *axiōmata* or statements are *lekta* which are true or false, as opposed to commands, prayers, and so on.[14] Thus in a perception there is an appearance which contains or realizes content, and an assent in the person's soul to a statement which articulates this content. Perception is a taking in of, and recognition of, information; to have a perception is to assent to the truth of a statement which is true or false, and thus to have a corresponding belief.[15]

13. Stob. *Ecl.* 2. 88.2–6, esp. 4.
14. Sext. Emp. *Math.* 8. 12 (= *SVF* 2. 166). But this is not the Stoic definition of statement, which is that of a complete utterance (the texts are problematic; see Frede 1974, 2. A. 1).
15. Belief has an uncertain role in Stoic philosophy of mind and epistemology (see Annas 1990), but a reasonable view of all the evidence allows us to say that all assent produces belief, though only some produces knowledge.

Assent, which occurs in every perception, is obviously not a conscious act, or literally articulated in words. The Stoics are committed to our mental life consisting in large part of the making of statements in a mental language or language of thought; insofar as this occurs in every perception, we are obviously not aware of it, and its nature cannot be indicated phenomenologically. It is perhaps best conceived by comparing an animal's instinctive reaction to a stimulus with a reaction to the same object on the part of a human, who conceptualizes the object more or less accurately and for whom it can have many different kinds of significance. Indeed some of our sources overstate this point by claiming that for humans perceptions *are* assents.[16] This is a way—an unnecessarily paradoxical way, as we sometimes find with the Stoics—of putting the point that perception essentially involves assent. By excluding factors other than assent at times, the Stoics are making the point that perception is not a two-stage process: reception of an uninterpreted sensory given *plus* a separable conceptualization of it. There are no perceptions which do not involve conceptualization and thinking: a Kantian kind of thesis, for which Kant was, again, to provide far more complex arguments.

It is central to the Stoic analysis that when I perceive an object, one and the same item, the appearance, is both a physical alteration of my soul-*pneuma* and an item realizing propositional content, which can be assented to and produces a true or false belief. There have to be items with both these aspects; otherwise we could not give an adequate account of human, as opposed to animal, perception. Modern philosophers of mind who see the matter in broadly this way divide on the deep question of whether we may assume that there are items with both these aspects or whether the part of the story involving content should ultimately be reduced to a purely physical story. The Stoics are not tempted to any reductive

16. Cic. *Luc.* 108 (= *SVF* 2. 73).

program and do not have any worries about the role of *lekta* in their philosophy of mind in particular.

However, there is a problem in principle with *lekta*, which arguably becomes more salient in the philosophy of mind. The Stoics are physicalists: everything that exists is physical. However, as we have seen, they allow that some things "subsist" without existing, like time and place and *lekta*. What does "subsistence" come down to? It is best thought of as a device for enabling us to explain the fact that we make statements, which appear to be true statements, about things which do not exist, since they are not physical particulars. Places subsist in that we can talk truly about things that do exist being in places, although places do not exist. Similarly, *lekta* or sayables subsist in that we can talk truly about people saying (commanding, praying, and so on) things, although *lekta* are not physical particulars. These items are not like fictional entities in that they have a legitimate place in our attempts to describe and explain the world; but since they are not physical, they do not exist, and, since they do not exist, they can have no place in a causal story.

But how can items with no causal power themselves make the very real difference between animal and human perception? Is this not a difference that has to be spelled out causally, in terms of a physical process? The Stoics meet one aspect of this problem; the mind or *hēgemonikon* of humans can be affected by *lekta*, they say, although it is not a direct causal influence, since the human mind is the kind of thing that can respond, without physical contact, to the content of an appearance. A pupil can imitate or represent the movements of a drill instructor, without being physically manipulated by the instructor but just by responding to the instructor's own movements in a way that produces representations of them. Similarly, the human mind can respond to physical stimulations in a way which produces representations of their content, although the content does not itself produce a physical effect.[17]

17. Sext. Emp. *Math.* 7. 409 (= *SVF* 2. 85).

The Stoic position thus seems to be analogous to that of modern theories which hold that our ability to represent content to ourselves is not to be explained causally, but rests on a fact of a different kind. There is a basic isomorphism between two structures: the structure of causal interrelations, in which the physical states of the world and of the perceiver are embedded, and the structure of semantic interrelations, in which is embedded the signification of the content of the physical states. Thus our minds represent the content of the physical states involved in perception, but not because of causal interaction. Similarly, the Stoics say that our minds are affected "not by (*hupo*) *lekta* but in relation to (*epi*) them."[18] This is a highly important point, and it is a great pity that our extant sources are not more forthcoming on it; the Stoics themselves do not seem to have found the point as problematic as they should have.

The Stoic account of perception is strikingly more adequate and interesting than that of, for example, Aristotle, who recognizes only in a sporadic and unenthusiastic way the articulable content of perception.[19] Not the least advantage is that the objects of perception are not tied to Aristotelian special sensibles—color, sound, and so on—and common sensibles,

18. It is tempting to refer to the modern slogan, "Take care of the syntax and the semantics will take care of itself."

19. Aristotle's lengthy accounts of perception in the *De anima* and *De sensu* concentrate on the physical processes of perception and fitting perception into the general account of change, together with discussion of sensory media and the special and common objects of perception. Only with the fleeting and marginal appearance of "incidental perception" do we find any recognition of the role of conceptualization in perception. Both this and the scrappy parts of book 3—that recognize that we perceive *that* such and such—are unintegrated with Aristotle's wider concerns and also with his scattered comments in the *Parva naturalia* that suggest a representative account of perception and an account of the self that lays more stress on its unity. It is instructive to see Alexander's struggles when he restates Aristotelian psychology in Stoic-influenced terms. He drops incidental perception and tries to squeeze far-reaching points about appearances out of Aristotle's limited and idiosyncratic account of appearance in *De anima* 3. 3.

like shape. We can perceive values, for example, since these certainly appear to us, and the imprint of them can be realized in a proposition and assented to in a statement.

In Stoicism our mental acts are, just as much as the rest of the world's events, part of the continuous chain of causes which is Fate. Assent will be a product of character and habit and one's past up to that point. The Stoics do not infer from this that perception is just something that happens in us, without being up to us to bring about or modify. Rather, because they think that the "principal cause" of what we do is ourselves, our present state and the way this has developed into our character, they think that there are differences between what people can perceive, and that these differences are due to the people themselves, who can be held responsible for them. Two people can look at the same object—for example, a tree. But one observer merely sees a tree; the other, who knows more, sees a silver birch. In a perfectly good sense, they are seeing the same thing, but they see it differently, in ways that reflect differences between them. (And note that the one with more knowledge has a better claim to be seeing the world as it really is; the tree really is a silver birch, not just a tree.)

Different people, then, will have different perceptual beliefs when faced by the same objects, because they have different thoughts which reflect their different degrees of understanding of what is given them in the appearances. This explains why the Stoics put so much stress on our developing good habits in the way we deal with appearances. "Nonprecipitancy is knowledge of when one should assent, and when not. . . . Nonfrivolity is a state of referring appearances to right reason."[20]

"Some appearances are expert (*technikai*), others inexpert; at any rate a picture is observed differently by an expert and an inexpert person."[21] A nonexpert will just see figures; the expert will see figures that represent gods. The expert is right— there really is that significance—and the nonexpert is missing

20. D. L. 7. 46–47 (= *SVF* 2. 130). Epictetus lays constant stress on our ability to accept or reject appearances.
21. D. L. 7. 51 (= *SVF* 2. 61).

something.[22] What is more surprising to us is the claim that the appearance is itself "expert." The expert is not seeing anything that is not there for the ignoramus to see. It is the fault of the ignoramus that he fails to see what is there to be seen, because he fails to understand the content of what is presented to him.

Some appearances are "expert"; others are "credible." The Stoics also think that some are "apprehensive" or kataleptic: they represent their object faithfully and could not fail to do this, so that if you have one, you grasp its object and could not be wrong about it. Scholars have been troubled that the appearances themselves have these properties; should it not depend on us whether an appearance is, for example, credible?[23] But the Stoics operate with an assumption defended in their metaphysics: this world is the richest possible. Objects really do have all the properties that we can perceive them to have: the tree really is a silver birch, not just a tree; the figures in the picture really do represent gods. The appearances they imprint on us reflect this richness: the tree gives us the appearance of a silver birch; the picture gives us the appearance of figures that represent gods. We may, of course, have confused and inadequate thoughts, and if we do, we will have confused and inadequate perceptions. More knowledge, and the exercise of the intellectual virtues, will enrich and clarify our thoughts, and we will see the tree and picture more clearly and knowledgeably. There is a sense in which we are seeing the same things, but there is also a sense in which we are seeing them for the first time.

The Stoics say disappointingly little about the exact relation between the appearance and the statement assented to, which contains the content of the appearance, and there are two different models each of which can capture the above position,

22. The ancients would not, I think, be likely to use *technē* of an appreciation of purely painterly qualities; I suppose that iconographical information is what is meant.

23. See Pohlenz (1965a); Sandbach (1971b); Frede (1984); Annas (1990).

namely, that perception is partially dependent on the perceiver. One is this: we all take in the same appearances, but the ignorant and the knowledgeable will assent to different statements on the basis of them. The ignoramus takes in the appearance of a silver birch; her resulting meager belief that she is seeing a tree results from her assenting to only part of the information contained in the appearance. This picture does justice to the realist side of the theory: we all perceive the same world. Nonetheless, it in effect introduces two stages of a kind: reception of information and selective assent to it.

The alternative picture stresses the point that perceptions are assents: to have a perception just is to receive an appearance and to assent to all the information in it. Thus the relation between the appearance and the statement is very direct: an appearance contains a single statement, and having that appearance just is assenting to the information contained in the appearance and expressed in that statement. On this model, the differences between the ignorant and the knowledgeable are accounted for by their having different appearances.

How is this compatible with the thought that appearances themselves are expert, kataleptic, and so on? Indeed, if they are, there must be something about the perceivers themselves which explains their ending up with different perceptual beliefs. Appearances, on this view, will be the same for everyone in the journey from object to sense organ; but in the further journey from sense organ to mind they will be affected by the perceiver's overall state, which expresses itself in pneumatic tension. The ignoramus assents to a vague or wrong statement because only a vague or wrong appearance has made its way to the *hēgemonikon;* information has been lost en route from sense organ to *hēgemonikon* which in a person with more coherent and firmer beliefs, and thus stronger tension, would have been retained. Thus my perceptions, and hence my perceptual beliefs, are a function of two factors: the way the world impinges on me, and my overall psychic state.

Appearances thus underdetermine the perceptual beliefs that perceivers will come up with. Difference in degrees of knowledgeability will make least difference with gross physical objects like trees and tables. However, we can see that in the case of values, for example, differences might be larger and matter more. The case of values also shows us that differences will not always come down merely to degrees of determinateness; the Stoics think that most people are radically wrong in their moral judgments and that this is because in their deliberations they see quite the wrong things as being morally salient.

The evidence does not really compel us to either of these interpretations. Nor, unfortunately, is it precise on another important matter: the exact form of perceptual belief-statements. Presumably these are the same in form as ordinary statements which we normally utter. If so, then the truth values of the compound statements will be given by the truth conditions of the atomic statements together with the rules for the logical constants in Stoic logic.[24] What of the truth conditions for the atomic ones? For the Stoics, an atomic statement is true if one of two conditions is fulfilled. One is that it is a definite statement, one in which the referring term is a singular term making direct reference, such as "He (that man) is walking." (And, of course, that the world is as the definite statement says it is—that he is in fact walking.) The other is that there is a true corresponding definite statement. For example, "Somebody is walking" is true if "He is walking" is true. If we are to think of our inner perceptual belief-statements on the same model, then it would appear that the truth of our ordinary perceptual claims will depend straightforwardly on the truth of definite statements reporting perceptual ostensions, pointings out of perceptual properties. However, no extant Stoic text explores this aspect of the theory.

So far we have been examining standard, normal perception. The Stoics are not very interested in abnormal perceptual experiences nor in investigating the phenomena of sleep,

24. Stoic logic is propositional. See Frede (1974); for some texts see Long and Sedley (1987, 34 and 35).

dreams, and the like. Sleep is brusquely said to be a "slack-ening of the perceptive tension round the *hēgemonikon*."[25] There is a difference between appearance (*phantasia*) and mere appearing (*phantasma*): the latter are "seemings in the mind such as happen in sleep."[26] Madmen have appearances which do not come from any real object.[27] For the Stoics these form a collection of not very interesting facts, which can easily be explained in a wholly naturalistic way: the sensory apparatus of sleepers and the mad is not functioning properly, and it leads them to take as the appearance of an object what is not so. Nothing philosophically significant hangs on it.

It is easy to see why this is so. For the Stoics, these cases are not epistemologically important. (The sceptics think they are; but that is part of another story.)[28] The Stoics think that their naturalistic theories give them every right to say, with Chrysippus, that the appearances of the waking just are clearer than those of the sleeping.[29] This is not to be construed as an epistemological claim, nor is it a report on the phenomenology of the experiences. It is at bottom a scientific claim about the unified system of *pneuma* and how it works in ordinary and abnormal circumstances.

Further, the Stoics do not feel the interest in these cases for their own sake that, for example, Aristotle does; and reasonably. Once the entire life of the mind is to be explained in terms of the operation of *pneuma*, it is obvious that there is nothing to say about sleep, dreams, and so on except that they are due to whatever turns out to be the appropriate tautening or relaxing of pneumatic tension.[30]

25. D. L. 7. 158 (= *SVF* 2. 766).
26. D. L. 7. 50.
27. Sext. Emp. *Math.* 7. 249 (= *SVF* 2. 65).
28. See Frede (1984); Annas (1990).
29. Cic. *Div.* 2. 61.126 (= *SVF* 2. 62).
30. If we take the Stoics to be gesturing toward what we see in terms of the functioning of the nervous system, the modern analogue would be an account of these phenomena in terms of the workings of different parts of the brain and nervous system, and the ways in which there can be interference to these. Both accounts appeal to

b) Thinking

The Stoics have no separate account of thinking; after perception, interest shifts to the epistemological notions of apprehension and knowledge. From the account of perception
we can see why; to understand what perceiving is, is already
to understand what thinking is. Thinking is the articulation of
content in perceiving.

This is what we would expect from thoroughgoing empiricists, and there are two important corollaries. One is that the
Stoics have no conceptual room for *pure* thinking, where that
is taken to be thinking that is in no way reliant on experience.
In opposition to the Platonic and Aristotelian traditions, they
take all thought to be developed through experience and by
reflection on experience. Such a view faces problems in accounting for mathematical thinking; indeed for the Stoics
mathematics can only be very abstract science. They say almost nothing about it and fail to explain why most mathe-
maticians (and philosophers influenced by mathematics, like
Plato) believe that mathematical thinking does not depend on
experience. In keeping with this, they reject, in their ethics,
the Platonic view that philosophy is a peculiarly abstract kind
of thinking like mathematics, and do not think that the only
appropriate life for a philosopher is the "contemplative" life
so valued by Plato and Aristotle, the life devoted to abstract
study.

Another corollary is that they give a highly empiricist account of concept formation. The mind or *hēgemonikon* is at
birth like blank paper, and experience writes on it. Single
experiences build up memory, and in the normal course of
events we will naturally build up both preconceptions (*prolēpseis*), ways of conceptualizing what we perceive, and concepts (*ennoiai*), which are theoretical and rely on teaching.
Concept formation is explained entirely in terms of our ability

---

science, though in the case of the Stoics it is a rather primitive science.

to interpret and generalize from the particular data of sense which confront us. The Stoics here self-consciously oppose an empiricist account to one which holds that something like Platonic Forms is required to explain how we can employ concepts.[31]

In a brutally abbreviated passage in one of our sources we find an even more starkly empiricist picture:

> Things thought of are thought of like this . . . by contact, perceptive things; by resemblance, analogous to what is present, for example, Socrates from his picture; by analogy, either by increase, like Tityos or the Cyclops, or by lessening, like the Pygmy. (The center of the earth was thought of by analogy from smaller spheres.) By transposition, for example, eyes on the chest; by composition the Hippocentaur is though of; by opposition, death. Some things are thought of by a kind of transposition, like *lekta* and space. It is by nature that just and good are thought of; also by privation, for example, handless. (D. L. 7. 53 [= *SVF* 2. 87])

This is not a crude empiricism, for the mind is not thought of as passively accepting or mechanically shuffling around the data provided by experience. Rather, the mind is completely involved all along the line. We have seen formulations such as that rational appearances are thoughts, and that perceptions are assents. These are conscious attempts to avoid two-stage analyses which posit first the sensory given and then rational reflection on it.

---

31. Aët. *Plac.* 4. 11 (= *SVF* 2. 83). For some texts see Long and Sedley (1987, 30) on universals. Plato's actual theory of Forms is not primarily a theory of universals at all, and indeed it is not clear whether Plato even accepted at any point that there was a Form for every general term. But it seems that by the time of the Stoics the theory was taken to be a crude theory of universals, as it often is today.

4

Action

The soul is defined by perception and also by impulse, the active and reactive power in the soul which enables the animal not only to take in information about the world but also to move around and act in it. "Impulses are the origin [or origins] of action."[1]

We have seen (in chapter 2, section d) that the Stoic account of the scale of beings laid great stress on the increased complexity and flexibility of movement in the case of things which have increased pneumatic tension, and thus increased functional unity. In particular, there is a great difference between animals and humans in the matter of impulse. In animals impulses are called forth automatically and instinctually, as with the spider which spins a web because that is the way it is built to function. Humans, however, have a choice as to whether and how they react to stimuli. Nature gets the credit for what animals do, "but reason having been given to rational beings, living rightly according to nature becomes for them what is according to nature; for reason supervenes as the craftsman

---

1. Plut. *Anim. an corp.* 501c. For texts on action see Long and Sedley (1987, 33, 57).

of the impulse."[2] Hence we are responsible for our actions as animals are not, and are praised and blamed accordingly.

This sharp line between animal and human action is one that we all draw, more or less uncomfortably, but the Stoics certainly went farther than needed in their insistence on a difference of kind between humans and animals. Since animals lack reason, they claimed, they do not have emotions or desires, which require reason, and have merely an analogue of these things. The Stoics were unimpressed by the complexity of some animal behavior,[3] continuing to hold that however similar animal behavior might be to human, its explanation had to be completely distinct. Thus Chrysippus held that when a dog sniffs down two out of three tracks and then goes off after its prey down the third without sniffing, something is going on in the dog of the form "Either p or q or r; but not p and not q, so r." But he denied that any thinking was going on in the dog; the impressive nature of the case merely underlines how impressive nature is in the way it works in nonrational animals. Chrysippus is not in the least tempted to query the absolute nature of the distinction he draws between rational and nonrational beings.[4] This is unconvincing; in the Hellenistic world there was a continuing debate on "the reason of animals," and the Stoics were not universally thought to have the better case. Further, the Stoics seem to have been affected for the worse by holding to such a sharp line between humans and other animals. Like the later Cartesians who held that nonhuman animals were mere machines, they moved too readily from the view that humans are different in kind from nonhuman animals to a detachment from the feelings and needs of those animals. The Stoics openly regarded them as resources for humans to use, even saying notoriously false and silly things such as that the pig's soul is like a kind of salt to

2. D. L. 7. 86 (= *SVF* 3. 178).
3. Cleanthes noticed the complex coordination of ant behavior (*SVF* 1. 515); we have seen (in part 2, chapter 2, section e) that Hierocles drew attention to exotic and complicated animal behavior.
4. For the dog see chapter 2, section e.

keep the flesh from going off, so that we can eat it.[5] The Stoics'
account of human mental life makes a great advance in stress-
ing its rational, language-involving nature. It is a pity that it
has a shadow side, of contempt for nonrational animals, which
do not use language. The Stoics are at any rate interested in
impulse only as regards its role in human action. What we
lose in biological realism we gain in a theory of impulse and
action which is closely tied in with questions of responsibility
and action.[6]

What then distinguishes a human impulse? We have a useful, though jargon-ridden, summarizing account of impulse in
one source:

> They say that what moves an impulse (*hormē*) is nothing
> but an impulsory (*hormetikē*) appearance of what is then
> and there appropriate, and that impulse is in general a
> movement of the soul toward something. The species of
> impulse, they say, are observed to be that which come
> about in the rational animals, and that in the nonrational
> ones; but these have no [distinct] names; for desire (*or-
> exis*) is not rational impulse, but a species of rational
> impulse. As for rational impulse, it would properly be
> defined by saying that it is a movement of the mind toward
> something involved in acting; and to this is opposed
> counterimpulse (*aphormē*), a kind of movement [of the
> mind away from something in acting]. In a special sense,
> they say that *orousis* is also impulse, since it is a species
> of practical impulse. *Orousis* is a movement of the mind
> toward something in the future. So up to now "impulse"
> is used in four ways and "counterimpulse" in two. "Im-
> pulse" is used in five ways if one adds the impulsory state
> (*hexis hormetikē*), which they actually call impulse in a

5. This remark is attributed to Cleanthes (Clem. *Strom.* 7. 6.33 [=
SVF 1. 516]). *SVF* 2. 723 collects various versions of it. We might
dismiss it as a bad joke were it not for other evidence, such as Philo
De mund. opif. 66 (= *SVF* 2. 722), which reports the view that fish
are "in a way animals and in a way not animals" because they do not
breathe air (and so are presumably short on *pneuma*).

6. See Inwood (1985) for a thorough account placing it in the
context of Stoic ethical theory.

special sense, and from which impulses come about. Of practical impulse there are several species . . . including *prothesis,* an indication of accomplishment; *epibolē,* an impulse before an impulse; *paraskeuē,* an action before an action; *encheirēsis,* an impulse toward something already in hand; *hairesis, a boulēsis* from reasoning by analogy; *prohairesis,* a *hairesis* before a *hairesis; boulēsis,* a reasonable desire (*orexis*); *thelēsis,* a voluntary *boulēsis.* (Arius Didymus apud Stob. *Ecl.* 2. 86–88 Wachsmuth [= *SVF* 3. 169, 173, 171])[7]

From this unprepossessing passage several points emerge. One is that impulses are correlated with "impulsory appearances"; here we should understand "impulsory" from impulse, not the other way round. The impulsory appearances are just those that do in fact produce an impulse, and there is no interesting independent categorization of these. The Stoics are not operating with a picture of the world in which all facts about the world are inert, and so need the addition of some mysterious extra ingredient before action can be produced in response to them. They accept the commonsense picture, namely, that some facts do, on occasion, lead some people to act. There is no special mystery about these cases; this is just the kind of fact that they are. Another is that the Stoics appear at least to have been consciously distancing themselves from Aristotle's account of action; Aristotle's favored terms *orexis* and *prohairesis* appear in very trivial roles. But if the Stoics were consciously distancing themselves, it was not a success; the terms reappeared in Epictetus in something like Aristotle's usage.[8]

7. See Inwood (1985) for detailed discussion of this passage and the numerous textual and interpretative problems it presents.
8. See Bonhoeffer (1890, 118–19, 232–61); Pohlenz (1970, 328–32); Inwood (1985, app. 2). *Prohairesis* is Aristotle's term for deliberated choice; the Stoics give it less room because they downplay the role of deliberation. *Orexis* is Aristotle's widest term for desire in general; the Stoics reject this (along with Epicurus; see part 3, chapter 8), substituting the term *hormē,* which did become established philosophical usage. We cannot say with certainty whether the Stoics had

Two highly important points emerge from the passage. On the one hand, there are many very different kinds of impulse to action—in particular, one only touched on here, but crucial to the Stoics, that between desire for virtue (the only thing that is good) and desire for other things (which are worth having, but by comparison with virtue, are "indifferent"). But, on the other hand, all these different kinds of motivations can be given a single analysis, for they can all be explained as an impulse. This is a unifying analysis—however complex an intention, however tortured a decision, there is something in both which we can isolate as "the impulse"—but it is not reductive. We are finding a common form, not a lowest common denominator.[9]

How does reason, characteristic of human impulse, enter in? Diogenes talks of reason as "crafting" impulse; Origen of its choosing between impulses.[10] Clement tells us that reason helps us to discriminate among appearances and not be carried away by them.[11] Chrysippus with characteristic overstatement calls impulse "a person's reason prescriptive of acting."[12] What holds these characterizations together?

It seems as though there is a certain parallelism between action and perception; in both cases there is an appearance, and what is up to the rational agent is to accept or reject it. We find indeed that reason in the action case functions in the form of assent.[13] Our best source tells us in more detail:

> They say that all the impulses are assents, but that the practical ones contain the motive element. Actually, assents are to one thing, and impulses toward another; as-

---

Aristotle in mind; their theory is certainly more systematic than his fragmentary remarks on the "practical syllogism" and had little to learn from those remarks.

9. Compare the similarly nonreductive analysis of all kinds of desires in terms of "pro-attitudes" in the work of Donald Davidson on action theory.

10. In the long passage in part 2, chapter 2, section d.

11. *Strom.* 2. 487 (= *SVF* 2. 714).

12. Plut. *De St. repugn.* 1037f (= *SVF* 3. 175).

13. See Plut. *De St. repugn.* 1057a (= *SVF* 3. 177).

sents are to statements (*axiōmata*) of a kind, and impulses are toward predicates (*katēgorēmata*), those that are somehow contained in the statements to which they assent. (Arius Didymus apud Stob. *Ecl.* 2. 88 Wachsmuth [= *SVF* 3. 171]).[14]

Thus to understand how an impulse can either be an assent or involve one, we first have to look at Stoic predicates.

A predicate is not a bit of language, but something expressed in language; it is technically an "incomplete sayable (*lekton*)," which can be completed in various ways to form what is expressed in commands, prayers, and so on; and when combined with a subject term produces a statement (*axiōma*), expressed in an utterance.[15] "A predicate is what is said of something; or an item which can go into a construction with one or more subjects, as Apollodorus says, or an incomplete sayable [*lekton*] which goes into a construction with a subject term to produce a statement."[16] Predicates are obviously not to be identified with words on the one hand or with items like properties on the other. There is no very intuitive account of a Stoic predicate; to get the idea we do best to think of a complete *lekton* expressed in a statement, and think of what remains when one removes the subject term, the referring element in it. When talking about predicates the Stoics tend to use the standard form "to A," the infinitive form of the verb, a form which shows incompleteness in that it cannot be used on its own to make a statement. When the predicate is completed by a subject term to produce a complete *lekton* expressed in a statement, I shall say that the predicate is satisfied.[17]

14. This is a continuation of the long passage above.
15. D. L. 7. 64 (= *SVF* 2. 183). See the discussion of types of statement at D. L. 7. 69–70 (= *SVF* 2. 204) and Sext. Emp. *Math.* 8. 96–103 (partly in *SVF* 2. 205).
16. D. L. 7. 64. "Subject term" is *orthē ptōsis*. Long and Sedley (1987, 200–201) argue that it should be translated "nominative case," but the result, which they accept, is that a sayable is partly composed of a word, and this cannot be right; the Stoics distinguish sharply between language and sayables, and rightly, since a word is not the kind of thing which can satisfy a predicate.
17. This is not Stoic terminology, but is, I think, suitable, and makes subsequent discussion easier.

Predicates have an important role in the Stoic analysis of causal statements:

> Every cause is a body which is the cause to a body of something nonbodily; for example, the knife is a body, and is the cause to a body, the flesh, of the nonbodily predicate *to be cut*, and again the fire is a body, and is the cause to a body, the wood, of the nonbodily predicate *to be burnt*. (Sext. Emp. *Math.* 9. 211 [= *SVF* 2. 341])

Presumably we are to understand "The knife is the cause to the flesh of a predicate" as follows: the action of the knife will result in a true statement produced by completing a predicate with the appropriate subject term. In this case the knife causes it to be true that the flesh is cut, that there is a true *axiōma* "The flesh is cut." Only bodies have causal efficacy; so the causal relation holds between two physical items, which have to make physical contact. But the causal relation is a three-termed relation; we have not understood that this is a *causal* relation until we bring in a predicate that is satisfied as a result of the holding of the causal relation. The predicate is satisfied when one item acts on another. In our examples it is always described in terms of the effect of this action, rather than the cause (the flesh's being cut, not the knife's cutting), presumably because it is more natural to describe causal activity in terms of what it brings about, rather than what brings it about. It is uninformative to be told that the knife is the cause to the flesh of the knife's cutting, although in principle this would seem to be as good an example of a satisfaction of a predicate as is the more familiar statement that it is the cause of the flesh's being cut.

Acting and doing are a kind of causal activity; and we can see the schema for action as a particular case of the causal schema. Every action will involve an impulse, and impulses, we are told, are directed toward predicates. Intuitively put, we do not want *things*, we want *to bring things about*. As Clement puts it (in terms of desire), "no one desires drink, but to drink the drinkable; not inheritance, but to inherit; likewise not knowledge, but to know, not good government, but to be well governed."[18] Suppose that I desire a drink. On the Stoic view, what I strictly desire is not the drink, considered as a physical object. Rather, I desire to bring about the satisfaction by me of the predicate *to drink*. That is, I desire that it be true that I drink. We can see how it can be said that I desire the predicate itself; for the verbal expression of Stoic predicates is the infinitive, *to drink*, and it can be said of me that I desire to drink, though more strictly what I desire is my bringing about my satisfaction of the predicate *to drink*. Thus I fulfill the causal schema; for I am the cause to myself of the predicate *to drink*, that is, I bring it about that I satisfy the predicate *to drink*. What makes this a case of action rather than mere causality is the fact that I bring this about by having an impulse.

Impulse involves assent. What I assent to seems to be, in Stoic sources, a statement as to what I ought to do to bring this about. Thus Arius says (see p. 91 above) that the appearance that moves the impulse is of something as being then and there "appropriate," the word being cognate with the Stoic term for kinds of action which one ought to do. And Seneca tells us, "I ought to walk; I walk only when I have said this to myself and approved this belief of mine."[19] Assent thus seems to be given to statements of the form "I ought to F."[20] The "ought" here is of course general, and has no suggestions of special moral force. Virtuous actions are a kind of action; but

18. *Strom.* 7. 7 (= *SVF* 3. 176); cf. Cic. *Tusc.* 4. 21 (= *SVF* 3. 398); Stob. *Ecl.* 2. 97.22–98.2 (= *SVF* 3. 91).

19. *Ep.* 113.18 (= *SVF* 3. 169).

20. Inwood (1985) argues that at this point the Stoics bring in imperatival forms; the agent responds not to "I ought to do A" but to something like "Do A, you!" self-addressed. Certainly some of our sources talk of reason commanding and forbidding (cf. n. 12 above). But imperatives are not specifically demanded by the evidence, and they complicate the resulting picture considerably. Instead of the fairly simple picture presented below, we would need something like a sentence-radical common to the relevant statement ("I ought to A") and the resulting self-addressed imperative ("A, you!"); otherwise we would not seem to get the right imperative. But there is no evidence for such a complication in our sources.

the general Stoic schema for action covers them together with ordinary cases of nonmoral action. They are all cases where the agent accepts that she ought, here and now, to do A, since A is the appropriate thing to do, here and now.

The picture is simply this. I desire to drink. That is, I desire the bringing about by me of my satisfying the predicate *to drink*. I assent to the statement "I ought (here and now and so forth) to drink"; for unless I assent to this, I am not really having an impulse for *my bringing about* the satisfaction of the predicate; I am merely hoping that it will happen, or the like. If I assent, however, I act, and so drink.

What exactly, in the above picture, is the impulse? There appears to be a conflict in the evidence here. We have seen the claim that impulses are assents, which implies that they are assents to statements; but this claim is at once modified to the claim that impulses are directed toward predicates which are somehow contained in statements which are assented to. How are these very different claims supposed to fit together? Further, we seem to get mutually conflicting claims about the relation of impulse and assent, supposing them to be distinct. One picture is that assent precedes impulse, and is necessary for it, while the other is that impulse precedes assent.[21]

Possibly the Stoics were confused here, or different Stoics held different views which were later conflated. There is, however, a fairly simple solution to these problems, which is to assume that "impulse" is here being used in two distinct, but easily conflated, ways. Let us distinguish impulse 1, a broad sense, from impulse 2, a narrow sense. Impulse 1 is the entire phenomenon consisting of impulse 2 and assent. This makes sense of the evidence as follows. Impulse 2 is a wanting or a desiring to do something, and so is directed at a predicate. When this is followed by assent to a statement of the form "I ought (here and now) to A," then we have impulse 1, which involves assent to a statement part of which is the predicate

---

21. For the former see Plut. *De St. repugn.* 1057a (= *SVF* 3. 177); for the latter, Cic. *Fat.* 40 (= *SVF* 2. 974).

to which impulse 2 is directed. This explains why the Stoics can say that impulses 1 are acts of assent; this is not all that they are, since they also involve impulses 2, but the formulation saying that they are acts of assent emphasizes the point that only when we have assent do we have an impulse 1. Impulse 2 is part of impulse 1 in just the way that the predicate is part of the statement. The problem concerning the order of impulse and assent can also be solved. Impulse 2 precedes assent, for I have to want to drink before assenting to the statement that I ought here and now to drink. But assent can be said to precede impulse 1, since impulse 1 requires assent to the relevant statement, namely, that I ought here and now to drink. It seems, then, that there is no confusion in the Stoic account of impulse, and while the Stoics would have avoided even the appearance of confusion if they had explicitly distinguished impulse 1 from impulse 2, they are not led into any confusions about them.

As with perception, assent is the point at which things are "up to" the agent. It is not up to me how the world appears to me; as a result of past habits and so on I cannot help it that some things now appear desirable to me and others not. So I cannot help desiring my bringing about the satisfaction of certain predicates and not others. But what I can help is assenting to the corresponding statements of "I ought to F"; for without such an assent there may be a mere desire to bring about a certain state of affairs, but there will not be the full impulse to bring it about, and so there will not be the action.

The position of assent generates an interesting problem within Stoic theory of action; for is assent not itself an action? On the one hand, we are drawn to say no, for an analysis of action ought to be normative about previously disputed cases; surely actions are *defined* as the effects of impulse and assent, so that assent cannot itself be an action.[22] If we are impressed by this, we are likely to think of assent as an antecedent of action, something like an intention. On the other hand, assent

22. See Inwood (1985, chap. 3 and app. 4).

is the first item in the chain which is clearly "up to us." If it is an action, it is a very special kind of action; we are not normally aware of it, and it seems absurd to say that an action takes place within the body, in the *hēgemonikon*. But there is an isolated, but very significant, passage indicating that the Stoics were happy with the idea that actions are within the body. Seneca says that Cleanthes and Chrysippus disagreed on what walking is.[23] Cleanthes said it was *pneuma* sent to the feet by the *hēgemonikon;* Chrysippus said that it was the *hēgemonikon* itself. The dispute is less important than the fact that both say what walking is without bringing in the movement of the feet. Walking, the action, and not just the antecedents of action, takes place in the soul-*pneuma*.

In fact it is not so implausible to locate actions within the body. The Stoics' interest is in what is, and what is not, "up to me"; and we would expect this to show up in a concern over what I can properly be said to *do*. Suppose I order the cavalry to charge, but the message goes wrong, the cavalry stays put, and the battle is lost. In a sense I have lost the battle, and will accept responsibility for that, but in a strict sense this is not what I *did;* what I *did* was to send the message. So what I do if it succeeds can be described in terms of its effects, but not if it does not succeed. This line of thought can easily be extended to messages that fail to arrive within the body as well as outside it. Thus, if all goes well, I move my legs; if I am suddenly paralyzed, I have still assented to what normally brings about the movement of the legs. We lack enough information to say exactly what Chrysippus' position was, but the Seneca passage suggests the following: "walking" is described in terms of the motion of the legs, that is, of the normal effects of assenting to the content of the object of impulse. Still, what I properly *do* when I walk is just to *assent*—that is, what I really *do* is the event in the *hēgemonikon*, not its effects in the legs. On this view, actions are all really in the *hēge-*

23. *Ep.* 113. 23 (= *SVF* 2. 836); cf. *Ep.* 85. 33–40 on one's action being unaffected by failure of the consequences.

monikon, since they are really assents, and they are differentiated by being described in terms of their normal effects: "walking," "riding," "charging," and so on are actions described in terms of nearer or remote effects. All we ever *do* is assent; the rest is up to nature. And that may let us down even within our bodies, never mind outside them.[24]

This view is more attractive than we might at first suppose. Firstly, it locates action where responsibility is. We are not normally responsible for the causal effects of our actions, only for the actions. The Stoics are simply counting as effects of the action the bodily movements which we might normally count as part of the action. This is, furthermore, something which we might well expect them to do, given their views that pain resulting from damage to the foot, for example, is felt in the *hēgemonikon*, not in the foot. The view of action just described is the obvious counterpart to this. Further, the problem of whether assent is an action or not can be neatly solved. It is not an action like others, since it is not caused by impulse and assent. But then this is exactly what we would expect. For assents are the actions by doing which we do all other actions; if they did not crucially differ from all other actions, we would have an infinite regress. Thus they occupy exactly the conceptual room taken up by *basic* actions in some modern theories of action.[25]

Because of the position of assent, it is clear that the Stoics do not have a simple model whereby my actions are those of my bodily movements that are produced by my beliefs and desires.[26] Rather, for the Stoics, beliefs and desires are the causes of *assent*. More strictly, beliefs are the causes of assents to various perceptual beliefs, whereas beliefs and desires in

24. Compare Prichard's notorious claim that all we ever do is *will*, or set ourselves to act; the rest is up to nature. Prichard's view has been uninfluential, because of its dualist form, but has been restated by more recent theories in physicalist forms.

25. See Annas (1978–79).

26. This is an advantage; such theories run into problems, notably over the status of bodily movements brought about by beliefs and desires, but in a causally deviant way.

combination are the causes of those assents that are identified with actions. Two people can assent to the same perceptual beliefs in front of a cold drink; only the one with a desire to drink will assent to "I ought here and now to drink that" and reach for the glass.[27] Assent is what distinguishes free human agency from instinctive animal behavior. It is nonetheless caused by desires and beliefs and is just as much a physical state as these are. If there are problems here, they are problems with Stoic compatibilism in general.

The Stoics do not give special attention to the step whereby assent brings about action, that is, the actual getting moving. This is because of their thesis that the soul is unified in being rational; once reason has been exercised in giving assent, there is no further, distinct element in the soul that could resist, so action must follow—unless, of course, external factors of an everyday kind intervene. Why then do we not always act as we see that we should? The Stoics analyze such cases as cases not of assent which is not followed by action, but as cases of incomplete or shifting assent.[28]

The Stoic theory of action plays an important role in Stoic ethics in the theory of *oikeiōsis* or familiarization. The Stoics believe that our initial natural impulses for self-preservation are what develop into our abilities to reason practically, and also into our ability to reason morally.[29] The theory also figures in one of the Stoics' debates with the sceptical Academy. Ancient forms of scepticism claimed that the result of adopting a critical, sceptical attitude was suspension of belief. A common objection was that living without beliefs is impossible, so that the sceptical self-description is incoherent. The sceptics appealed to the Stoic account of action to make their reply. Sceptics, of course, cannot appeal to beliefs of their own; rather, they always have to meet their opponents on their own ground.

27. Is "assent" then used ambiguously, since only certain assents are actions? No; assents are actions only when brought about in a certain way, namely, by desires as well as beliefs.
28. These cases will be discussed further in the next chapter.
29. See Inwood (1985, chap. 6).

The sceptics may have appealed to the Stoics' own theory because the criticism had come from Stoics in particular.[30] Arcesilaus, the head of the sceptical Academy, claimed that perception and impulse are in fact sufficient for action, and assent, presupposing belief, is not required. "Impulse, aroused by sensation, moves us in the shape of the action directed toward a suitable goal; a kind of casting weight has been put in the scale of our governing part, and a directed movement is set afoot."[31] The Stoic reply is obvious: this is not *action* but what goes on in spiders and dogs. In humans there has to be assent, because that is what defines human, as opposed to animal, action.

The argument can go several ways. One could call into question the Stoics' sharp cutoff line between human and animal action and demand more adequate defense of it. Or one could explore the idea that a human life could be lived without beliefs, like that of an animal. If it could, there is a further question, How can the sceptics defend it using rational means like arguments? But that takes us into a different area.[32]

30. Or it may be that the Stoic theory was regarded as widely acceptable, so that replying on its terms served to meet a variety of opponents more generally.

31. Plut. *Adv. Col.* 1122bff.; trans. Einarson and de Lacy.

32. On scepticism and the life without belief see Burnyeat (1980); Annas (1986); McPherran (1989).

5

The Emotions

Few Stoic doctrines have been as criticized as the Stoic theory of the *pathē* or emotions;[1] from antiquity the theory has been attacked as counterintuitive and even absurd. Much of this is due to misrepresentation; parts of the theory have been ripped from their context (especially the thesis that emotions are beliefs) and criticized in isolation from other theses that make sense of them. But it is also true that the theory to some extent redefines the original phenomena, as we can see from the claim that the ideal moral agent will not have *pathē*. This runs against the normal usage of *pathos* in Greek, according to which the *pathē* are in themselves neither good nor bad: what matters is how one handles them. Because of this, some have

---

1. *Pathos* does not mean "emotion"; it is a more general term, which can cover a wide range of what one "suffers" or what is done to one (*pathein*). However, what the Stoics (and Epicureans and a wide range of ancient philosophers) are discussing is clearly, from the key examples and key theses, emotions such as anger, fear, and joy. The discussions also cover some cases of what we would call feelings that do not amount to emotions, such as desires and feelings of pleasure or repulsion. However, "emotions" seems a better general term in English than "feelings," and it is certainly more suitable for the Stoics, although the Epicurean account makes feelings more central (see part 3, chapter 9).

preferred to translate *pathē* as "passions" or the like;[2] but this risks missing the way that the Stoics mean to be talking about the emotions, as we understand them, although they are revising commonsense beliefs about them.

An emotion is a kind of impulse; thus much that has been said about impulse (in chapter 4) carries over. An emotion is a motive cause bringing about action; it is an impulse to bring about a state of affairs, taking effect via the agent's assent to a statement that she ought to bring about that state of affairs. Still, it is an impulse "in excess," and this raises special problems. The main features of the theory are brought together in a summary by Arius that follows, and are best laid out together and then discussed individually.

> An emotion (*pathos*), they say, is an impulse which is excessive (*pleonazousa*) and disobedient to reason which is dictating; or an [irrational] movement in the soul contrary to nature (all emotions belong in the soul's *hēgemonikon*); so that every upset (*ptoia*) is an emotion, and again every emotion is an upset. Emotion being of such a kind, we must suppose that some are primary and lead the way, while others have their reference to these. Primary in the genus are these four: desire (*epithumia*), fear (*phobos*), pain (*lupē*), and pleasure (*hēdonē*). Desire and fear take the lead, desire being directed toward apparent good, and fear directed toward apparent evil. Pleasure and pain supervene (*epigignesthai*) on these, pleasure when we get what we were desiring or escape what we were fearing, and pain when we fail to get what we were desiring or happen on what we were fearing. With all the soul's emotions, since they call them beliefs, the belief is understood as a weak supposition, and the "fresh" [part]

2. For example, Inwood (1985, chap. 5) in his excellent discussion translates *pathē* as "passions." He rightly criticizes Cicero, who, finding translation in Latin difficult, renders *pathos* as *morbus*, "disease," thus confusing the *pathos* with the faulty state giving rise to it (*Tusc.* 4. 7–11; cf. *Fin.* 3. 35, where Cicero gives up and transliterates *pathos*). See Sen. *Ep.* 75 for the difference.

as what moves an irrational contraction [or] elation. (Stob. *Ecl.* 2.88.8–89.3 Wachsmuth [= *SVF* 3. 378])[3]

All the elements here are echoed in other sources, though not always together.

What makes an emotion an "excessive impulse" is its being disobedient to the dictates of reason. This cannot mean that the agent's practical reasoning results in decision, but an impulse conflicts with this. An impulse is itself rational; Chrysippus called impulse "a person's reason prescriptive of acting."[4] Since an impulse brings about action by way of its content, the action is thus far rational. An impulse "disobedient to reason" cannot be blocking the reasoning that leads to action; it *is* the reasoning that leads to action. It must, then, be disobedient to reason in a normative sense: *right* reason, the reasoning that *should* have been followed. We always act for *a* reason, but we can always ask if it was a *good* reason, the result of intelligent reflection and developed rationality.

Galen in his polemic against Chrysippus' theory of the emotions in *On the Doctrines of Hippocrates and Plato* 4 and 5 preserves a quotation from Chrysippus in which he elucidates the sense in which an emotion is an excessive impulse and a movement in the soul:

First one must keep in mind that the rational animal is by nature such as to follow reason and to act with reason as his guide. But often he moves in another way toward some things and away from some things in disobedience to reason when he is pushed too much. Both definitions refer to this movement: the unnatural motion arises irrationally in this way, and also the excess in the impulses. For this irrationality must be understood as disobedient to reason and rejecting it; and with reference to this motion we say in ordinary usage that some persons are

3. For other texts on the emotions in Stoicism see Long and Sedley (1987, 65).
4. Plut. *De St. repugn.* 1037f (= *SVF* 3. 75).

pushed and moved irrationally, without reason and judgment. For when we use these expressions it is not as if a person is carried away by error. (*PHP* 368–69K, 241 de Lacy [= *SVF* 3. 462])[5]

Our normal talk of "irrational" impulses suggests that they are not rational at all; but for the Stoics ordinary language is just wrong here, for there can be no such thing as a totally nonrational impulse, at least not in undefective humans. We grasp the phenomenon, but it is not what we think it is, namely, reason versus something devoid of reason, but rather good reason versus bad, inadequate reason.

a) Emotions as Irrational Movements in the Soul

An excessive impulse is not just a movement in the soul, but an "upset," a hiccup in the "even flow" of the good life. The physical specification of this can only be an upset in the right overall pneumatic tension of the *hēgemonikon*. But there is more to say, because the emotions, being impulses, are complex phenomena; they have content, as all impulses do, and they are an especially important kind of impulse, since they affect our lives greatly, for good or bad, and they are educable.

Just as the body has good or bad tension, so does the soul. In the body, this takes the form of fitness and taut muscles, enabling the body to perform what is needed. In the soul it takes the form of firmness of character; like an underexercised body unable to perform physical tasks which it should be capable of, the soul with poor tension will respond weakly when it should be responding firmly. We have already seen that this idea plays a role in the theory of perception; someone with perfectly functioning sense organs may nonetheless assent to vague or wrong perceptual beliefs because only a vague or wrong appearance has made it to the *hēgemonikon*. With impulses, and especially with the emotions, the state of one's

5. Trans. de Lacy, with "impulse" substituted for "conation." Cf. *PHP* 393–94K, 206–7 de Lacy (= *SVF* 3. 479).

overall pneumatic tension affects not only what one takes in but how one reacts. Chrysippus used the example of Menelaus confronting Helen at Troy, determined to kill her but then feebly giving in because he felt overcome by her beauty. The result of his seeing Helen was his assenting to the impulse to embrace this lovely woman, which made him fail to act as he had resolved was right.[6] Emotional behavior is thus due to a weakness in the soul as a whole. Menelaus acted on what he saw to be a bad reason because his whole character was weak; an impulse was excessive in him which a stronger character might have resisted. Thus the state of soul allowing the emotion to have its way (not the emotion itself) is a weakness; the person is mentally flabby and should shape up. We can recognize, of course, the metaphor of mental health, developed in Plato's *Republic*.[7]

From this comes the thought that emotions are disorders which can be cured: one of Chrysippus' books on the emotions was called *Therapy and Ethics*.[8] Acting on emotion is acting for a bad reason through weakness of character. Because emotions are reasons, this involves a conflict in practical reasoning;[9] and further and better reasoning will remove this. Looked at from the physical point of view, the result is a literally strengthened character, with stronger pneumatic tension.

Chrysippus in fact put considerable energy into restating Plato's psychology in terms of the Stoic physical, unitary soul. Health in the soul, for example, he declared to be like health in the body: a matter of proportion, harmony, and blending.[10] This clearly recalls the *Republic*; and in his first book on emotions Chrysippus wrote a kind of epitome of Plato's views on the training of children and their motivations.[11] Unfortunately,

6. *PHP* 404–6K, 270–72 de Lacy (= *SVF* 3. 473).
7. Chrysippus developed this at length (even the prolix Cicero finds it too lengthy; see *Tusc.* 4. 23).
8. *PHP* 443K, 302–4 de Lacy.
9. Cf. *PHP* 456–58K, 314–16 de Lacy.
10. *PHP* 439–41K, 300–301 de Lacy (= *SVF* 3. 471).
11. *PHP* 466K, 324 de Lacy. We know that he also criticized Plato extensively in a work *On Justice* (see Plut. *De St. repugn.* 1040a–41b

our source for this is Galen, who fails to understand Chrysippus and is concerned to defend Plato, so we have little helpful idea as to how Plato's talk of parts of the soul was transposed into Stoic terms. Presumably, harmony between parts of the soul was restated as something like harmoniously unified functioning of the whole soul in a way appropriate to all the diverse workings of its different parts and capacities. We have one rather opaque comment from Chrysippus: "They are parts of the soul through which its reason and disposition of its reason are constituted. And a soul is beautiful or ugly by virtue of its *hēgemonikon* being in this or that state with respect to its own proper division."[12]

b) Emotions as Beliefs

The Arius passage does not make much of the theory's most controversial feature: emotions are beliefs (*doxai*) or judgments (*kriseis*). Our most extensive discussion of this comes from the hostile Galen, who has injected into many interpretations two of his own claims which are patently wrong. One is that the thesis that emotions are judgments is a willfully ludicrous and farfetched idea; the other is that it was an innovation by Chrysippus, replacing a more reasonable view held by Zeno and Cleanthes.[13]

[= (in part) *SVF* 3. 157, 313]). Note that since for the Stoics emotions involve reason, neither animals nor children have them (*PHP* 392K, 260 de Lacy; 431K, 294 de Lacy); hence moral education is, strictly, training children to come to have rational impulses.

12. *PHP* 444K, 304 de Lacy (= *SVF* 3. 471a); trans. de Lacy with slight alterations.

13. This latter claim has had great influence through its defense by Pohlenz (1965a, 1970), as part of his more general thesis that Chrysippus produced a new and more "intellectualist" Stoic psychology. Pohlenz was effectively criticized by Philippson (1937). The earlier account by Bonhoeffer (1890, esp. 262–84) is much sounder than Pohlenz's account; after long neglect it is beginning to be influential again. See also Ioppolo (1972); Glibert-Thirry (1977); Lloyd (1978); Inwood (1985).

Emotions can be said to be beliefs in just the same way that any impulse can; thus there is no problem, as Galen pretends there is, with combining the thesis that emotions are beliefs with the thesis that they are excessive impulses. Assent to a statement articulating the content of the "impulsory" appearance is part of every impulse;[14] in assenting to the statement the agent is committing herself to a corresponding practical belief. We have seen that impulses could actually be called assents, and this is clearly why they are sometimes called beliefs.

Galen more than once claims that Chrysippus contradicted Zeno on this issue,[15] and that Chrysippus said that emotions are judgments whereas Zeno thought them "contractions," "relaxations," "elations," "depressions," and the like, which "supervene" on judgments. But we can see from one incautious passage that Galen is being dishonest here.[16] We shall shortly see that Zeno's account of the "fresh" opinion actually demands that emotions be judgments. It is clear that for the Stoics emotions have to be interpreted in many ways: as movements, as impulses, as beliefs. Clearly, Zeno laid less stress than did Chrysippus on the belief element; but we have no grounds to suppose a change of doctrine.

14. Of every impulse 1, that is, the broader conception that includes impulse 2 and assent. Could one perhaps defend what look like blatant mistakes or misrepresentations on Galen's part by arguing that he is sometimes thinking of impulse 1 and sometimes of impulse 2, and that this is legitimate, since the Stoics do not explicitly distinguish them? I do not think that this is any excuse. The Stoic position is quite clear: they have in mind impulse 1, the whole phenomenon, and in different contexts emphasize one or another part of it. The only confusion seems to be Galen's own.

15. *PHP* 367K, 240 de Lacy; 377K, 246 de Lacy; 429K, 292 de Lacy; cf. *SVF* 1. 209.

16. *PHP* 478K, 334 de Lacy. Zeno's view, Galen says, can be interpreted more than one way, either as Chrysippean or as Platonic. Galen himself is obsessed with conforming the views of everyone but Chrysippus to Plato's, and his view here is almost certainly not reasonable; but at least we find him admitting that it is possible to interpret Zeno and Chrysippus as holding the same view.

Some phenomena will cause trouble for a theory that emotions are beliefs; for sometimes we feel fear, elation, or depression, while lacking any appropriate belief. We may even have a firm belief that there is nothing to fear, and still wince. But this familiar phenomenon is not a real difficulty for the Stoics; for the absence of belief precisely disinclines us to think that here we have an emotion. These are distinct, though related, phenomena, which came at some point to be called *propatheiai*, "pre-emotions."[17]

c) Emotions as Involving a "Fresh" Belief

The Arius passage preserves this point in obviously incomplete form, but it can be pieced together from other sources. The belief aspect of the emotion was analyzed into two parts. As Cicero puts it, "it has been adequately stated that distress is a belief about a present evil, a belief including this: that it is right to feel distress."[18] This is, he adds, Zeno's addition of a "fresh" (*recens*) belief to the belief about evil. This fits with Arius' statement that the "fresh" (*prosphatos*) part of the belief gets moving the irrational contraction or elevation. Arius describes the causal history; Cicero describes it from the viewpoint of the agent's reasons. It seems that the belief part of an emotion contains one part assenting to something being a

17. See Bonhoeffer (1890, 307–11); Inwood (1985); Epictetus frag. 9 (apud Aul. Gell. *Noct. Att.* 19. 1.14–20); Cic. *Tusc.* 3. 83; Plut. *Vir. mor.* 449a–b (= *SVF* 3. 439). Seneca is very interested in the *propatheiai* (*Ep.* 11, 57. 3–5; *Ira* 2. 1–2; *Ep.* 71. 29, 74. 31–32). Pohlenz (1970, 307–10; 2: 154) sees this as an attempt to mitigate the "intellectualism" of Chrysippus. But Seneca clearly takes a Chrysippean line on the *pathē*: see *Ep.* 85. 5–12 (the *pathē* are always wrong; *Ira* 1. 2.3–4; 1. 8.3). (*Ep.* 92. 8 talks of an irrational part of the soul, but this can be interpreted in Chrysippean, rather than Posidonian, fashion, pace Modrze 1932.) Seneca regards the *propatheiai* as properly belonging to the *body* (*Ep.* 71. 29) since they do not involve the belief, crucial for a *pathos*, that anything is good or evil (cf. *Ep.* 74. 31–32).
18. *Tusc.* 3. 74–75.

good (or bad) thing and another assenting to something like "I ought to rejoice (or cry) over it." This is the part that produces action, like smiling or crying; indeed it is just the part that has the form of a belief that normally leads to action. So, however tragic I think something is, unless I take it to be something I should cry over, I will not actually cry; this is the part of the thought (not, of course, a conscious thought!) that gets the tears flowing.

Cicero adds the obviously right point that "fresh" here has nothing to do with time. Artemisia thought her husband's death not just sad but something to mourn over all her life; her "fresh" belief lasted years.[19] However, Chrysippus discussed the "fresh" belief in some connection with time, since Galen preserves part of his comments on why people eventually cease to feel emotions with the original force, although retaining their original beliefs about the emotions' objects.[20] Chrysippus admits that this is hard to account for; time alone cannot make a difference, so there must be some alteration in the belief. The passage is tendentiously presented and cut off by Galen, but the solution seems to be that while we continue to think the thing bad, for example, we cease to find it something to cry over.[21] He mentions causes of laughter and may have in mind something like the following point. On hearing a joke for the first few times we find it funny and laugh at it. After the twenty-sixth hearing, we still find it funny (nothing has happened to change our opinion of that) but no longer laugh at it. We have lost the "fresh" belief that this is something to laugh at, the belief that actually gets us to laugh. So the "fresh" part of the belief will be one that we tend to lose with time, though it is not just its recentness in time that gives it its force.

19. Galen retails (*PHP* 416K, 280 de Lacy [= *SVF* 1. 213]) Posidonius' attack on Chrysippus over the "fresh" belief, in which it is interpreted in a purely temporal way, but this is clearly wrong.
20. *PHP* 419–20K, 284 de Lacy (= *SVF* 3. 466).
21. Cf. Bonhoeffer (1890, 262–84, esp. 266–73); Inwood (1985).

d) The Taxonomy of the Emotions

Many sources list the basic four emotions; Arius adds that desire and fear are prior to the other two and are directed at apparent good and evil—the apparent good, because impulses directed at the real good can never be excessive, and so emotions.[22] Pleasure and pain are secondary: they "supervene" on the other two. "The Stoics say that pleasure, if it exists, is a supervention, when nature seeking by itself finds what suits the animal's constitution."[23] We do not know exactly what the Stoics took supervenience to be. The intuitive conception of supervenience is something like this: certain conditions will produce pleasure, but there are no general necessary links between types of condition and production of pleasure. Thus pleasure results from engaging in certain types of activity in certain ways; but there is no guarantee.

There is a problem here, however; pleasure so construed is an "indifferent"; that is, it is something which is not morally good or bad and so does not add to or detract from the agent's happiness.[24] Can this be the same as the pleasure which is a *pathos*, and thus always morally bad?[25] A *pathos* is an impulse, and so something which involves the agent's assent, which does not seem to be true of a supervention. The simplest solution is that the Stoics do not think that there are two fundamentally different kinds of pleasure, but that pleasure can play either of two roles in our lives. If it simply supervenes on what we are doing, then it is morally neutral. But if our getting pleasure depends on our assent to some belief, then the pleasure itself is a *pathos*, and so bad. Pleasure is all right when it comes unbidden, as it were; but not if an impulse is required for us to have it.

22. There is an obvious asymmetry here between good and evil. Compare the point that there are only three *eupatheiai* (below).
23. D. L. 7. 86 (= *SVF* 3. 178).
24. D. L. 7. 102 (= *SVF* 3. 117).
25. Gosling and Taylor (1982) argue that the Stoics have a univocal account of pleasure; Long and Sedley (1987, 1: 405) disagree.

The Stoics made much use of definitions, and many of our sources contain long lists of subsidiary definitions of ever more finely grained emotional states, unified by the basic taxonomy which derives excess in impulse from wrong attachment to the apparent good or evil, with pleasure and pain resulting from this. The Stoic definitions are intellectualist by comparison with the accounts in the Aristotelian tradition; they lay weight on assent and thus on the agent's conception of the state of affairs, rather than on the less intellectual aspects of emotion.[26]

e) Good Feelings

So far we have not examined the thesis which was usually found to be the most startling: all *pathē* are morally bad, and the good person would be *apathēs*, without them; for, striking as this thesis is, it does not emerge from any of the considerations we have looked at so far, which have been considerations from philosophy of mind. Had Stoic ethics been different, the Stoics would not have held this thesis; but as it is, it derives from fundamental considerations in their ethics.

The Stoics hold that reason, when developed properly in a natural way (something that nobody actually achieves in our conventional and perverted societies) leads the agent to have a clear grasp of the difference between the value of virtue and the value of any other kind of aim. Thus at a certain point the rationally developed person will see that everything that he has hitherto held to be a reasonable object of pursuit is valuable, indeed, but in a way that is simply overridden by the claims of virtue. We can compare this to our distinction between moral and nonmoral value. Thus the person whose reason is right or correct, the standard of the virtuous person, will value virtue in a way which ensures that the claims of

26. This emerges clearly from a comparison of the sections on the emotions in Arius Didymus' account of Stoic ethics in Stobaeus with the corresponding sections in the Peripatetic account.

virtue will always override claims deriving from other things
that we normally consider good, such as health, wealth, power,
and so on. He will not lose interest in these things, but his
pursuit of them is always strongly conditional on their consistency with what virtue requires. The Stoics put this by saying
that the rational person realizes that only virtue is good, everything else being "indifferent."

It is this position which implies that all emotions are bad;
for emotions such as anger, fear, and so on all presuppose an
attachment to nonvirtuous aims; I cannot be angry at an insult
unless I think that social humiliation is a bad thing, getting
one's own back a good thing, and so on. But all such thoughts
involve commitment to mistaken values. Hence the emotions,
although they are rational in that they all involve commitment
to beliefs about things, are in conflict with right reason in that
they get in the way of our accepting and living by the moral
point of view which reason reveals: the point of view from
which nothing but virtue and vice matter. Emotions thus are
not good, since they do not encourage us to become attached
to moral value. They are not even neutral, but positively harmful, since they encourage us to become attached to values
which militate against giving moral value the supremacy that
reason demands.

Nothing in this picture demands that the virtuous Stoic
would or should be affectless, and this would be a misinter-
pretation of *apatheia;* for while *pathē* are always bad, there
are some corresponding good states, *eupatheiai.*[27] If you are
virtuous, and thus your impulses are all in accord with right
reason, you will not feel fear, but you will feel something; you
will be in the affective state of precaution (*eulabeia*). Similarly,
you will feel wish (*boulēsis*), not desire, and joy (*chara*), not

27. Difficulty has been felt over how a *pathos* state can be good.
Clearly in *eupatheia* the *pathos* element has its everyday neutral
meaning, and in *apatheia* its negative connotations within Stoic theory. But this is easy enough to recognize; the Stoics may be deliberately making the point that *only* for the wise person is any form of
pathos not a bad thing. In any case, little weight seems to have been
laid on the term; Cicero uses *constantia.*

pleasure. There is no rational analogue to feeling pain. *Eupatheiai* are achieved only by the virtuous person, whose impulses are not excessive; they are the states you will be in if you are attached in the right way to moral value, and thus, while caring in the normal way for things with nonmoral value, do not wrongly value them in a way which could lead you to give morality less than its proper, overriding place. Since *eupatheiai* are defined via ideal conditions, it is not very surprising that we have no very intuitive idea of what they would be like.

f) The Unity of the Soul

This theory of the emotions is marked throughout by tremendous stress on the soul's unity. The soul is diversified, but functions as a whole; it has no part which could conflict with the centralized rational *hēgemonikon*. Our emotions and feelings, turbulent and dysfunctional though they can be, cannot be ascribed to an irrational part of the soul over which the agent has only indirect control. They are something *done* by the whole soul, just as much as wise and considered actions. Chrysippus' most famous example for a person acting emotionally was a man running instead of walking:

> When a man walks in accordance with an impulse, the motion of his legs is not excessive but is in some way commensurate with the impulse, so that he may stop when he wishes, or change his pace. But when persons run in accordance with an impulse, this sort of thing no longer happens. The movement of the legs exceeds the impulse, so that they are carried away and do not obediently change their pace [as they did before] the moment they set out to do so. I think that something similar to these [movements of the legs] happens also in impulses because of an excess beyond the rational measure, so that when a man exercises the impulse he is not obedient to reason; and whereas the excess in running is termed contrary to

the impulse, the excess in impulse is termed contrary to reason. (*PHP* 369–70K, 240–42 de Lacy)[28]

Emotional behavior is seen not as internal conflict or break-down, but as the whole unified person being out of control. The walker can adapt to circumstances, the runner cannot; but the runner is just the walker going too fast, not the walker afflicted by lack of coordination. From this stress on unity flows the other striking feature of the theory: we are responsible for our emotions, just as we are for our more considered actions. We cannot shove them off on a conveniently non-rational part of us and say that an emotional outburst was "not really me" or the like. Excessive impulses have been assented to, just as much as the ones that accord with right reason.

Common sense, boosted by Platonic and Aristotelian the-ory, tends to the alternative, inner-conflict model of emotion, with a soul divided between rational and irrational parts. One thing this tends to lead to is a distancing of oneself from the part labeled irrational; it and its impulses come to be seen as "lower," and for Plato at least as the "bestial" part of oneself; one identifies, as we put it, with the rational part, which has the other part (mostly) under control. But if the whole soul is rational and undivided, we are indissolubly identified with our emotions and their expression. The Stoics, in a way in-terestingly like early Sartre, insist that emotions involve the whole soul and are expressed in all its activities; they are not produced by a subordinate and potentially alien force within us. If I get angry, I am, says Chrysippus, like the out-of-control runner: what makes me do it is "outside me, not inside."[29] A later passage makes clear that the outside force is "the con-vincingness of appearances, and instruction."[30] Acting emo-tionally is not being overcome by my "lower self"; it is being overimpressed, through weakness of character, by the way the

28. Trans. de Lacy, with "impulse" for "conation."
29. *PHP* 412K, 276–78 de Lacy.
30. *PHP* 463K, 320 de Lacy.

situation appears. I am fully responsible for assenting to that appearance instead of thinking things through more fully.[31]

Throughout antiquity the Stoic theory was wrongly taken to imply an extreme intellectualism about the emotions. Yet we have from Chrysippus vivid descriptions of irrational behavior: when in a passion we bite the keys and kick the door when it fails to open quickly enough and take out our anger on inanimate objects like balls of wool.[32] Chrysippus also discussed *akrasia* and its most famous literary exemplar, Medea, at length.[33] For the Stoics, of course, these phenomena show not that there are warring parts of the soul but rather that we can come to identify with bad, as well as with good, reasons. As Plutarch puts it,

> they say that the emotion is not distinct from reason, and that there is no dispute or civil war between two things, but a turning of one and the same reason to both sides, which we do not notice because of its suddenness and speed; for we do not grasp that it is the nature of the same aspect of the soul to desire and to change one's mind, to feel anger and feel fear, to be carried toward what is shameful by pleasure and to be carried back again and get a hold of itself. (*Vir. mor.* 446f [= *SVF* 3. 459])[34]

But Plutarch states the theory only to complain that it is ludicrously false to the facts; whereas of course it is claiming to redescribe those facts.

31. Cf. Bréhier (1950, 258): "La passion vient de nous, au même titre que l'acte raisonnable; on a tort d'y chercher la trace d'une force irrationelle qui est en dehors de nous, et que notre vrai moi doit comme dompter du dehors; notre ennemi est en nous-même, et il est l'expression et le résultat de ce que nous sommes; nous ne sommes pas dans la vie morale comme des spectateurs d'une lutte entre deux principes; nous devons nous transformer nous-même."

32. *PHP* 414–15K, 278–80 de Lacy (= *SVF* 3. 478). This clearly memorable passage is discussed by Philodemus in the very fragmentary frag. 2 of *On Anger*.

33. See the excellent discussion of this in Gill (1983).

34. Plutarch also makes the telling point that the Stoics have difficulty giving a convincing account of *enkrateia*, self-control, as well as of *akrasia*.

Even the more favorably disposed can accept the wrong picture of what the Stoics are doing. Cicero in *Tusculan Disputations* 4 makes a gallant attempt to compromise by combining Stoic accounts of the emotions with a Platonic division of the soul into rational and irrational parts. The result is merely edifying muddle: Cicero persists in treating the Stoic ideal of banishing *pathē* as a more rigoristic version of other theories' demand to moderate the *pathē*, failing to see that within the different theories *pathē* have quite different implications. The Stoics emerge as edifyingly high-minded, but comically unrealistic, about the emotions; and this was the caricature that survived in most popular, and even philosophical, discussions.[35]

One Stoic, Posidonius, made a real and unexpected modification to the theory.[36] He criticized Chrysippus and appeared to revert to a Platonic picture of distinct rational and nonrational faculties in the soul. Unfortunately, our information here comes from Galen, who uses him as a stick with which to beat Chrysippus, and it is hard to know how much of the Platonizing is read in by Galen.

Galen preserves only one (oft-repeated) argument, one agreeing with Posidonius' character as an indefatigable searcher for causes.[37] When an impulse is excessive, what makes it so? The cause cannot be reason, for reason is against the action and cannot be responsible for its own defeat. So it must be a further, irrational element in the soul. However, we already know the cause—it is weakness of character, weak tension in the whole soul. Galen takes this as an argument for ascribing emotions to a part of the soul distinct from reason, but as so considered, it is feeble.

It is possible, of course, that Galen is unfairly representing Posidonius as much more of a Platonist than he was, and that

35. See Dillon (1983) for failure to understand the theory in the Platonist tradition.
36. See Theiler's (1982) collection of the fragments; also Kidd (1971); Cooper (forthcoming).
37. *PHP* 378K, 248 de Lacy; 398–403K, 264–70 de Lacy; 463K, 320 de Lacy.

his real view was consistent with orthodox Stoicism, and much less extreme.[38] We know that Posidonius' interest in the emotions was connected with an interest in their educability, and he seems, as far as we can glimpse his position through Galen, to have been concerned with general patterns of predisposition to emotions. His claim may have been that humans have stable patterns of nonrational "emotional movements" (*pathētikai kinēseis*) which make us inclined to emotions.[39] Thus we might be said to come already equipped with "emotional movements" of a reactive and aggressive kind, which predispose us to anger. This does not make anger itself irrational (thus Galen is wrong in assimilating Posidonius to the Platonic view which places anger in a distinct, nonrational part of the soul). So Posidonius may well have kept to the orthodox Stoic view of what emotions are: they are judgments and so on, and thus rational. But he thought that he could give a better and more convincing account of the emotions if he allowed that we had certain "emotional movements" in the soul which were not themselves emotions but explained why we tend to be prone to commiting ourselves to wrong values and thus to feeling emotions. Thus his view would be orthodox at core but would allow more weight than Chrysippus did to factors which encourage some philosophers to posit a nonrational part of the soul, and to ascribe emotions to it.

This is an attractive interpretation; it would explain what is otherwise puzzling, namely, why Posidonius thought of his view

38. See Cooper (forthcoming). As Cooper points out, it is clear that Galen's presentation of Chrysippus' view is thoroughly marred by incomprehension, and we have no very good reason to expect him to give us a more respectable picture of Posidonius.

39. Cooper's article claims that Posidonius is misrepresented by Galen as holding that emotions themselves are irrational or belong to a part of the soul distinct from reason. One aspect of this is that Galen identifies *pathē*, emotions themselves, with *pathētikai kinēseis*, "emotional movements," which on the present account are only a predisposing condition. Cooper points out that there are passages which suggest, despite Galen's bias, that for Posidonius emotional movements were distinct, and functioned as suggested: *PHP* 464–65K, 322 de Lacy; 463K, 320 de Lacy; 422K, 286 de Lacy; 424K, 288 de Lacy.

as a Stoic view. Overall, however, its advantages are balanced
by disadvantages. Posidonius can certainly give a more plausible account than Chrysippus of why I may continue to feel
depressed and grieving, for example, long after I show every
other sign of having lost the belief on which the grief was
based.[40] And he can give a better account of why people in
general are inclined to get angry, feel fear, and so on: this is
for him an aspect of our common human nature, not a consensus in the kind of mistakes that we make. However, Chrysippus' account can give a better account of something very
important for the Stoics, namely, our responsibility for our
emotions. Indeed, on Posidonius' account it would be possible
partly at least to reject responsibility for having an emotion,
on the grounds that one was burdened with emotional movements that were not under one's control to have or not, and
which made it unreasonably difficult to refuse to have the
emotion in question.[41]

40. Chrysippus can of course appeal to the distinctness of the
standing belief that the thing is or is not valuable, and the "fresh"
part of the belief that gets us to grieve, rejoice, and so on. But Posidonius can give a far better account of the kind of case where I
continue to be emotionally affected when I seem to have lost the
belief about the value of the object: I have ceased to have the emotion
but continue to be affected by the emotional movements.
41. Cooper suggests that it is because of this implication that Posidonius' account was not generally accepted by later Stoics, even
where they might well allow that he gives an account superior to
Chrysippus' of the phenomenon of emotions in isolation.

Part Three

The Epicureans

6

Atomism and Agents

a) Physicalism and Reductivism

Epicurean and Stoic theories of the soul are often structurally very similar and sometimes also similar in detail. The two theories have very different metaphysical backing: the Stoics have a continuum theory of matter and hold that the universe is animate and runs by laws which reveal the workings of providence, while the Epicureans have an atomic theory of matter and reject all appeal to providence and any kind of teleology. They also have different ethical contexts: the Stoics think that rationality is what is crucially important in our ethical development, while Epicurus holds that our final end is pleasure, and that this is revealed to us directly by our feelings. However, the two theories share a common physicalist framework of thinking about the soul and in many ways have far more in common with each other than either does with a theory like Aristotle's. The chief differences are due to the fact that the Stoics are heavily influenced by contemporary medical and scientific theories, whereas Epicurus is less impressed by scientific results and more reliant on a combination of commonsense folk psychology and straightforward philosophical argument.[1]

1. Epicurus is clearly influenced in his physics by Aristotle's criticisms of atomism, and we know from a papyrus fragment that he

"The soul is a body of fine parts, spread over the whole assemblage."[2] Epicurus has one brisk argument for the soul's physicality, which appeals to the principles of Epicurean physics: everything in the world must be explained in terms only of Epicurus' meager ontology of atoms and void.[3] This applies to the soul in just the same way that it applies to everything else. Thus, he says, we cannot conceive of anything existent that is not body, except the void. The void can neither act nor be acted on. But soul clearly does both. The soul therefore must be body. The crucial premise here is that only body (ultimately, atoms) can act or be acted on. Lucretius develops a different argument, from interaction: the soul moves the body, and what happens to the body affects the soul.[4] Hence the soul is a body. Lucretius relies on the more roundabout premise that interaction requires touch and that this requires body.

We have seen the Stoics use versions of these arguments;[5] they are part of shared Hellenistic philosophical currency. They make it clear that Epicurus is a physicalist, as defined in part 1. Study of the soul is part of *phusikē*, enquiry into the natural world; Epicurean *phusikē* recognizes only two kinds of basic item, atoms and void, so the soul must be accounted for, in some way, in terms of atoms and void.

Epicurus is sometimes thought to have abandoned physicalism (or, alternatively, to have made his version of physicalism untenable) because he modified Democritean atomism by allowing a random "swerve" among the atoms; the swerve is connected in our chief sources with our having freedom of

---

read the *Physics* and *Analytics* (Philodemus *Pap. Herc.* 1005; Arrighetti 1973, 473). But claims that his philosophy of mind and particularly action are heavily influenced by Aristotle seem to me exaggerated (see Diano 1974a; Furley 1967; Englert 1988).

2. *Ep. Herod.* 63.

3. For his argument for the soul's physicality see *Ep. Herod.* 67. For some texts on the basic principles of Epicurean physics, see Long and Sedley (1987, 4–13). Texts on the soul can be found on pp. 14 and 15. Some passages discussed in this section, on free agency, are on p. 20.

4. 3.161–76.

5. In part 2, chapter 2, section a.

action,[6] and it is often concluded that free human actions are, for Epicurus, due to events which breach regular Epicurean physical laws.

The swerve will be discussed in chapter 8; for now it is enough to note that the above conclusion would be confused. The swerve introduces an indeterminate element into physics, but this is a thesis within physics,[7] not an abandonment of physicalism. It complicates the physical picture but is not a breach of it. It is not defined in terms of solving a problem of free agency; it is just a factor in the physical world, which operates in us, and also enables the production of worlds to get going.

It is often assumed that Epicurus was not only a physicalist but a reductivist. Possibly the tone of some of his writings may have given a handle to this: Epicurus is sometimes aggressively philistine, and we find Sextus asking the Epicureans how plea-sure can exist in "the heap of atoms" they call the soul.[8] But it is clear that Epicurus is not a reductivist from a striking passage in book 25 of *On Nature*, fragments of which we pos-sess.[9] Epicurus argues in this passage against the thesis that all events in the world, including our actions and thoughts, come about "of necessity." He allows that the truth about the physical world is given by atomic theory, which is (apart from the swerve, which is not mentioned in this text) determinist. So at the atomic level, events do happen "of necessity." But it is a mistake to conclude from this that, at the macro-level, my actions happen of necessity. It seems as though they must; for my action of arguing, say, *is* atoms moving in various ways

6. Diogenes of Oenoanda frag. 32; Lucr. 2. 256–60. See chapter 8 below.

7. And is so introduced by Lucretius (2. 216–93).

8. *Pyr.* 3. 187.

9. That this is the number of this book has been argued by Laursen (1987). See also Diano (1946); Sedley (1974, 1983, 1989). The text can be found in Arrighetti [34]; there are sections with translation in Sedley (1983); in Long and Sedley (1987, 2:20 B and C; 1:20 j); and in Laursen (1988). I have had the benefit of seeing Laursen's new readings for much of this book; I am very grateful. A new edition by Laursen of the entire text (which exists in fragments from three pa-pyri) is forthcoming.

which come about of necessity: so how can it not come about
of necessity that I am arguing? Against Democritus Epicurus
argues that this involves one in a blindness to oneself that lands
one in a self-refuting position.[10]

He begins from the fact that we have practices of praise,
blame, and the like, which make sense only on the assumption
that we are agents capable of choice between perceived alternatives, and not just nodes in causal chains. He contrasts
these practices with the way we treat wild animals, which we
do not treat as agents but merely handle as best we can.[11]
Epicurus then addresses the reductivist opponent who claims
that these beliefs and practices are undermined by the truth
of deterministic atomism, since all our actions are "merely"
movements of atoms, so that even our very praising and blam-
ing are "of necessity." Epicurus maintains that

> such an argument refutes itself [lit. turns itself upside
> down] and never can establish that everything is such as
> the things which are said to happen according to neces-
> sity. Rather, he combats a person on this very point as
> though it were because of himself that the person were
> being silly. And even if he goes on *ad infinitum* saying
> that the person is doing *that* according to necessity, al-
> ways from arguments, he is failing to reason in that he
> ascribes to himself the cause of having reasoned correctly

10. Democritus is not named explicitly, but there are Epicurean
precedents for seeing him referred to here as "the great man"; see
Sedley (1983). For Epicurus' argument see Arrighetti [34.30]; Sedley
(1983, 20, 29–30 with n. 28); Long and Sedley (1987, 20 C [13]). This
passage has been extensively discussed; see Laks (1981); Gigante (1981,
56–62).

11. Arrighetti [34.30]; Sedley (1983, 24 n. 18); Long and Sedley
(1987, 20 j); Laursen (1988, 17). In contrast to admonition (*nouthe-
tikos . . . tropos*), we exonerate wild animals instead of admonishing
them or trying to reform them, or indeed regarding ourselves as
retaliating against them. We treat them not as agents whose developments are up to them, but "conflate their developments (*apoge-
gennēmena*) and their makeup (*sustasis*) alike into a single thing."
Elsewhere in the book Epicurus denies that we do this in the case of
responsible agents.

and to his opponent the cause of having reasoned incorrectly.[12] (Arrighetti [34.28]; Sedley 1983, 19; Long and Sedley 1987, 20 C [5]–[6])

Epicurus is using a standard ancient "overturning" argument.[13] It involves what we would call pragmatic self-refutation. There is no formal self-contradiction, but what the person says or puts forward is, it is claimed, undermined by her way of saying it or putting it forward. An example would be proving that there is no such thing as proof. If I prove to you that there is no such thing as proof, then what I prove (that there is no such thing as proof) is pragmatically refuted by the fact that I prove it. If I win, I lose. Epicurus claims here that reductivists like Democritus fall into a trap of this form and that they are "blind to themselves" because they fail to notice this point.

The reductivist holds that because all human actions are movements of atoms, human actions are "necessitated"; thus they are not really up to us, as we suppose them to be, and there is really no such thing as free human acting. If so, of course, there is really no such thing as arguing, criticizing, and so on; what we think to be such is "nothing but" atoms moving in the void in ways that they have to move. However, the reductivist *argues* against Epicurus to this effect, *states* and *defends* his view, *criticizes* Epicurus for getting it wrong, and so on. And all this undermines his thesis, since it presupposes that the thesis is mistaken. Hence he is landed with a conflict between his thesis and what he is doing in stating and defending his thesis. He can of course retreat, admitting of what he says that it was necessitated. But the retreat can never be quite fast enough; in *admitting* this he is presupposing the falsity of his thesis. As Epicurus points out, at every stage of his retreat what he does is in conflict with the thesis he holds.

Epicurus does not here meet the more sophisticated determinist who claims that the necessitation appropriate to atomic

12. Cf. *Vatican Sentence* (hereafter *VS*) 40: "The person who says that everything comes about according to necessity cannot criticize the person who denies it—for he says that this too comes about according to necessity."

13. For this kind of argument see Burnyeat (1976).

motions is not in conflict with human agency because it is compatible with it. Epicurus is here concerned only with the opponent who tries to undermine our everyday concept or *prolēpsis* of agency. The opponent, he says, is trying to change our concept of what it is to act. But he has not succeeded in doing this unless he can evade the self-refutation argument, and otherwise he is in effect just changing a word by calling "necessitated" what we call free agency, and this is futile, since it makes no real difference.[14]

Epicurus' is the first in a long line of arguments to establish nonreductive physicalism by showing that reductivism (at least in a determinist version) cannot be consistently stated. So, there are facts about atoms and facts about human agency, and each set of facts will be real; it will be wrong to treat the latter as a mere appearance of the former.[15] We should note that this argument does *not* show that Epicurus is not a determinist. It shows that he thinks that, properly understood, determinism must be compatible with our commonsense understanding of ourselves and of the world. The argument is thus more properly antireductivist than antideterminist.[16]

Epicurus is thus justified in distinguishing between what happens by necessity or by chance from what depends on us

14. Arrighetti [34.(28)19–(30)7]; Long and Sedley (1987, 20 C [8]–[12]).

15. There is also a specifically Epicurean argument; see Arrighetti [34.28–30]; Sedley (1983, 20; cf. 27–28); Long and Sedley (1987, 20 C [8]). If the reductivist claims that talk of "necessity" does not conflict with, but rather has proper application to, what we do "through ourselves," by our own agency, then he is merely changing the word; our "conception" (*prolēpsis*) of our own agency precisely contrasts with being necessitated. This argument also has modern analogues.

16. As Sedley (1983, 1989) recognizes, though he conflates reductivism with eliminativism and takes the argument to be stronger than it is, claiming that it shows that Epicurus was not only not a determinist but not a physicalist either. Given our total evidence about Epicurus, it is impossible that a breach in his physicalism should have gone unnoticed in the ancient world (see the end of this section), and the argument does not even show that Epicurus is not a determinist; it shows only that if he is (as he seems to be) he must be a compatibilist.

(*par' hēmas*).[17] It is noteworthy that Epicurus does not claim that things are up to us (*eph' hēmin*) but that they depend on us (*par' hēmas*). He is defending the intuitive idea that we are agents, and seems not to want to defend a very strong and possibly unintuitive version of the idea.[18]

In particular, moral development is real; Lucretius insists that by reasoning the individual can overcome handicaps of inherited temperament.[19] In several unfortunately fragmentary and difficult parts of *On Nature* 25 Epicurus insists that our atomic constitution is to be distinguished from our "development" (*apogegennēmenon*), which depends on us. It depends on me, not just my atoms, how I develop and what kind of a person I become; even though it is a truth of physics that I *am* atoms. This is a defense of common sense: my physical makeup and the experience I have put some constraints on what I can become, but still how I develop depends on me. As Epicurus explains,

> from the first beginning we have seeds directing us, some toward some things, others toward others, others toward both—in every case seeds, which may be many or few, of actions, thoughts, and dispositions.[20] Thus it depends on us at first absolutely what becomes of what is already a development, whether of one or another kind, and the things which of necessity flow in from the environment through the pores depend on us when they come about at some time, and depend on our beliefs that come from ourselves. (Arrighetti [34.26]; Sedley 1983, 36–37; Long and Sedley 1987, 20 C [1])

17. As he does at *Ep. Men.* 133.

18. Epicurus does not use *epi* with the dative with the meaning "up to the person," an idiom common among other philosophers. He prefers *para*, which has the force of "depending"; there is a parallel in the fourth sceptical Mode (see Annas and Barnes 1985, chap. 7).

19. 3. 307–22.

20. The Greek is syntactically ambiguous, and Sedley translates with actions, thoughts, and so on being what the seeds direct us toward, not what they are seeds of.

Epicurus clearly has great reliance on our commonsense view of ourselves as free, developing agents.[21]

In this passage, which is unfortunately both highly technical and very fragmentary, Epicurus talks of, on the one hand, the self ("we") and the development and, on the other, of the atoms, the nature, and the constitution. Sometimes the development seems to depend on the self (as in the above passage), but the text as a whole supports the view that Epicurus is simply talking about an agent who develops. Sometimes the agent is identified with her development, sometimes the development is discussed separately, as being an aspect of the agent as a whole. On the other side, the constitution (sometimes the original constitution) is distinguished from the development. The development changes the original constitution and gets it to change or "grow" in some respect. The nature is simply the nature of the constitution; and likewise the atoms are the atoms of the constitution. There is no implication that the self or the development are nonatomic, but the atoms of the constitution can be contrasted with the atoms which impinge from the outside and help to produce the development.[22]

Epicurus thus sees us, commonsensically enough despite the jargon, as developing agents, indeed as agents who develop ourselves. Although humans are atomic compounds like any other, they differ from other kinds of atomic compounds in that their growth and functioning is not to be explained solely in terms of automatic response to stimuli from outside. How they develop depends to some extent, though not totally, on themselves, on what they do with the information they take in, how they decide to react selectively to it, and what kinds of character and dispositions they build up.[23] Thus Epicurus

21. On the argument of these difficult texts see Sedley (1983, 1989); Laursen (1988); Annas (1991 and forthcoming).
22. Sedley (1983, 1989) claims that the self is distinct from *all* atoms, and that Epicurus is thus not a physicalist (see above n. 16). For arguments against this as a reading of this text see Annas (forthcoming).
23. The last clause goes beyond anything explicitly in the papyrus,

is concerned to do justice to folk psychology's belief that we are agents who move and develop ourselves. This point on its own does not determine either the outline or the detail of any metaphysical conception of the self; it is a minimal basis compatible with a number of different kinds of theoretical explanation. As to how such self-development is possible we find in the fragments only the point that we have from the very start "seeds," potentials for developing one way rather than the other. This is taken for granted and not further defended.

The only hint we find in the remains of this book as to how we develop ourselves lies in the reference to the information we take in from the environment depending on the beliefs we have. It is because we have reason and can form beliefs that we develop as agents; this is clear already from the passage from Lucretius which tells us that by developing our reason we can order the rest of our nature and overcome the tendencies we are born with.[24] Reason, however, takes many forms; we shall see in the next section that they are not all limited to humans.

There is one passage of book 25 which seems to suggest something stronger than the commonsense picture:

Many [developments?][25] which have a nature which is capable of becoming productive of both this and that through themselves do not become productive, and it is not because of the same cause in the atoms and in themselves.[26] These in particular we combat and rebuke . . .

---

but the opening and concluding fragments make it fairly clear that the book was concerned with ethically right development.

24. See p. 129 and n. 19 above.

25. Long and Sedley (1987) take the subject here to be *zōia*, that is, the agents or selves themselves. Laursen (1988) argues that the subjects must be the developments themselves.

26. The Greek is syntactically ambiguous; Long and Sedley take "through themselves" with "do not become" rather than with "becoming productive."

in accordance with[27] their nature, which is disturbed from the beginning, as is true of all animals; for in their case the nature of the atoms has contributed nothing to some of their actions, and to the extent of their actions and dispositions, but the developments themselves contain all or most of the cause of some of these things. As a result of that nature some of the atoms' motions are moved in a disturbed way, not in every way through the atoms, but through what enters . . . from the environment into the natural . . . combatting and advising many people together, which is opposed to the necessary cause of the same kind. Thus when something develops which has some distinctness among the atoms[28] in a differential way which is not like that from a different distance,[29] it acquires a cause from itself, then transmits it at once to the primary natures and in some way makes all of it one.[30] (Arrighetti [34.21–22]; Sedley 1983, 36–38; Long and Sedley 1987, 20 B [1]–[6]; Laursen 1988, 17–18)

This passage has been made the basis for claims that Epicurus holds that we are not just agents in the commonsense understanding of self-developers, but selves in a way that transcends atomism altogether.[31] However, it is important to note that this passage concerns *disordered* people, in whom something, though it is not clear just what, has gone wrong. Furthermore, even in these people it is only some of their actions to which the atoms contribute nothing,[32] and even then we are told that the development accounts for all or most of the

27. There is a participle here, but the verb is uncertain. Long and Sedley read "hating them" (*misountes*).
28. Long and Sedley (1987) read "distinctness *from* the atoms." See Sedley (1983). For the present reading see Laursen (1988, 12–13).
29. See Sedley (1989, n. 45); on "differential" see Laursen (1988, 13–14).
30. See Laursen (1988, 14–15) for difficulties in identifying the subject here. Long and Sedley (1987) translate "he," importing a hitherto unmarked subject.
31. See Sedley (1983, 1989) and the commentary on Long and Sedley (1987, 20 B, C, and j).
32. The atoms of the constitution, that is; see p. 130 above.

cause of what they do. This is, therefore, not an account of normal agency, and so cannot give us Epicurus' own view of human agency.

However, it is interesting to us even as an account of deviant agency, and it is a pity that it is so hard to see just what has gone wrong. Epicurus says that the condition of "all animals" is disturbed from the beginning; this may well include humans, and seems to embody the idea that we achieve the desirable Epicurean ethical end of untroubledness (*ataraxia*) as we mature, by imposing order on our initially disorderly nature. What is wrong with the agents here is that they are like immature, disorderly agents. However, this does not seem to be what they are themselves, since the passage suggests that they are perverse or deviant, rather than immature. Perhaps the nearest we can get to a general interpretation of what is going on is that two things are true of these agents. The way they are developing is at odds with their constitution. They are developing, or trying to develop, in ways that do not fit the way they have developed hitherto. Secondly, their constitution is, as a result, disorderly, like the initial state of immature agents.

However we interpret the details of this passage, the overall picture which emerges is that of an Epicurus who is impressed by the fact that humans are a self-moving kind of thing, with potential to develop in diverse ways, but who does not react by abandoning physicalism. We shall see further that he is quite ingenious in working out details of a thoroughly physicalist account of the soul. He is aware that there is a tension between reductive physicalism and our commonsense view of ourselves, which he wants to preserve, and he responds with an argument to show that reductivism cannot, in principle, be true. It is clear even by this point that Epicurus' account is answering to a number of constraints. His philosophy of mind must be physicalist, and in particular must be developed within his version of atomism. It is also, as we shall see, an empiricist account. But it also takes very seriously what we believe about ourselves, and where this conflicts with a possible way for his theory to develop, it is the theory he rejects and not our intuitive picture of ourselves as developing agents. We have to wait until later to find out what makes us *free* agents.[33]

b) Soul in the World

The Stoic cosmos is animate, designed by providence, and permeated by reason. The Epicurean cosmos is none of these things, and this makes a big difference to the place in it of human beings.

The motions of atoms in the void give rise to compounds among which are animate, sensing, beings; but the atoms themselves are inanimate;[34] Epicurus rejects the panpsychist demand that life be present in the ultimate constituents of what has life. Hence there is no Epicurean world soul; living beings do not display in themselves the workings of principles of life also at work in the universe as a whole.

Further, Epicurus rejects providence and any teleology, both for the world as a whole and for its parts.[35] Since the world is not an ordered whole, humans have no particular place in it; there is no scale of beings. "The soul is a peculiar kind of thing, like nothing else."[36] For Epicurus there is also nothing like Stoic rationality which permeates the world and gives it (in many senses) significance. Rationality does not cut humans sharply off from animals as it does for the Stoics. Animals as well as humans act freely; at least Lucretius illustrates the existence of free impulse (*libera voluntas*) from the example of horses in a race.[37] Further, a passage in *On Nature* 25 distinguishes between wild and tame animals by the extent

33. See chapter 8.
34. As Lucretius argues at length (2. 865–990).
35. Lucr. 4. 823–57.
36. Philodemus *On Signs* 25. 3–4.
37. 2. 263–71. Huby (1969) finds this problematic and contrasts the *On Nature* passage about wild and tame animals. But the problem is greatly lessened once we realize that *libera voluntas* is not "free will" but the capacity for free action (see chapter 8).

to which their reaction is straightforwardly caused by input from the environment, or depends on the animal itself.[38]

The Epicureans in fact have a position strikingly different from the Stoics' on "the reason of animals." Not only does Lucretius talk of horses having *libera voluntas,* he talks of horses and deer as having a mind.[39] However, Hermarchus, an early Epicurean, denies, in a discussion of justice and animals, that animals have *logos* or reasoning. That is, he says, why we can make no contracts with them.[40] Humans, as opposed to animals, have advanced in civilization because they can reason about what is in their interests, whereas animals have only "irrational memory."[41]

Are these mutually contradictory views on the part of different branches of the school? They seem rather to be a matter of differences of emphasis. We find a more nuanced view in a later head of the school, Polystratus.[42] Animals, he says, share broad general features with us but are importantly different. They take in, but do not understand as we do,[43] certain things: prudential concepts (healthy, expedient), ethical concepts (fine, base), religious concepts (sacred, profane), and signs (*sēmeia*). The last amounts to the claim that animals have no inferential reasoning; this explains, for Polystratus, why they cannot foresee problems, learn from the past, assess their own

38. Arrighetti [34.25]; Sedley (1983, 24 n. 18); Long and Sedley (1987, 20 j); Laursen (1988, 17).

39. Horses: 2. 265, 268 (*mens*), 270 (*animus*). Deer have a *mens* at 3. 299.

40. Frag. 34 Longo Auricchio (= Porph. *Abst.* 1. 7–12, 26, 4) 12. 5–6.

41. Hence the rather bleak conclusion that the rise of human society is at the expense of animals, who are "expelled" from it, and to whom we owe no duties of justice.

42. In the opening columns (1–8) of his *On Irrational Contempt for Popular Opinions.*

43. *Sunoran:* they cannot "see them together." It is tempting, though speculative, to connect this with passages in *On Nature* 25 that talk of thinking of oneself, and seem to be discussing the idea of holding together different experiences as experiences of the same self: Arrighetti [34.14–16].

interests, or reflect on their lives as wholes.[44] So animals "do not share in reasoning, or not one like ours."[45] Yet Polystratus thinks it ridiculous to deny that we are in general ways like animals, as the Stoics do.

The obvious way to make all this consistent is to recognize that animals have some reasoning capacities, but not others; in particular, not the ones that distinguish humans, which we inevitably call the higher ones. This is a commonsense conclusion, but it has an important, though overlooked, consequence: for the Epicureans rationality is not a single kind of thing but a cluster of capacities, some of which animals share with us and some not. We shall see that Epicurus frequently falls into difficulties over the status of the rational part of the soul, and much of his philosophy of mind would have benefited from taking more to heart this consequence of denying a sharp cutoff between humans and other animals.[46]

Kuria doxa 32 encapsulates the Epicurean attitude to what divides us from animals: "As for those animals that cannot make contracts about not harming one another or being harmed—toward these there is no just or unjust; and similarly with those nations that cannot or will not make contracts about not harming or being harmed."[47] We do not owe duties of justice to animals; but this is merely because they do not have enough reasoning capacity to make and keep contracts—something true of some humans also. And we can see from book 5 of Lucretius how deeply ambivalent the Epicureans are about the "progress" of civilization and the ways in which

44. Polystratus seems to be denying animals some kind of memory; possibly he would allow, with Hermarchus, that they have "irrational" memory.

45. Polystr. 7. 6–8.

46. Epicureans are often willing to see specifically human capacities as more developed forms of what we can see in other animals. They hold this for human language (Lucr. 5. 1056–90), sexual desire (4. 1192–1207), and dreams (4. 986–1010).

47. We find the content of this and associated *Doxai* expanded by Hermarchus, Epicurus' successor, in the work paraphrased by Porphyry in *De abstinentia* 1. 7–12. Cf. Clay (1983).

we have used our reasoning to differentiate ourselves from animals.

c) The Nature and Structure of the Soul

"The soul consists of the smoothest and roundest atoms, greatly superior [sc. in these respects] to those of fire."[48] The soul animates the entire body without depending on bulk or brute force, merely because of the nature of its composition. "The soul provides nature with the reason for the [presence or absence of] life. For even though it does not possess the same number of atoms as the body, being placed in it with its rational and irrational elements, nevertheless it encompasses the whole body and, being bound by it, binds it in its turn, just as the shortest dash of acid juice curdles a vast quantity of milk."[49]

The soul is a combination of four kinds of soul atom. It is puzzling that Epicurus' own *Letter to Herodotus* 63 so understates the doctrine as to be seriously misleading,[50] but we know from other sources that the soul is constituted of atoms of four kinds: firelike, airlike, *pneuma*-like, and nameless.[51] The claim that the first three kinds of atoms are *like* the atoms of fire, air, and so on presumably amounts to something like the following. The soul does not contain just the kind of fire that we find in fireplaces, but something which is like that in basic

48. Schol. in *Ep. Herod.* 66 (= Usener 311); cf. Lucr. 3. 177–230.
49. Diogenes of Oenoanda frag. 37, col. 1; trans. Chilton, with slight alterations.
50. Kerferd (1971) ingeniously avoids the problem by denying that the relevant sentence of Epicurus refers to the composition of the soul at all.
51. See Plut. *Adv. Col.* 1118d–e; Aët. 4. 3, 11, p. 388 Diels (hereafter D) (= Usener 315); Lucr. 3. 231–322. Sharples (1980) argues that Lucretius is talking about ordinary fire, air, and wind, not atoms that are fire*like* and so on. But our other sources give the more cautious view. Plutarch has *ek tinos thermou kai pneumatikou;* Aëtius has *ek poiou purōdous, ek poiou aērōdous, ek poiou pneumatikou.*

respects, but more refined (it does not burn the rest of the soul, for example). The idea we have of it comes from our idea of fire, indeed for Epicurus it has to, since he is an empiricist and holds that our concepts are built up from what we encounter in experience. Thus our concept of it is simply something fire*like,* since we have no direct access to it in experience; all we can do is simply extend the experiential conception that we do have.

The basis for this account of the soul's composition is just the commonsense observation that "a certain thin breath mixed with heat leaves the dying, and heat, further, brings air along with it."[52] It is notable here that *pneuma* has retained its commonsense meaning of "breath," in contrast to its dramatic theoretical development in Aristotle and the medical writers. So far is Epicurus from what was to become the scientific mainstream, in which *pneuma* is essentially warm, that his *pneuma* is characteristically cold.[53]

Lucretius develops a theory about differing contributions made by the first three elements.[54] Fierce lions have a preponderance of heat; timid stags illustrate the dominance of cold *pneuma,* and placid cows that of stable air. He goes on to apply the idea to explain differences of temperaments between individual humans; it is not clear whether this is his own contribution, or how it is to be extended from the idea of type differences.

The fourth, nameless element has a privileged position. It greatly exceeds the other elements in the fineness of its parts (*leptomereia*) and "thus is more sensitive to (*sumpathēs*) the entire assemblage."[55] According to Plutarch it is from this nameless element that there comes about "that by which the agent judges and remembers and loves and hates, and in gen-

---

52. Lucr. 3. 232–33.
53. Lucretius translates it as *aura,* "breeze," or *ventus,* "wind." In Diogenes of Oenoanda new frag. 82 *pneuma* is ordinary wind, which is "cold and high" when there is hail.
54. Lucr. 3. 288–322.
55. Epicurus *Ep. Herod.* 63.

eral the intelligence and reasoning."[56] According to Aëtius the fourth element is the only one that can produce sensation.[57] So the fourth atom type seems to be responsible for sensation, thought, emotion, and memory.

Why is the fourth element nameless? Epicurus is hardly reluctant to coin new jargon elsewhere. Here he is constrained by his empiricism about concepts and language. We have some idea of what the firelike atoms in the soul are like from our experiences with fire, which have led us to produce the word "fire"; our concept of the ingredient in the soul works outward from this. But in the case of the fourth kind of atom there is nothing in our experience capable of giving us any, even partial, idea of what it is like. Not only do we never encounter it, we never even encounter anything that stands to it the way fire in fireplaces stands to the firelike atoms in the soul. The nameless kind of atom is the only purely theoretical entity in Epicureanism. Even in the case of atoms and void we can conceive both by extension from things in our experience which are indivisible and empty.

Many have found the anomalous nature of the nameless atoms an embarrassment. Critics ancient and modern have claimed that here Epicurus is driven back upon a something he knows not what, and that this really amounts to an abandonment of physicalism; for the nameless kind of atom is physical, but, in appealing to something that has no experiential basis whatever, Epicurus is just providing a stand-in for everything that is hard to explain, given a physicalist position.[58] It is undeniable that Epicurus is weakening his empiricism here to a great extent; we have to rely on there being a theoretical entity which does a great deal of work in the theory but of which we have no idea at all from experience. But this need not be seen as objectionable; indeed it can be seen as merely realistic. Our idea of the soul goes far beyond what we can

56. *Adv. Col.* 1118e.
57. Aët. 4. 3, 11, p. 388D (= Usener 315); cf. Lucr. 3. 237–42.
58. Cf. Bailey (1928, 392), who sees a "thin disguise for the abandonment of the materialist position."

readily extrapolate from the natures of fire, air, and *pneuma*. Nor is there any reason to think that Epicurus is abandoning physicalism, thinking of the fourth kind of atom as in effect a magic addition which will bring to life something that physicalist principles cannot account for.[59]

The role of the fourth element emerges from Lucretius.[60] The motions of the atoms, he says, so interpenetrate that they cannot be separated, nor can their properties be divided off. The atoms (the kinds of atom, presumably) are like the many powers of a single body. A living creature is one thing, although it has many properties like smell, heat, and taste; similarly, the kinds of atom form "a single nature." We are reminded of the comparison of the Stoic unified soul with its different powers to an apple with its different properties. The fourth element is the power that makes the soul into a unity— without it, Lucretius says, the other three kinds of atom would not hold together and be enabled to function as they in fact do in an animate body.[61]

The fourth element is "hidden deepest" in the soul, as the soul is in the body; it is "the soul of the soul" and "runs things in the entire body." Clearly the fourth element is not spatially farthest inside, boxed in by the other three.[62] The soul, after all, is not boxed in by the body. Rather the soul is "hidden" in the sense that we do not encounter it in experience. We see clearly enough the effects of having a soul: it animates and directs the body. But the soul itself is not open to observation. Similarly, the fourth element is what "animates" the soul. Although we cannot observe the soul, we can make inferences

59. This rules out theories that treat the fourth element alone as responsible for the soul's activity or that of its rational part (for a survey of theories on these lines, see Kerferd 1971, 84–87). One persistent version of this point is that the fourth nature is a transformation of Aristotle's "fifth element"; there is no reason to think this, and it is equally misguided to think of either as "wholly spiritual and non-material" (Bailey 1928, 392).
60. 3. 258–87.
61. 3. 285–87.
62. As Diano (1974a) sees.

as to its nature, and in particular infer the existence of a kind of atom which gets the soul to function as a whole, and which is distinct from the other soul elements whose nature we can partially describe from experience.

Soul and body, as Lucretius says,[63] are mutually dependent: soul is like the scent in a perfume which you cannot remove without destroying the substance. And the fourth element stands to the soul as the soul stands to the body; it and the other soul elements are mutually dependent in that without them it would have nothing to "animate," and without it they would not hold together as a single kind of thing. How does the fourth element do this? It cannot be by operating, in a seemingly magical fashion, on its own. Rather, it must, by its particularly fine nature, enable the other elements to come together in a new sort of compound. It makes the soul a unity in the straightforward sense that its nature forms the necessary basis for the other atom kinds to cohere in a compound that has the properties of a soul. The introduction of the fourth element marks an insistence that there is a *physical* difference between souls and other kinds of body.

In one way this fits well into Epicurean theory: the soul's operations are supposed to involve particularly fine, invisible processes, and the fourth element serves to explain how the soul, though physical, can have a peculiarly fine structure enabling these to occur. But in other ways the move seems undermotivated. Epicurean physics and cosmology operate with atoms and void: atomic motions and the resulting compounds they give rise to are all we have to explain the varied phenomenal world. Faced by a complex and self-reproducing kind of thing like a tree, an Epicurean has to admit that the way it grows and reproduces is accounted for by its pattern of functional organization, which is stable enough to establish trees as things with persisting natures. Given an ontology as meager as that of atoms and void, and a rejection of teleology, patterns of functional organization are required to explain a world

63. 3. 323–32.

where things fall into species with stable behavior. But why will the approach deemed adequate to explain the species-specific behavior of trees not suffice to explain the behavior of people? To reverse the point, if we need a special kind of nameless atom to explain what souls are, why do we not need another kind of atom to explain what trees are?

It may be that Epicurus simply thought that animals and humans are so different in their complexity from things like trees that the same type of explanation would leave something out in their case. More likely, he may have thought that appealing merely to patterns of functional organization in the case of humans to explain what is characteristic of them was problematic from the point of view of atomist methodology. It is all right to say that a tree is the kind of thing it is because its atoms are organized in a particular stably functioning way. But to say this of humans might sound dangerously close to Aristotle, and would verge on recognizing a metaphysical principle like form as being as basic for explanation as matter. If it really provides an explanation to say that I perceive and act because there are stable perceptive, reactive, and so on patterns of functioning which my soul enables my body to carry out, these patterns seem to have a large explanatory role. And we can see why Epicurus would find this problematic; large differences of explanatory role ought, in a physicalist system, to have a physical basis. Thus the nameless atom type, far from signaling a retreat from physicalism, reveals confidence in the adequacy of physicalism as a theory of the soul. There is a physical difference between souls and other kinds of thing; so we do not need anything like Aristotelian forms to explain the way the soul functions.

Is this move successful? Aristotle argues that ignoring the role of form leaves us unable to explain functioning. Is the postulation of a physical difference, a new kind of ingredient, adequate to meet this kind of challenge? We might feel unhappy when we recall that the ingredient is nameless, since theory postulates something of which experience gives us no idea. A successful challenge to Aristotle would rely on achieved science and point to acknowledged complexity of structure to do the explanatory work assigned to form. But not only is Epicurus not in a position to appeal to such science, he is in general not very interested in low-level, working science. He accepts atomism as the best available scientific theory and tends to assume that what is needed can be worked out within atomism, without waiting for actual research. Thus in his appeal to nameless atoms there is a considerable element of faith—the kind of faith in science which philosophers often have who do not do any actual science.

Epicurus' account of the soul tries to interpret common sense in terms of atomic theory. Unlike the Stoics, he does not try to push the interpretation of soul in the direction of the mental. He accounts for much of what we call the mental by the rational soul, but the rational soul is merely a part of the whole soul, and that is clearly taken to be the physical basis of all the functionings of a living thing. We can see from a fragment of Diogenes of Oenoanda how closely Epicurus stays to common sense:

> Often when the body has been brought to surrender by a long illness, and reduced to such thinness and wasting that the dry skin is almost adhering to the bones whilst the nature of the inward parts seems empty and bloodless, nevertheless the soul stands its ground, and does not permit the creature to die. And this is not the only indication of supremacy: the severing of hands, and often the removal of whole arms or feet by fire and steel cannot undo the bonds of life. So great is the sway of life held by that part of us which is soul. (Frag. 37, cols. 2–3)[64]

Soul is what makes us alive, and so functioning. This is a commonplace, but Epicureanism stresses the importance of rightly understanding the commonplace.

64. Trans. Chilton; cf. new frags. 20, 94.

d) Parts of the Soul

The soul is not uniform; "the rational part" (*to logikon*) is located in the chest, while the rest, "the irrational part," is diffused through the whole body. This part of the theory, surprisingly absent from the *Letter to Herodotus*, is well attested in a scholium on the letter and, in the same words, in Diogenes of Oenoanda.[65] Lucretius makes much of it; he calls the parts *animus* and *anima*, elegant Latin which unfortunately loses the point that the *animus* is the rational part and the *anima* the irrational one.

The rational part is responsible not only for reasoning and cognition but for emotions such as "fears and joys." Lucretius says that in it are located both the understanding (*consilium*) and the governing (*regimen*) of life.[66] In fact the irrational soul tends to be thought of as responsible solely for perception, in which role it has some independence: the eyes themselves see, rather than being windows through which the rational soul sees.[67]

There is a clear contrast with the Stoics, who put perception and impulse together as characterizing the whole soul, and who take thinking to be involved in all the soul's activities. In fact, while the Epicurean rational soul is bound to remind us in some ways of the Stoic *hēgemonikon*—it centralizes all the soul's activities, for example—there are striking differences. For the Epicureans sensation is registered in the sensing organ; for the Stoics the sensation is registered in the *hēgemonikon*. Thus the Epicurean rational soul is not involved in all events in the soul in the way that is true of the *hēgemonikon*. And while the Stoics come to use "the *hēgemonikon*" to refer to the soul as a whole, this is not the case with the Epicurean

65. Schol. in *Ep. Herod.* 66 (= Usener 311); Diogenes of Oenoanda frag. 37, col. 1.
66. Schol. in *Ep. Herod.* 66 (= Usener 311); Lucr. 3. 95, 140–42.
67. Lucr. 3. 359–69. Cicero refers to the "window" theory at *Tusc.* 1. 46.

rational soul. In fact Lucretius says explicitly that when he refers to the soul as a whole he will use *anima*, the word for the irrational soul.[68] This is surprising, and in many ways unfortunate. One wonders whether he would have done so as readily had he been using words which reflected the fact that the parts are introduced by Epicurus in ways that make clear their relation to rationality.

The rational soul is located in the chest, because this is the region of emotions.[69] This is reminiscent of Chrysippus' insistence that the *hēgemonikon* is in the chest and not the head. Two interesting fragments of Demetrius Lacon show that later Epicureans had to contend, much as Chrysippus did, with the discovery of the function of the brain and the nervous system.[70] Demetrius mentions Epicurus' view that the location of the soul's reasoning part allows of enquiry that is both practical (*pragmatikē*) and rational (*kata logon*). There is a claim that it is obvious that movement and emotion "drag" toward the chest. "Many doctors" are mentioned, who use some inductive reasoning (*sēmeiōsis*) to establish that reasoning is in the head. We seem to have a fragment of a confrontation very similar to the Stoic one.[71] Scientific research points to the role of the brain; but the philosophers refuse to abandon folk psychology.

However, the Epicureans' response differs in two ways. Firstly, they are in general not much impressed by the lower levels of science. Secondly, they do not have Chrysippus' reluctance to divide the soul; for the Epicurean rational soul is not the rational aspect of the whole soul. The whole soul is not rational; the rational soul is a part of the whole, as much a part as is a hand or an eye.[72] It organizes and so dominates

68. 3. 421–24.
69. Schol. in *Ep. Herod.* 66 (= Usener 311); Lucr. 3. 140–42.
70. Pap. 1012, cols. 29–30, pp. 38–39 de Falco (= Usener 313). See Croenert (1906, 117). De Falco thinks that some followers of Herophilus and Erasistratus may be meant, such as Demetrius of Apamea. Croenert identifies the doctors only as Empiricists.
71. See part 2, chapter 2, section f.
72. Diogenes of Oenoanda frag. 37, col. 1; Lucr. 3. 94–97.

the soul's activities, so that it can function as a relatively independent part, while the irrational soul depends on it.[73] It is located in a specific part of the body, and damage there is more destructive to life than damage to other parts.[74]

Two questions suggest themselves. Is the rational soul itself a unity? We have already seen that the conclusion suggested by Epicurean views of humans and animals is that it is more like a cluster of capacities.[75] Rationality is shown in a variety of ways and comes in different kinds.[76] It cannot be said, however, that the Epicureans recognize this point explicitly, as one might expect them to do.

Secondly, how does the division of the soul affect the thesis that it is the fourth, nameless kind of element that makes it function as a unity? This thesis has to be rendered consistent with the partially independent workings of the *animus* and *anima*, and the obvious solution is that the effects of having the fourth element must be differentiated. Since it is associated with the soul's exceptionally fine structure, it is tempting to take it as located primarily in the *animus;* its most prominent activity is thinking, the activity most likely to require fine, rapid processes.

If the fourth element were located only in the *animus*, however, it would be the working of the *animus* that accounted for the unity of the whole soul. This Stoic kind of picture is arguably what Epicurus needs, and what he implicitly assumes much of the time. But it sorts ill with the relative independence of the *anima*, and the state of our sources makes the safest conclusion the disappointing one that Epicurus had not thought the point through. In fact Epicurus faces a difficulty over the unity of the soul. The whole soul is a functional unity; but the only part competent to unify it is not involved in all the soul's activities.

73. Lucr. 3. 147–60.
74. Lucr. 3. 396–416.
75. See section b of this chapter.
76. Compare the distinction between wild and tame animals (in section a of this chapter).

Does this matter? Epicurus is concerned to do justice to common sense; does that take for granted that our whole soul, rational and irrational, is strongly unified? One might think that common sense is actually inclined to deny the unity of the soul; the Stoic theory of the emotions, for example, is commonly taken to be highly counterintuitive, and more generally the Stoics might be taken to flout common sense in holding that information reaching the eyes and damage reaching the foot are registered in the *hēgemonikon* rather than in the eyes or in the foot. So perhaps in making *animus* and *anima* partially independent of each other Epicurus is deliberately answering to folk psychology.[77] This may well be true; certainly the Epicurean soul is much more weakly unified than the Stoic soul, and this may be due to a conscious desire to conform with common sense. However, we also find Epicurean claims that the soul is a unity, rather than two linked systems: Lucretius claims, for example, that rational and irrational soul together form "a single nature," and cannot be separated without mutual destruction.[78] The very fact that Lucretius is content to use *anima* to cover the whole soul suggests that he is not taking really seriously the partial independence of the irrational soul. And in his account of the soul-body relation, and in his arguments about death and its importance, Epicurus seems to be presupposing a unified soul and failing to take due account of the differences between its parts and the ways they function.

e) The Soul-Body Relation

There is a tension in Epicureanism over the soul-body relation. On the one hand the body is emphatically said to be the container or vessel of the soul. Epicurus uses such language repeatedly; Lucretius even bases his first argument for the soul's

77. On this issue I am indebted to comments by Rob Cummins.
78. 3. 136–37.

mortality on the comparison of the body with a vessel.[79] It is the body that holds together the soul and thus enables unified animate functioning—a reversal of the Aristotelian and Stoic view that what makes the agent alive and functioning is the soul's holding the body together.

Such language is, however, surprisingly inappropriate for the soul-body relation as Epicureanism actually develops that idea. Lucretius adds that the soul is the body's "guardian and cause of preservation; for they cling together like common roots and it is seen that they cannot be sundered without destruction." The soul is "in" the body like scent in perfume; it cannot be removed without destroying the substance. "So interwoven are their elements between them from their first beginning; they are endowed with a mutual life."[80] Diogenes of Oenoanda insists that the soul, which is "bound" by the body, "binds" it in turn.[81] Soul and body are two bodies which, in a living thing, are mutually dependent.

Epicurus presses the point for sentience: strictly speaking, it does not belong to the soul alone but is a joint product of soul and body. Lucretius puts this point more elegantly,[82] but here Epicurus' famously rugged Greek reveals an interesting conceptual struggle:

> We should keep in mind that soul has the greatest share in causing (*aitia*) sensation (*aisthēsis*). However, it would not have had this if it had not been enclosed in a way by the rest of the assemblage. The rest of the assemblage, which provides it with this causality, itself has, derived from the soul, a share in just such a property—though

79. Epicurus *Ep. Herod.* 63–66 contains three uses of forms of *to stegazon* for the body, and one of *ta periechonta*. Cf. 65: "When the whole assemblage is broken up the soul scatters." Lucr. 3. 425–44 is the passage in question; cf. 555. Cf. also Usener 337, where the soul is said to be in the body like wind (*pneuma*) in a wineskin (and thus to scatter at death).
80. Lucr. 3. 323–32; cf. 337–49: "A body is never born by itself."
81. Frag. 37, col. 1.
82. 3. 331–36, 350–58.

not in everything the soul possesses. Hence when the soul departs it lacks sensation. For it did not itself possess this power in itself; something else connate with it provided it, and this, through the power brought about in connection with it depending on movement, at once achieved for itself a property of sentience and supplied it to the other also, depending on juxtaposition and mutual sensitivity, as I said. Therefore while the soul is indwelling it never lacks sensation through the removal of any other part—whatever of it perishes along with the breaking up of the enclosure, in whole or in part, if it remains, it will have sensation. The rest of the assemblage, whether it survives in whole or in part, will not have sensation when it is gone—that is, whatever quantity of atoms is needed to hold together to constitute the soul's nature. Further, when the whole assemblage is broken up the soul is scattered and no longer has the same powers, or moves; so it does not possess sensation either, for we cannot think of it as sentient unless in this composite and using these movements, when the enclosing and surrounding parts are not such as these in which [the soul] now is and has these movements. (*Ep. Herod.* 64–66)

The point which Epicurus has such trouble getting across is not that the soul requires the body for sensation, nor that sensation is the product of soul and body interacting, nor even that this is necessarily so. All these claims are quite compatible with dualism. Rather, Epicurean soul and body need each other to exist and to function *as soul and as body*. Without the body, the soul no longer exists or functions as soul, but is just scattered atoms; without the soul, the body no longer exists or functions as a body, but is a mere corpse. Sentience brings this out: it is the product of the mutually dependent soul and body, for the soul needs the body to exist as the soul of a sentient agent, and the body needs the soul to exist as the body of a sentient agent.

Why does Epicurus have such a struggle to express this? The problems are due largely to his clinging to the inappropriate conception of body and soul as vessel and contents.[83] Epicurus often states a thesis in unnecessarily and sometimes misleadingly polemical and crude form; when we examine the thesis we find the crude formulations fail to do it justice. We can only put this down to an imperfect fit between Epicurus' philosophical activity and his pedagogical approach. The latter sometimes requires shock tactics to shake people out of their set views and prejudices. If and when they get involved in studying Epicurean philosophy, they may find that the initially controversial appearance was misleading; but by that time it will probably no longer matter, at least to the convinced Epicurean. Sometimes, however, Epicurus' cruder statements turn out to make trouble for his more sophisticated thoughts.[84]

What brings out the closeness of the soul-body relation is sentience, which characterizes the irrational soul. We find elsewhere, however, that the Epicureans tend to *contrast* soul and body, and that when they do they have a different contrast in mind, namely, that between the body plus the irrational soul on the one hand and the rational soul on the other. "The pains of the soul," for example, "are worse than those of the body; for the flesh suffers only for the present moment, but the soul for past, present, and future. Similarly, the pleasures of the soul are greater."[85] Here "the body" clearly refers to the sentient body, closely linked to the irrational soul, and "the soul" clearly refers to the rational soul.

Further, many themes in Epicurean ethics stress not only this distinction, but the superiority of the soul, which by drawing on past, present, and future experiences can more than counterbalance what happens to the body. The star example here is Epicurus' dying letter to his friends, where he says that his present agonizing pains are more than counterbalanced

83. Diano (1974, 146ff.) suggests that this may be an inheritance from Democritus, who calls the body a *skēnos* (frags. A152, B37, B223 DK).

84. This is particularly the case with his account of pleasure, where his crude and shocking slogans are quite misleading.

85. D. L. 10. 137.

by the joy in his soul from memories of philosophical activity.[86] Epicureans from Polystratus to Lucretius tirelessly urge on us that only the rational activity of philosophy will make us happy, for we need the exercise of the rational soul in order to organize our lives and make sense of the products of the irrational soul.

There is potentially a tension here. For Epicurus it is crucial that I think of my soul as something dependent for its existence and functioning on the existence and functioning of my body. He has shown this for the irrational soul, the source of sentience. But, given the stress on the importance of our identifying with the rational soul, and the contrast between the rational soul on the one hand and the body with the irrational soul on the other, the question is bound to arise whether Epicurus has adequately shown that the soul as a whole is indissolubly linked with the body. It could be objected, of course, that all he needs to show is that the sentient, irrational soul is indissolubly linked to the body, and the rational soul in turn indissolubly linked to the irrational soul; if the soul's unity is weak anyway, we would not expect an argument to show directly that the rational soul was linked indissolubly to the workings of the body. But, while that is arguably what Epicurus needs, we do not find explicitly either any acknowledgment that this is what is to be shown or any arguments to show it.

f) Survival

A famous and fundamental Epicurean teaching is that "death is nothing to us; for what is broken up has no sensation, and what has no sensation is nothing to us."[87] At greater length:

> Get used to the idea that death is nothing to us, since every good and evil lies in sensation, and death is the deprivation of sensation. . . . So death, the most fearful of all evils, is nothing to us, since when we are, death is

86. D. L. 10. 22.
87. *Kuria doxai* 2.

not present, and when death is present, then we are not. It is therefore nothing to the living, nor to the dead; for the former it is not, and the latter are no longer. (Epicurus *Ep. Men.* 124–25)

Lucretius puts this point forcefully: what happens after I am dead will be of no concern to me, since there will be no me, just as the Punic Wars were of no concern to me when they happened, since there was then no me to be concerned. "And even if the nature of the rational soul and the power of the irrational soul go on having sensation after being torn from our body, still it is nothing to us, who are made into one united compound by the mating and marriage of body and soul."[88] It is possible, he adds, that in the past my soul and body atoms came together in just the way they do now; but any such past union was not *me*. *I* could not be around before the conception which brought me into being as an ensouled body, and in the same way *I* cannot be around after the death that breaks up the mutually dependent functioning of soul and body. So what happens after my death is like what happened before my birth— nothing to me.

The argument has raised controversy, ancient and modern. The important point here is the need for the premise that all good and evil lie in sensation. For sensation is, of course, characteristic of the irrational soul; and we have seen that in sentience the body and irrational soul are indeed mutually dependent. But the claim that for us *all* good and evil lie in sentience seems to neglect the role of the rational soul. This comes out in at least two ways. It is because of the activity of the rational soul that we are able to identify our good with projects whose content goes beyond our own personal pleasures, and which may be fulfilled only after our death. Epicurus himself stresses the value of friendship, and concern for friends and their activities for their own sake. But this will involve an agent in perfectly rational concern for projects and activities whose fruition does not depend on her being alive.

88. Lucr. 3. 830–69, esp. 843–46.

It is hard to see how death is nothing to such a person just because she knows she will not be aware of these projects: her concern for the projects did not depend on her being aware of them.

Secondly, because the rational soul can, as Epicurus puts it, compare past, present, and future, it is what gives an agent a sense of himself as an agent continuing through time, a being with a whole life. And this means that though death is nothing to me when it arrives, since it removes the agent in question, it is not necessarily irrational to worry about its happening in the future. Both Epicurus and Lucretius deny this: since death will not concern me when it comes, it is irrational for me to worry about it now.[89] But why are they entitled to this? That death is not an evil when it comes does not imply that it is not an evil in someone's life as a whole (by coming sooner rather than later, for example).

It might be urged that these objections come from unfairly pressing Epicurus' language of good and evil lying in *sensation*. Surely he did not mean to limit sensation in this connection to the activity of the irrational soul. Is he not more fairly understood as claiming that nothing is a good or evil for an agent unless that agent can *experience* it—where "experience" is taken to refer to the activity of the whole soul, rational and irrational? It may be that something like this is what Epicurus did mean. But however generously we interpret "sensation" here, we shall not get out of the problem. Death is not an evil at the time it occurs, but this does not show that it is not an evil in one's life as a whole. But the rational soul is what gives the Epicurean a notion of her life as a whole. Nor does it show that death is not an evil in frustrating concerns that go beyond one's life and do not depend on one's experiencing the results. But the rational soul is what gives the Epicurean her concern for projects and activities that go beyond her life and matter whether she experiences the results or not—for example, the concerns and activities of friends.

89. Epicurus *Ep. Men.* 124–25; Lucr. 3. 870–977.

Epicurus has an answer to these objections. They all involve in some way the claim that death, while it may not be an evil when it occurs, is nonetheless an evil by depriving us of goods which we would otherwise have; for, thanks to our rational soul, we have a conception of our lives as wholes, and of projects that go beyond the reach of our own sentience; yet it is just this which enables us to commit ourselves to there being goods which, so it seems, death can deprive us of. Epicurus can say that only a non-Epicurean will be concerned by this, because she has a faulty conception of what these goods are. An Epicurean will realize that our highest good is pleasure and that all the goods that we can reasonably recognize in our lives are means to, or ways of, achieving this pleasure. We even seek friendship, and goals that extend beyond our own lives, for the sake of pleasure. Epicurus' own theory of what this pleasure, rightly conceived, actually is, is complicated, and the evidence difficult, but some things are clear. It is not to be identified with good feeling: it is a condition of "untroubledness" or *ataraxia*, which one achieves by following only natural desires and avoiding courses of action which will predictably lead to worry and trouble.

An important aspect of this is that the Epicurean will have achieved equanimity about goods that can be lost; for what she is after, in seeking *ataraxia*, is not the external results of action, but the inner result, the pleasure that lies in having the right attitude toward things that make other people upset. The pleasure that is our goal of life is radically internalized. One remarkable result of this is the thesis that pleasure is not increased by duration: once you have achieved Epicurean happiness, you have all that you need for happiness, and further time spent doing actions can merely vary what you have, not add to it.[90] Hence death does not deprive the good Epicurean of goods after all.[91]

90. This idea, that one's happiness is "complete," embracing everything worth having, in a way that takes no account of the natural

The limitation of this response is clear: it works only for the committed Epicurean, who already accepts Epicurean ethics in full. It will not convince the non-Epicurean, who has a different idea of what it is rational to consider good. And it seems a weakness that a thesis about the soul should depend so directly on a very controversial ethical thesis. Unless one is an Epicurean on other grounds, therefore, the death arguments contain a gap, one that makes more obvious Epicurus' lack of an explicit discussion of the nature of the soul's unity, and the relations of the rational and irrational parts of the soul.

Epicurus' argument does not depend on the premise that my soul is mortal; as Lucretius makes clear, it would hold even if my soul did survive the breakup of its union with the body—and even if it were immortal, since death is nothing to me even if there will be a qualitatively identical *Doppelgänger* constituted of the very same atoms that constitute me. In principle, the Epicurean soul could be immortal without endangering the survival arguments.

It is therefore surprising that Lucretius prefaces his great declaration that death is nothing to us with nearly thirty arguments to prove that the soul is mortal.[92] Lucretius may be confused.[93] But possibly these arguments are meant to play an important subsidiary role; for the belief that my soul is immortal, while not as crucial as the belief that death is a bad thing for me, does play an important role in the various beliefs that make up fear of death and a negative attitude toward

---

contours of a human life, is highly controversial. See Nagel (1979); Furley (1986); Mitsis (1988a, 1988b); Striker (1988); Rosenbaum (1990).

91. Of course this would still leave imperfect Epicureans rationally wanting to live longer, so as to get nearer the goal of *ataraxia*. It is only the fully wise Epicurean who has no more to gain from another forty years than from another four minutes.

92. 3. 425–829.

93. He says that death is nothing to us because the (rational) soul's nature is mortal, and this just misstates the argument.

dying. Lucretius' flood of arguments is best understood as a sustained attempt to remove mistakes and to enable us to have a correct *prolēpsis* or conception of the soul. Their unsophisticated nature is deliberate—Lucretius hammers home simple and undeniable facts, such as that disease affects us psychologically as well as physiologically, and brings them into direct conflict with the notion of the soul as immortal. In Epicureanism it is important that we start from a right conception of what we are investigating;[94] in the case of the soul this involves the removal of confusions, and an effective way to do this is to appeal repeatedly to our basic intuitions. For Epicurus our awareness of something clear and concrete in our lives is not likely to be corrupted by bad theory. Diogenes of Oenoanda ridicules belief in survival after death in the same down-to-earth and unsophisticated way.[95]

For Epicurus both the belief that my soul is immortal and the belief that death is a bad thing for me are not just false but unhealthy, pathological. As long as we hold them, we will not be happy, for they deeply corrupt our conception of what we are and how we should live. We will be tempted, for example, to locate the significance of our lives in something supposedly waiting for us after death.[96] Lucretius devotes passionate rhetoric to showing us that this is perverse; the desire to survive death is based on failure to face reality. Those who regret dying are merely rebuked for clinging to immature fantasies.[97]

94. See Asmis (1984, pt. 1).
95. New frag. 2; frags. 34, 35.
96. See Konstan (1973) for the claim that when Lucretius says that the terrors of hell are in our own lives, he means that hell is a projection onto the supposed afterlife of false beliefs about this life.
97. Cf. the end of Philodemus *On Death*. See Gigante (1969a).

7

Perception and Thought

Perception figures extensively in both ancient and modern accounts of Epicurus' theory of the soul. What has attracted most attention has been the strange account of perceptual mechanisms, and the controversial epistemological doctrines. Less attention has been paid to the way in which perception involves conceptualization and thought, a feature not stressed in our main sources, Epicurus' letters and Lucretius.[1]

The physiological account of perception is an extension of atomist physics. For Epicurus, physical solid objects are collections of atoms temporarily unified. Their cohesion is impressive at the macroscopic level, but even a stable object is constantly giving off a stream or effluence of images (*eidōla*), contact with which is necessary for us to perceive or to think.[2] Epicurus devoted great attention to the image theory, writing a book *On Images* and devoting book 2 of his *On Nature* to them. The theory dominates Lucretius' account of perception; Diogenes of Oenoanda discusses images at great and detailed

1. For texts relevant to perception and thought see Long and Sedley (1987, 15, 16, 17, 19).
2. "Effluence" is *aporrhoia* or *rheusis* (D. L. 10.46, 48); images are also called *tupoi* or *simulacra*. See Aët. 4. 8, 10, p. 395 D (= Usener 317).

length. Whatever its faults, the theory does try to meet the challenge of accounting for our sensitivity to the world in terms of nothing but atoms and void. For the basic point, that objects are always shedding atoms, neither Epicurus nor his successors do any better than to claim that it is consistent with the phenomena and the rest of Epicurean theory.[3] The theory is presumably to get any stronger support than this merely from the adequacy with which it accounts for the phenomena.

Even solid bodies contain void, and there is a "vibration of the atoms deep in the solid body" which results in a constant detachment and shedding of films of atoms at the surface.[4] These images, retaining the body's appearance because the film retains its coherence, move at tremendous speed.[5] The flow of images from an object is constant and uninterrupted, and they travel straight ahead from their source.[6] Both Lucretius and Diogenes appeal to empirical analogues, like the phenomenon of mirroring, to aid our acceptance of the theoretical claims.

3. Epicurus *Ep. Herod.* 46–48; Lucr. 4. 54–71; Epicurus *On Nature* 2, cols. 17. 5–18. 1 (Arrighetti [24.41–2]). Consistency of this kind is for Epicurus a kind of justification.

4. Epicurus *Ep. Herod.* 48. This seems to be what Lucretius has in mind at 4. 192–98 as the "tiny cause" (*parvola causa*) which gets the atomic films moving. Cf. the difficult and technical passage in *On Nature* 2 (Arrighetti [24.42–44]) where Epicurus says that if only solid objects, and not images also, could *[ex]ōseis p[oieis]thai* (make displacements), then only the former, and not the latter, could move *kata ton [exō]stikon t[r]opon* (in the displacing way). Arrighetti (584) argues that here *exōsis* is the same as Lucretius' *parvola causa*. He also argues that it means "thrust" and refers to the effects of the central vibration, rejecting Barigazzi's (1958) view that the *exōstikos tropos* is just the common-sense phenomenon, transferred from visible to theoretical entities, of one thing striking another with a knock-on effect.

5. Lucr. 3. 176–216; Epicurus says that they are created "as quick as thought" (*hama noēmati* both at the end of *On Nature* 2 [Arrighetti (24.50)] and at *Ep. Herod.* 48), and most of the extant parts of *On Nature* 2 concern the images' speed of travel.

6. On the flow of images see Epicurus *Ep. Herod.* 49–50; Lucr. 4. 143–75, 217–38; Cic. *Nat. d.* 1. 109. On their direction of travel, Lucr. 4. 609; Diogenes of Oenoanda new frag. 5.

The images are not themselves solid; Epicurus calls them "hollow and thin things" and emphasizes that they are "full of void" (*polukenon*).[7] Lucretius and Diogenes of Oenoanda stress that they are fine and thin but nevertheless have the normal powers of body.[8] "The flow from the bodies . . . preserves for a long time the position and order of the atoms in the solid body."[9] The images have the same color as their parent bodies, and the same shape.[10]

We may find this hard to make sense of. What is "the" color or shape of the parent body? Presumably what is meant is the color and shape as seen by the perceiver at the time of perception. Further, the size of the images is an embarrassing problem. The visual image of the Taj Mahal that reaches my eyes can hardly be the same size as the Taj Mahal; yet it started life that size.[11]

The Epicureans meet these difficulties by claiming that in transit between object and percipient the images are damaged and altered. Being very fine, they are liable to collision and thus to all kinds of fusion and reformation. Even an image of an object that gets to us whole has been greatly modified in passage. For one thing, it has collapsed in size; the image of the Taj Mahal, when it reaches me, has shrunk down to the right size to enter my eyes, though it has retained all the orig-

7. *Ep. Herod.* 46, *On Nature* 2 (Arrighetti [24.48–49]). They are, however, three-dimensional rather than flat; see Manuwald (1972, app. 2).

8. Lucr. 4. 110–28; Diogenes of Oenoanda frag. 7, new frag. 1. He solves a false dilemma: the Stoics do not give the images enough power, Democritus gives them too much. Like many of Diogenes' other reports on non-Epicurean philosophy, this is idiosyncratic, and the problems artificially engineered to make the Epicurean solution sound better motivated.

9. Epicurus *Ep. Herod.* 48.

10. Epicurus *Ep. Herod.* 49; Diogenes of Oenoanda new frag. 13; Alexander *In Arist. sens.* 2. 438a (= Usener 319).

11. Epicurus says (*Ep. Herod.* 49) that the images have the same color and shape as their parent objects and enter vision or thought "in the appropriate size" (*kata to enarmatton megethos*). It is not clear whether the size is appropriate to vision or to thought, nor what appropriateness consists in.

inal proportions and color.[12] Further, long and difficult passage through the air can modify the image's color and shape, as the atoms' configuration is changed. The classic case of this is the square tower which from a distance appears round; the image reaching the viewer is in fact rounded, since the corners have been knocked off the sharp atoms by the friction of the air.[13] These expedients have always seemed bizarre; that Epicurus accepts them underlines the fact that he wants the images themselves to have shape, color, and size of a kind adequate to represent the shape, color, and size of the parent bodies in a straightforward sense.

Images which encounter sentient beings enter the body through "pores" via the organs of the five senses. Diogenes of Oenoanda says strikingly that "our nature has its pores opened (*poroporeitai*)" in perception.[14] The different sense modalities are distinguished by the aptness of the atomic structure of the sense organs to receive different kinds of atom.[15] Epicurus is scanty on differential detail about the senses. He says some things about sight, hearing, and smell in the *Letter to Herodotus* 50–53 (and wrote books on the first two), and Lucretius deals

12. Avotins (1980b) denies that the Epicureans were committed to this view. He relies on two passages of Alexander of Aphrodisias to suggest that images do not collapse, but that the eye, for example, takes in a stream of *parts* of the images and reassembles a "scale-model" as a result. (See also Asmis 1984, 131 n. 23.) Avotins admits, however, that the Alexander passages have to be treated with caution; they contain sections which cannot refer to Epicurus.

13. Lucr. 4. 353–63; cf. Diogenes of Oenoanda new frag. 9; Sext. Emp. *Math.* 7. 209.

14. New frag. 5, col. 3.

15. Lucretius calls the pores *viae* (4. 344) and *foramina* (350). They are "commensurate with" and "fitted to" the appropriate atoms (Epicurus *Ep. Herod.* 47, 61), an idea ridiculed by Plutarch (*Adv. Col.* 1109c). In frag. 8, col. 4, of an unplaced book of *On Nature* (Arrighetti [36.23]) Epicurus may talk of the pores having tension—*suntonia* (Gigante 1969a, 93; Arrighetti, however, reads *sum[m]etria*). The irrational soul can literally escape through the pores, presumably when they are slackened (Lucr. 3. 252–55; Philodemus *On Death* 37.31–33; see Gigante 1969a, 77–82 and 93: *[t]ēs psuchēs hetoi[mo]tatous p[o]rous eis [e]kpnoēn echous[es]*). Philodemus sees this as one reason why we are so exposed to death.

with these and taste; but we find them both merely fitting atomic theory mechanically to requirement. When the images encounter the soul atoms, we have sensation. Lucretius tells us that the "sense-bearing motions" are first picked up by the most sensitive "fourth nature" and then passed on to the body through the other types of atom in an order corresponding to the relative fineness of the atom type.[16] Presumably, what is meant is not a relay race, with something being passed on from one type of atom to another. It makes more sense to think of the whole soul being more and more fully involved at each stage, as more of the types of atoms making it up are involved.

In atomic theory there can be no purely qualitative change; Lucretius is right to insist that touch is fundamental for sensation. The effect of the image atoms on the soul atoms can only be to rearrange them, or more likely their patterns of motion,[17] for the image I have of the Taj Mahal started life literally as part of the Taj Mahal; there is no need to suppose that my soul can absorb such a detached part of the world, however fine it is. Presumably having made its impact, the image passes out of the body in some broken-down form. Epicurus calls this impact of the images imprinting: external objects "stamp themselves" on us.[18] The images are in constant flow; the impression made on us is "according to the continual solidification (*puknōma*) or remnant (*enkataleimma*) of the image." A continual barrage of images makes an imprint in the soul by building up a new pattern of atomic movement in the soul. Perception is, on the physical level, a change in the perceiver that consists in having some of her atomic movements changed. A single perception will do this fleetingly; it takes continued perception to build up something more permanent in the perceiver's soul. The general idea is clear enough, though we do not know how Epicurus would deal

16. 4. 241–51.
17. Lucr. 2. 434. Cf. Furley (1967).
18. *Ep. Herod.* 49: the word is *enaposphragizein*, reminiscent of Stoic talk of sensation as imprinting.

with the case where the perceiver retains a memory of a single, fleeting, but vivid, image.[19] The physical account of perception is a totally receptive one; no room seems to be made for aspects like awareness.[20]

The person whose sentient soul is impressed by images receives an "appearance," *phantasia*.[21] Epicurean appearances are, as we have seen, conceived in very visual terms. They are unlike Stoic appearances in that they do not carry articulable content. Epicurus indeed tends to assign perception to the irrational soul, as we have seen.[22] Nonetheless, his account of knowledge prominently demands that all perceptions are true.

19. The obvious retort would be that a perceiver cannot retain a single image just because of its vividness; if one image produces memory, that must be because it reminds the perceiver in some way of other retained images. With some ingenuity this could be rendered plausible.

20. Epicurus occasionally speaks of *epaisthēsis* (e.g., *Ep. Herod.* 52), and this has been held to mark a kind of awareness over and above mere receptivity. But the interpretation of *epaisthēsis* is disputed. See Glidden (1979); Lee (1978), who sets out alternative interpretations, leaning to the view that it marks directional awareness of the object perceived; Asmis (1984, 162–64), who claims that *epaisthēsis* is synonymous with *aisthēsis*, the prefix marking only the immediate and direct nature of perception.

21. Epicurus wrote a lost book on *phantasia*. In the *Letter to Herodotus*, *phantasia* is used twice for the percipient's "appearance" resulting from the imprinting of the images on the soul. Elsewhere in the extant remains Epicurus uses it mostly of our pretheoretical impressions of things, which serve as evidence for theories. Hence it bulks largest in discussions of scientific matters: *Ep. Pyth.* 80; *On Nature* 11 (on cosmology), Arrighetti [26.11.5, 25.3, 40.11]; 14 (criticism of the *Timaeus* elements theory), [29.23.9, 24.5, 25.14]; 15 (probably on the same), [30.13.3, 35.19]; unplaced book on time, [37.15.3, 23.6, 31.1, 36.5, 37.9]. In one letter, [80.8], it means "external, i.e., social appearances." In the *Letter to Mother*, [72], *phantasiai* and *phazmata* are appearances of the absent. *Phantasma* is used for this at D. L. 10. 32 ("appearances of the mad"); otherwise it is used as a variant on *phantasia*, especially in scientific contexts—*Ep. Herod.* 75; *Ep. Pyth.* 88, 102, 110; *On Nature* 35 [34.32.3]—as is *phantasmos* at *Ep. Herod.* 51. Epicurus' epistemology (below) makes it clear why he is not concerned to use a distinctive word for veridical appearances: *all* appearances are veridical, and what we take to be differences in their veridicality are really differences in belief.

22. See chapter 6, section d.

We shall examine his reasons for this below, but it is in any case clear that a nonreductive physicalist like Epicurus has no desire to reduce perception to blank imprinting. He takes it for granted that in perception we receive and process information, indeed that this constitutes knowledge. If so, however, he seems at first sight to have produced a classically bad account: trying to explain how the perceiver sees a red square by getting something (smaller and) red and square into the perceiver. Such a mechanism by itself of course achieves nothing: to make this into an account of perceiving we have to supplement it with a little homunculus inside the perceiver who can interpret the little red square appearance inside the perceiver and acquire the perceptual belief that he is seeing something red and square. If Epicurus has nothing better than this to offer, his account is disappointing.

However, we do find material for supplementing the image theory in the Epicurean account of thinking and concept formation, though this is not brought into connection with it in the ancient sources, and we have to make the links ourselves. Although casting the material into this form takes us into speculation, it is worth doing, rather than resting content with the idea that Epicurus is producing an account of perception which reduces it to passive imprinting. In this, as in other areas of his philosophy, Epicurus is producing an elaborate atomic story not for its own sake, but to provide an explanatory account of an everyday phenomenon which is to be explained and supported, not reduced to something else. The atomic story itself hardly accords with common sense; large parts of it are extremely counterintuitive. But this does not imply that Epicurus was prepared to give a counterintuitive account of perception itself, and he has good reason not to want to do this, especially given his epistemology, which aims to be commonsensical. Thus it is worth seeing what Epicurus' resources are for producing an account of perception which answers to the basic point that in perception we acquire information.

Thought, according to Epicurus, is produced by images streaming off objects in a way analogous to what happens in perception; as Lucretius says, this explains how we can perceive and think of the very same things.[23] The thought images, however, are thinner and finer; hence they can affect the rational soul via the sense organs and irrational soul without having to affect these latter at the same time. As Diogenes of Oenoanda explains, "after the impingings (*enptoseis*) of the first images our nature has its pores opened (*poroporeitai*) in such a way that even when the objects which it at first saw are no longer present, things similar to the first ones are received by the mind."[24]

Lucretius makes the point that since the irrational soul is not sensitive to the images which produce thinking in the rational soul, the latter's activity is in many ways independent of the former. In sleep, for example, when we dream, a kind of thinking is going on while we are not perceiving. As Diogenes puts it, the soul is awake but unaware that the senses are asleep, and so does not refer to them to test the images it picks up from the uninterrupted flow from objects.[25]

Lucretius tells us that the mind is so tenuous that a single thin thought image can affect it; also that the thought images are prone to entanglement and confusion.[26] Thus atomic theory attempts to explain how we can think with much less external stimulation than perception requires, and how our thoughts are not limited by our range of perception. Memory seems to be explained dispositionally: some images affect us in such a way that we are prone to repeat the thought of their object.[27]

So far, thinking looks entirely parallel to perceiving; it requires an image just as the latter does, and it is only because thought images, being finer, are more prone to fission and

23. 4. 745–46.
24. New frag. 5, col. 3. Lucretius echoes this at 4. 973–83.
25. New frags. 5 and 6; Lucr. 4. 722–822. Diogenes does not actually specify the rational soul, but it must be this, since the senses are asleep and "extinguished." He is careless about specifying the rational or irrational soul: see Chilton (1971) on frag. 37.
26. 4. 745–47, 724–44.
27. Lucr. 4. 962–1036. See Diano (1974a, 161–62); Kerferd (1971).

reformation than sense images that thought can range farther than perception does. Like Aristotle, Epicurus seems determined to make perceiving and thinking parallel; both are explained in terms of impingings from what is outside the person. Epicurean physics, however, renders the result for the case of thinking very bizarre: thinking is not what the mind does, but the way it is affected by thought objects streaming in from the outside.

However, the mind also has in thinking some active power of concentrating, as we find from an important passage in Lucretius.[28] It can focus on any of the available images. What my mind focuses on will of course be determined by my interests, beliefs, and desires. Thinking involves a selective focusing of interest and seems to be rather like focusing one's eyes on something. However, it appears from this passage that unlike focusing one's eyes, focusing one's mind is the norm rather than the exception, since there is an enormous amount of thought images always available—so great an amount that if the mind were not cognitively active, it would be overwhelmed. We have to be active thinkers to make sense of things. Lucretius' account has no direct parallel in other sources, but this focusing ability, making us active, selective thinkers, may be what lies behind the curious point that in Epicureanism there is something called *epibolē tēs dianoias* or "grasp by the mind"; this is a factor of uncertain role and very disputed significance, but it seems to have something to do with the active aspect of thinking.[29]

28. 4. 794–815. Unfortunately, this passage is a very chaotic one, in which this topic is conflated with that of moving images in dreams. Asmis (1981) argues that the surrounding passage has suffered dislocation and should be reordered. She expels from the account of thought, however, the reference to the sheer quantity (*copia*) of objects of thought, which I take to be important.

29. This is a very controversial topic. Bailey (1928, app. 3) established the root meaning of *epibolē* and *epiballein* as suggestive of effort and attention (repeated by Asmis 1984 for the senses and thinking) but spoiled his thesis by the patently wrong claim that *epibolē tēs dianoias* is not merely selective, attentive thought, but infallible intuition. Faults in Bailey's account are trenchantly exposed in Furley

We know that Epicurus distinguished and gave technical names to various kinds of empirical and nonempirical thinking and was concerned with the different ways these could lead to error in our concepts.[30] He nowhere in the extant remains faces the question of how the mind's ability to focus actively on images can give rise to propositional, empirical, and ultimately inferential thinking. Like many empiricists he assumes hopefully that all the mind's powers of reasoning, however abstract, can somehow be developed from the ability to select among and reformulate empirical data.

It is because we are active thinkers that we can form concepts. It was Epicurus who invented the notion of a preconception or *prolēpsis*, a notion to become influential in Stoic and later philosophy.[31] As Diogenes Laertius relates,

> preconceptions they [Epicureans] speak of as being like apprehension or correct belief or concept (*ennoia*) or universal thought stored up, that is, a memory of what has often appeared externally, such as "Such and such is a man"; for as soon as "man" is spoken, at once, dependent on the preconception, its image (*tupos*) is thought of, with the senses leading the way. Therefore what is primarily brought under each word is clear. We would never have investigated the object of our investigation, unless we had previously recognized it; for example, "That thing standing far off is a horse or an ox"; for one has to recognize at some point the shape of horse and ox, dependent on the preconception. Otherwise we would not have named anything, not having learned its image (*tu-*

(1967, 206–8) who denies *epibolē* any importance, claiming that its main function is explaining illusory appearances. Furley is criticized by Sedley (1973, 24–25 n. 140), who restricts *epibolē* to "the visualization of perceptible objects." Manuwald (1972, app. 1) refutes Kleve's (1963) view of *epibolē* as an inferential act of thinking. I do not pretend to be able to improve on any of these suggestions; I think it may safely be retained that *epibolē* refers to the *active* aspect of thinking.

30. In *On Nature* 28, frag. 13, cols. 6–7.

31. Cic. *Nat. d.* 1. 44 tells us this.

pos), dependent on the preconception. Therefore pre-conceptions are clear (*enargeis*). (10.33)

Preconceptions are astonishingly like British empiricist "ideas," and fulfill two of their roles. We can come to generalize from the impressions made on us by experience and to express the results of this in language. We thus acquire general concepts drawn from experience, which are also the meanings of our words. There is a sense in which Epicurus does not have a theory of meaning, since he denies that there are such things as meanings construed as entities intermediate between spoken or written words and the things the words are of.[32] But again Epicurus has no desire to flout common sense; of course our words and utterances have meaning,[33] and his theory of concept acquisition shows how this is so. Like many empiricists he accounts for our ability to conceptualize and use language in terms only of the mind's ability to reformulate empirical data. Sometimes he clearly thinks of the concepts as being themselves a kind of image, abstracted and composite, like the images they are produced from by generalization. But this is fortunately not a settled view; *prolēpseis* can be derived from experience in all sorts of ways. We are told that a *prolēpsis* is a grasp (*epibolē*) of something clear, and of the clear conception (*epinoia*) of a thing, and that all *epinoiai* are derived from the senses by not only direct experience (*periptōsis*) but also analogy, likeness, and combination. Thus quite a lot of intellectual work can go into the

32. Plut. *Adv. Col.* 1119f; Sext. Emp. *Math.* 8. 13, 258, 336. Epicurus is compared with the Stoics, who do have such intermediate entities in *lekta*. Glidden in his articles defends the view that the Epicureans have a robustly "extensional" account of meaning, which rejects much of what we might expect from a theory of meaning. I have taken Epicurus' approach to be more conciliatory toward common sense and to be aiming at allowing for the phenomenon of meaningfulness, while merely avoiding what he sees as obscure and metaphysically undesirable intermediary entities.

33. This is the aspect of the theory of *prolēpsis* which has received most recent attention. See Sedley (1973) for the text; also Manuwald (1972); Long (1971); Glidden (1983, 1985).

development of a concept. We have a *prolēpsis* of justice, for example; and Epicurus makes some points about it which are relevant more generally.[34] The concept of justice has a clear central core: a law not leading to mutual advantage, claims Epicurus, is not just. But the concept can tolerate quite a lot of variation—for example, in the balance of advantage. And it can even tolerate fairly radical change of content if changed circumstances make different means necessary for the mutual gaining of advantage.

The objections to such an empiricist theory of concepts and meaning are familiar; here what matters is that *prolēpseis* are what are needed to fill out the Epicurean account of perception. We can easily see how a perception would involve not only a *phantasia* or appearance, but also an application of some *prolēpsis* to the appearance. The perceiver would thereby identify and classify what is perceived, and also, since *prolēpseis* function to give words meaning, would be able to articulate in language the content of what is perceived. Such an account would make perception a function of the whole person, involving both irrational and sentient and rational and cognitively interpreting soul.

However, although an account like this is what Epicurus needs for his theories overall, it is not explicit in the sources (which indeed tend to assign perception to the irrational soul), and we can only look for a diagnosis of its absence. Epicurus' theory suffers from a lack of clear relationship between the rational and irrational soul and clear demarcation of their functions. It also suffers from the fact that, unlike the Stoics, Epicurus has no very convincing location for perceptual content. Stoic rational appearances are items which convey content, and what the mind does is to articulate and interpret this, assenting to a *lekton* as a result. Epicurus, however, thinks that *lekta* are metaphysically objectionable entities, and that there are no such things; so he has to give an account of how we receive information in perception which lacks a mechanism

34. *Kuriai doxai* 37, 38.

for receiving content from the appearances. On Epicurus' view the mind somehow conceptualizes and articulates the informational content of perception as a result of sensory barrage by images and is able to do this because repeated experiences have built up patterns in the mind atoms which amount to the possession of concepts. It is undoubtedly the less satisfactory view.

Epicurus was notorious in antiquity for believing that "all perceptions are true." As an epistemological thesis, this seems to have been adopted for antisceptical reasons: since perceptual experience is the foundation for all our knowledge, some perceptions must be true, and we must accept that all are if we are not to get entangled in sceptical arguments which discredit some perceptions on the basis of others.[35] The obvious sceptical objections to the thesis are met by the obvious expedient: all perceptions are true, and falsehood is always due to added belief.[36] Perception never goes wrong insofar as it is the reception of information from outside; belief involves a reaction on our part which can go right, but can also go wrong. This arms the Epicureans against sceptics, and indeed we often find sceptics and Epicureans drawing different conclusions from the same material.[37] However, this role for belief is problematic. That we have a factor in ourselves accounting for error allows the process of perception itself to be a totally passive reception of data; but since thinking was supposed to be like perception in being just such a passive reception, it is hard to see how we get the error-permitting process out of

35. See Striker (1977, 135–38). For an account of Epicurus as a naturalistic epistemologist, who is not motivated by the challenge of scepticism, see Everson (1990).

36. D. L. 10. 32; Sext. Emp. *Math.* 8. 63–66. See Striker (1977) and Taylor (1980).

37. So Lucretius, on the basis of one short antisceptical argument (4. 469–77), feels free to put to Epicurean use quantities of material used in the later sceptical tradition (4. 324–468). This material is particularly prominent in Aenesidemus' Ten Modes, particularly the Fifth in Sextus' ordering (see Annas and Barnes 1985). Diogenes of Oenoanda (new frag. 9) seems to have a similar attitude. Cf. Gigante (1981); Fowler (1984).

thinking; indeed a parallel factor would seem required to account for error in thinking. How to account convincingly for error is a problem facing all empiricist accounts which make our information-receiving mechanisms conspicuously passive.

Problems arise when we press the question, What is the perception which is always true? The thesis is expressed in a great variety of ways. What is said to be always true is perception or appearance (*phantasia*) or perception and appearance or the appearances occurring through perception or "the senses" in general.[38] These differences matter, for if Epicurus is wavering between a wider and a narrower notion of what the item is which is always true, he is by the same token also wavering between a wider and a narrower notion of what the added belief element is which can produce falsity.

It is easy to see what gets Epicurus into trouble here. He wants a commonsense epistemology: we can rely on our perceptions. But the thesis that all perceptions are true is rapidly seen to be false at the commonsense level, for the "conflicts in perception" of which the sceptics made so much arise very obviously. I see the tower as square close up, round at a distance. The wine heats me and chills you. Epicurus did not have a satisfactory single answer to this. Plutarch preserves a passage which suggests a relativistic solution: we do not really have conflicting appearances about the same thing, the wine. Rather, because of its atomic constitution, the wine is heating to me, cooling to you.[39] Sextus suggests another way of avoiding the conflict: each of us truly reports how the thing in question appears to us, so we are not disagreeing about the object, but merely reporting its different appearances.[40] Both these answers are retreats from common sense. Inevitably, given his

38. Examples of each include the following: perception: Sext. Emp. *Math.* 8. 185; appearance (*phantasia*): Sext. Emp. *Math.* 7. 204; perception and appearance: Aët. 4. 9, 5, p. 396D (= Usener 248); appearances occurring through perception: Plut. *Adv. Col.* 1109b; "the senses" in general: Cic. *Luc.* 79.

39. *Adv. Col.* 1109b–1110e; cf. Lucr. 4. 642–72.

40. *Math* 7. 205–16; see Everson (1990).

commitment to the thesis that all perceptions are true, Epicurus will be driven back to the position that what is always true will be the agent's claims as to how the world appears to him to be. This result is somewhat embarrassing for three reasons.

Firstly, statements about ordinary physical objects become theoretical, a projection from the perceptual experience we rely on, and this is counterintuitive. This would not matter for some theories, but Epicurus makes large efforts to present his theories as intuitive (and other people's theories as ridiculously counterintuitive). There are obvious ways of saving the theory, though it is not clear that Epicurus followed any of them up. It might be, for example, that perceptual judgments should be analyzed in a way which makes them more non-committal than we normally assume; perhaps a perceptual judgment strictly claims merely that there is something there to be perceived, but does not reveal its nature. On this view, perception will tell us that there is something which appears square close up and round from a distance; but it is for theory to tell us that it is a tower. This view of course holds that everyday perceptual experience reveals far less than we normally take it to do, and does not really reestablish the theory as an intuitive one.

Secondly, the perceptions which are true will be our appearances; but we have seen why Epicurus has some difficulty in saying that the appearances themselves are true, for they do not themselves have content in the way that Stoic perceptual appearances do. Hence, perhaps, there is a standing complication in the evidence: perceptions are said to be true but are also sometimes characterized in ways that conflict with this; they are irrational,[41] and so simply record, and do not add or subtract anything. And Sextus says that everything perceived is "true and existent," but that here "true" does not differ from "subsisting."[42] Passages like this have led some to

41. D. L. 10. 31; Sext. Emp. *Math.* 8. 9.
42. *Math.* 8. 9.

the view that Epicurean perceptions are true in a special sense not involving propositional content. It is obscure, however, what this could be; if it means simply that they really occur, then far too many things get let in as being true—pains, for example. In any case, the evidence does not demand a special sense of "true," for Epicurus could, and almost certainly did, mean that they were true in a derived sense, namely, that on the basis of them true statements can be made. Pictures and images of many kinds can be said to be true in this sense, and Epicurus could quite well have thought that when I perceive a red square, for example, I receive an image which is red and square, and is not itself true, but that my perception can be said to be true because on the basis of it I can assent to "There is a red square here," which is true. The problem for Epicurus is simply that he has no mechanism for explaining how this is the case, as the Stoics do. For Epicurus it looks like sheer unexplained good luck that information in imagistic form gets transformed into something that can be said to be true or false.

Thirdly, the difference between a veridical and a nonveridical appearance—a straightforward perception and a dream image or illusion—turns out to depend on whether the agent has true or false beliefs about other things; and this again is counterintuitive. Despite the official commonsense epistemology, Epicureans feel that the phenomena of dreams, hallucinations, and so on are a serious problem for them; for the appearances presented to the sleeper and to the wakeful are equally "true." Lucretius, Epicurus, and Diogenes of Oenoanda discuss at some length the problem that we have visions and dream images and emotional reactions to them.[43] The official account given by Diogenes is that the mind is affected independently of the senses and fails to refer its images to the senses, which would declare them not to be images of real things.[44] But the test which the senses provide is problematic.

43. Diogenes of Oenoanda new frag. 6, frag. 7, new frags. 1, 12.
44. New frag. 6; see Clay (1980).

The Epicureans want to account for two facts: that some non-veridical experiences seem as convincing as veridical ones, and that they are nonetheless not experiences of the real world. But the Epicurean theory of perception does not give a robust enough account of the second fact, while the account it gives of the first is all too plausible.

8

Action and Freedom of Action

For the Epicurean account of the mechanism of action we are dependent on a brief and rather isolated passage in Lucretius.[1] He starts by saying that he will explain "how it comes about that we can carry our steps onward, and how it is given to us to move our limbs in various ways." What he perceives as the main problem here is how the soul, fine and small, can move so bulky a thing as the body, and he takes up most of his exposition explaining how this is no problem: force of movement is not in direct relation to bulk. He does not find anything particularly problematic in the initial stage, of how we have an impulse to move in the first place:

> I say that first of all images of walking (*simulacra meandi*) strike upon our rational soul (*animo nostro . . . accidere*) and hit upon the rational soul, as we said before. Thence impulse comes about (*inde voluntas fit*); for no one ever begins to do anything until the mind foresees what it

1. 4. 877–906. The passage is sandwiched for no obvious reason between a rejection of teleology and an account of sleep. Even allowing for the unfinished condition of much of book 4, this can be taken as an indication that for the Epicureans action is not as central and prominent a topic as it is for the Stoics.

wishes (*providit quid velit*); what it foresees, the picture (*imago*) of that thing comes about. Therefore when the rational soul so stirs itself that it wishes to go and to move forward, it forthwith strikes all the force of the irrational soul which is distributed in the entire body throughout the limbs and members. And this is easy to do, since it is held together in combination with it. Thence it in turn strikes the body, and thus gradually the whole mass is pushed forward and moves. (4.881–91)

Like the Stoics, Epicurus makes clear that in action the rational, as well as the irrational, soul is involved; action in human beings is more than a mere sensory reflex or reaction. He differs from the Stoics in being (if we infer rightly from this passage) comparatively uninterested in impulse as a phenomenon in its own right. We have some tantalizing bits of evidence here; it appears that he wishes to downplay the Aristotelian word for desire, *orexis*, or even discredit it, though it is unclear precisely what his grounds for this were.[2] However, Epicurus develops no new technical notion that we know of; there is nothing to compare with the careful Stoic treatment of *hormē*. Epicurus may have used *hormē* as a term for "impulse" in the analysis of action; we cannot tell, but it seems likely that that is the word which Lucretius translates as *voluntas*. By Lucretius' time, however, the Stoic

2. Nussbaum (1985, sect. 6) points to four striking instances of Epicurus' use of *orexis*, which occurs "always pejoratively and always in connexion with the empty desires associated with false beliefs about the good." These are *Kuria doxa* 26; Porph. *Ad Marc.* 27 (= Usener 202), 29 (= Usener 445); Stob. *Flor.* 17. 35 (= Usener 422). To these should be added Lucian *Par.* 12; Porph. *Abst.* 1. 49 (= Usener 456); also Usener 483, where love (*erōs*) is defined as intense *orexis* for sex, with frenzy and distress. There is an apparently neutral use of *orexis* in Plut. *Cont. Ep. beat.* 1088c, but this may be Plutarch's own wording. Epicurus may have been trying to combat the Aristotelian use of *orexis* in theory of action, but more likely is pressing the ordinary-language implication that *orexis*, which derives from a verb whose primary meaning is that of reaching for something, implies attempt rather than success.

term may have come into more general use even among Epicureans.[3] Epicurus' account of action also contrasts with the Stoics' in not standing in particularly close or helpful relation to his ethics.

"Images of walking" strike the rational soul and get it moving; this is Epicurus' analogue to the Stoic "impulsory appearance." Some appearances, the perceptual ones, permit us to take in information. Others produce reaction in us, either of attraction or of repulsion. As with the perceptual appearances, the ones which produce action are spoken of as images. Epicurus is again silent as to any mechanism whereby we could get from images striking the soul to content that can be interpreted and acted on. All we find is that an "image of walking" strikes the soul, which the rational soul in some way

3. *Voluntas* is sometimes translated "will," but the philosophical notion of "free will" has no place here. This mistake has encouraged attempts to link this passage with the swerve (see below). That *voluntas* translates *hormē* is simply my speculation; but if it translates a single Greek term at all, that is a good candidate. Cicero, writing prose and thus with more freedom of choice than Lucretius here, translates *hormē* as *appetitio* at *Off.* 2. 18 and *Luc.* 24 and 30, but also as *appetitus* at *Off.* 1. 101 (cf. Sen. *Ep.* 134.3) and *impetus* at *Off.* 1. 105 (cf. Sen. *Ep.* 113.18). Seneca translates it as *irritatio* at *Ep.* 9.17. Clearly there was no fixed translation. Epicurus uses *hormēma* for an agent's autonomous internal impulse in *On Nature* 35 (Arrighetti [34.29]; Diano 1946, 43–45); Sedley (1983, 22) translates this occurrence as "impulse." *Hormē* and *horman* seem to be used either for physical movements (comets, falling stars), as at *Ep. Pyth.* 111, 115, or of impulse to a way of life rather than to a single action: *epi philosophian hormēsas* (Usener 117), *epi strateian hormēse* (Usener 171), *epi to sophisteuein hormesai* (Usener 172). Hermarchus is reported by Porphyry (*Abst.* 1. 8) as using the phrase *tais hormais epi tas asumphorous praxeis*, but this may be paraphrase. Later Epicureans, possibly influenced by Stoic terminology, do use *hormē* for the impulse to a particular action. Cf. Diogenes of Oenoanda frag. 24, col. 1. 11–13 and new frag. 10, col. 2. 3–4 (*pros praxin* in both cases). Philodemus, who uses *hormasthai* in a logical sense (*On Signs* 19. 31, 30. 3, 22) uses *hormē* as an impulse to something as enjoyable at *On Anger* 44. 7, 46. 36–40 (*hoi de phusikōs phasin hēmas epi tēn orgēn hōsper epi tēn eucharistian horman*), and 48. 5–7 (*ei phusikōs hormōmen epi to suntonōs eucharistian*).

interprets and makes sense of; as a result an impulse is produced. There are two points where we might justifiably demand more of an explicit account if we are not to regard the
process as highly mysterious. One is the image that strikes the
soul: it is an "image *of walking*" (*meandi*). What can an image
of walking be? We can easily form an image of a person walking, or each person can picture himself or herself walking.[4]
But a definite image like this greatly underdetermines the
thoughts one could have about it. Why should a picture of
myself walking produce an impulse in me to walk, rather than
not to walk? Or an impulse to walk, rather than to take the
car? What is needed is rather an image which will plausibly
produce the reaction that the agent walks. Most likely this is
why Lucretius uses the odd expression "images of walking."
But this just lands us back with the problem of giving a sense
to the notion of an *image* of something as general as walking.
The problem can be summed up in general: a particular image cannot explain why one action is produced on the basis
of it rather than another. What is needed is the presentation
of something with generality. But an image cannot express
generality. An image theory cannot cope with any form of
abstraction, and hence cannot account for thoughts which
require it.[5] Maybe we should not concentrate so much on the
image but think rather of what the rational soul interprets from
the image. This requires considerable interpretative charity,
since Epicurus gives us absolutely nothing on this point.

The second problem arises with the impulse that is formed,
for it also is presented in imagistic terms, and similar difficulties arise for it. The impulse itself is a "picture" of what
the rational soul foresees as what it wants to do; thus if I form
an impulse to walk, I will presumably form a picture of myself

---

4. Bailey (1928) notices this problem, saying that Epicurus "should
more strictly have said 'images of us walking' or 'of one walking,
meantis.'"

5. I am grateful to Rob Cummins for pointing out that this is the
basic problem here.

walking. However, all the problems that arose for the first image arise again here. How can picturing myself walking lead to action? We need at least two ideas which the picture itself cannot express, namely, that the walking is in the future and that it is in some way desirable. Again, however, no image is competent to express these ideas, and anything that is cannot simply be an image.

Again, we might think that we are being uncharitable. Elsewhere Epicurus says that the person who walks has a "practical belief," *pragmatikē doxa*.[6] Perhaps Lucretius is simply telling us part of the story here. If so, then when a person resolves to do something, she forms a practical belief, and the image that Lucretius talks about is just the content of the practical belief as presented to the agent. We need not, then, take Epicurus to be trying vainly to extract a belief from a picture; rather, he is saying that when I resolve to walk, I form a belief, and part of what this involves is picturing myself walking. On this view, the image has a more plausible role. However, even this more charitable interpretation has its drawbacks. Firstly, we cannot tell a parallel story for the first image, which strikes the soul and leads to the formation of the impulse; so the two images in the story will function very differently. Secondly, even in its own terms this story will only be plausible for a selection of impulses, namely, simple cases of immediate action. It does not extend at all plausibly to large-scale resolves. Suppose I resolve to become a millionaire; this does not seem to bring with it the need to visualize myself doing anything concrete. Indeed, this seems inappropriate; I might visualize myself gloating over money-bags or ordering people around in a fancy office, but clearly no such picture is either necessary or sufficient for me to have the resolve. Here the problem is that a large-scale resolve is compatible with many different, and sometimes mutually exclusive, ways of carrying it out; so visualization of

6. *On Nature* 28, frag. 13, col. 9. 4.

these resolves can form no part of having the resolve. Even the more charitable interpretation, therefore, leaves Epicurus with a very unsatisfactory theory here.

Lucretius sees no difficulty as to how impulse produces action: once the impulse has been formed, we simply get the causal story of how the rational soul affects the irrational, and that affects the body. No attention is paid, in this context, to the possibility of blocking factors which might produce, for example, *akrasia;* it is hard to see where Epicurus could find room for them, and his answer to this problem is probably like the that of the Stoics: *akrasia* is not an extra blocking factor, but a case of shifting or unclear resolve.

Epicurus' account of action has often been compared to that of Aristotle in *De motu animalium*,[7] but the differences are more striking than the similarities, and Epicureans and Stoics have more in common with each other than either school has with Aristotle. Both analyze action in terms of impulse, including some kind of cognitive factor. For the Stoics this is clearly propositional. For Epicurus it is propositional, but not very clearly so; more weight is laid on the having of an image or picture of some kind. But neither school has anything remotely like Aristotle's account of deliberation as a kind of enquiry or search leading to action. For the Hellenistic schools impulse is partnered by only one "practical belief." Indeed, Epicurus says of the agent who has a practical, not merely a theoretical, belief, that if it is a universal (*katholou*) belief, then "he embarks [lit. 'walks,' *badizei*] immediately upon an action such as if he had also accepted empirically that in a particular instance something was or was not of a certain kind."[8] For Epicurus, deliberation or selection at the moment of action is not stressed. Rather, action is the product of the world's impinging on an agent who already has a character and reactive capacities of a certain kind. As with the Stoics, the answer to "Why did you do that?" will be given by ref-

---

7. See Furley (1967); Diano (1974a); Englert (1988).
8. *On Nature* 28, frag. 13, col. 11. 4–14; trans. Sedley.

erence to two factors. One is the way the world appeared to me at the time; the other is my overall state at that time, a state resulting from past choices and present endorsement of past development.

We have seen that Epicurus never doubts that we are free agents, and argues that reductive determinism is untenable.[9] We also know that the thesis that some things are in our power and that not everything is "by necessity" was at some point defended by reference to the theory of the "swerve" (*parenklisis, clinamen*) of the atoms. We have nothing extant from Epicurus himself on the swerve, but that it is his theory is clear from later references.[10] The idea is simple: atoms fall perpendicularly through the void at uniform speed, but now and then one may swerve, "at no fixed time or place," but only minimally.[11] Thus the motions of the atoms are not totally explicable, even in principle, by deterministic laws. This indeterminacy at the atomic level accounts for two things: the fact that in a "rain" of atoms moving at even speed in parallel perpendicular lines, we even get collisions leading to the forming of compounds, and of entire worlds in particular; and, more importantly here, that some things at least are "up to us."

We do not know if the swerve always had these two functions, or if either of them was more prominent for Epicurus, but the ancient evidence (much of it hostile) makes it clear that the swerve was in some way meant to explain how we are

9. See chapter 6, section a.

10. The swerve's absence from the extant letters of Epicurus has occasioned some surprise. The most plausible explanation is that these summarizing works were produced at a stage before Epicurus had worked on the swerve idea; this would make it a later development from his Athenian period. See pp. 187–88 and n. 26 below. For references to the swerve other than those cited below, which are mostly not very informative, see Cic. *Fin.* 1. 18–20; Plut. *De an. proc.* 1015b–c; August. *Contra Acad.* 3. 23. For these and other relevant Cicero passages see Usener 281. Philodemus mentions that Zeno of Sidon wrote a work on the swerve (see Croenert 1906).

11. For a good account of the swerve, see Englert (1988, chap. 2).

free agents. Cicero explains why the swerve was introduced: since otherwise "we would have no freedom" and "nothing would be in our power."[12] Philodemus says cautiously that the swerve must be shown to be consistent with experience—we must not just accept it "because of chance and of things depending on us."[13] And Diogenes of Oenoanda hails the swerve as grounds for confidence that we are free agents and are justified in our practices of praise, blame, and so on:

> If someone makes use of the theory of Democritus, saying that there is no free movement for the atoms because of their collisions with one another, from which it is clear that all things are moved by necessity, we shall say to him, "Do you not know, whoever you may be, that there *is* a kind of free movement in the atoms, which Democritus did not discover but which Epicurus brought to light, an inherent swerve, as he shows from the phenomena? The most important point is this: if destiny is believed in, all admonition and rebuke is done away with. (Frag. 32)[14]

Undeniable as it is that the swerve is in some way to explain free action, it is extremely puzzling how it could do so. Firstly, we have already seen that Epicurus can adequately defend our belief that we are free agents, and responsible for what we do, by arguing that a theory that denies this is untenable.[15] There seems no need for anything like the swerve. Further, it is not clear how a commonsense belief can be supported in the way that Epicurus needs by a controversial philosophical thesis. The whole thrust of arguments like Epicurus' refutation of determinism is that we are entitled to our folk psychology beliefs as they are; they cannot be undermined by philosophical theories such as determinism. The swerve theory seems

12. *Nihil liberum nobis esset* (*Fat.* 22–23); *nihil fore in nostra potestate* (*Nat. d.* 1.69).
13. *To par' hēmas* (*On Signs* 36. 11–14). Note that things depend on us, rather than being up to us. See chapter 6, section a, p. 129 above.
14. Trans. Chilton.
15. In chapter 6, section a.

to backtrack on this: the thought that our belief in our own free agency needs the swerve theory to support it suggests that we are really not, after all, entitled to our ordinary beliefs as they are.

Epicurus may, of course, have changed his mind about the kind of support that our belief in our own free agency demands. Or he may have thought that the refutation of determinism and the swerve theory serve two distinct ends. The first merely shows that we have no real alternative to thinking of ourselves as free agents; the second shows us not that, but how, this is possible: atomic theory can accommodate it. We may still feel discomfort. Why does atomic theory have to be shown to accommodate free agency, unless free agency is already thought to pose a philosophical problem? But the refutation argument proceeded on the assumption that it is the philosophical arguments against free agency that pose a problem, not free agency itself. By showing that atomic theory can be modified to accommodate free agency, the swerve theory can only encourage the thought that the refutation argument rejects, that atomic theory threatens free agency.

Apart from this, the swerve theory has internal problems. How can indeterminacy at the micro-level explain free agency at the macro-level? How can random swerves among the atoms explain the behavior of atomic compounds? The problem is worsened here by the point that what is to be explained is merely the behavior of some atomic compounds, namely, human agents. Trees and stones are not taken to exhibit results of swerves. But everything, inanimate as well as animate, is composed of atoms, and so the indeterminacy produced by swerves among the atoms should have any effects it has at the macro-level across the board. We need some intermediate stage to show how swerves at the atomic level produce effects at the macro-level, and further, effects which are limited to free agency in humans.

We get no satisfactory account of such a stage or process. One of our most important sources suggests one, but in a puzzling way. When Lucretius introduces the swerve in its cosmogonical role he then abruptly ascribes to the swerve "that free impulse torn from fate, by which we progress wherever pleasure leads each person, and swerving our motions not at a fixed time or in a fixed region of space, but where the mind itself has taken us."[16] Our freedom to do one thing rather than another is compared, somewhat grotesquely, to the swerving of the atoms. Lucretius goes on to give examples of free action, which introduce various considerations and are far from perspicuous. The first is an example of animal action, horses at the starting barrier of a race. The second is of a person being pushed and resisting the pressure, who is compared to someone moving without opposition.[17] Lucretius concludes that there is a special kind of cause in the atoms: "That the mind itself should not have necessity within it in all action, and should not be as it were conquered and compelled to endure and suffer; this is brought about by the elements' tiny swerve, in no fixed region of space and at no fixed time."[18]

Lucretius' passage suggests that swerves are responsible for free actions rather directly. Does he, however, mean that an action is free because a swerve is part of the immediately preceding causal chain? This interpretation, until recently indeed the orthodox interpretation, faces tremendous problems.[19] In his later account of action (see pp. 175–76 above) Lucretius never mentions swerves, and there is no obvious place to insert them in his account of how an action comes about. Further, since swerves are random, it is hard to see how they help to explain free action. We can scarcely expect

16. 2. 256–60; the complete passage is 2. 250–93. In the portion quoted *voluntas* is an emendation for *voluptas,* almost universally accepted; see Fowler (1983). The appearance of "free" here has unfortunately encouraged the translation of *voluntas* as "will," and the importation of modern problems.

17. Saunders (1984) argues that the crucial point about both examples is that they present particularly effortful actions. This feature of the examples has frequently been overlooked.

18. 2. 289–93; *mens* ("mind") is almost universally accepted here as an emendation for *res.* See Fowler (1983), who argues against Avotins (1979) and Kleve (1980).

19. The interpretation derives from Giussani (1896) and Bailey (1928).

there to be a *random* swerve before every free action. Free actions are frequent, and (fairly) reliable. Random swerves cannot account for either of these features. This problem would be lessened if we could assume that swerves are very frequent, so that there is always likely to be one around before an action. However, if swerves are frequent, we face the problem that stones and trees ought to be enabled to act freely. And even in the case of humans random swerves would seem to produce, if anything, random actions; we still lack any clue as to how they could produce actions which are free.

An influential modern line of thought avoids these problems by arguing that our evidence does not demand that there be a swerve for each free action.[20] Rather, swerves explain the fact that people have characters capable of change and reaction that goes beyond mechanical response to stimuli. We act freely because we have characters that are flexible and spontaneous, and this is because we are composed of atoms which swerve occasionally. On this account, swerves do not have to be frequent, since they are not part of any mechanism of action; one swerve in your soul is enough for the kind of character flexibility that is required. Such an account avoids the problems attaching to any account that brings swerves into free action, but at the cost of not answering very closely to the evidence; the Lucretius passage certainly suggests that swerves are in some way relevant at the point of action.

Another kind of suggestion is that swerves are not the causes of free actions at all. Rather, they come into the process whereby free actions are brought about. Swerves are supposed to explain something about the nature of free agency and how it works, but they do not cause free actions (by cutting across causal chains, for example). This suggestion can be developed in several ways. The boldest version holds that swerves do not explain the existence of free volitions at all;[21] rather Epicurus holds anyway that volitions are nonphysical, "emergent" en-

20. Furley (1967).
21. Sedley (1983, 1989).

tities. The role of swerves is to provide alternative possibilities for volitions to choose between, for there would be no point in having free will if there were no genuinely open possibilities between which to select. This suggestion depends on the strong thesis that Epicurus regards the mind as something nonphysical, which we have seen to be highly contentious;[22] and also it likewise does not really answer to the evidence, in which it is not merely the possibility of swerves, but actual swerves, which play a role at the level of action. A second kind of account gives the swerve a role in enabling the mind to focus on one thing rather than another by way of the mind's selective "grasp" or *epibolē tēs dianoias*.[23] A third sees it as parallel to Aristotle's use of the connate *pneuma*;[24] that is, it creates a new kind of physical substance which explains, within a physicalist system, how human minds can be active, and in particular can initiate action.

It is undoubtedly more attractive to find a role for swerves in the mechanism of free action, rather than as mysterious events enabling free action to come about. However, all such accounts face the problem of evidence: Lucretius, the only source who gives us much detail about the swerve in human action, associates it with the formation of impulse (*voluntas*), not with any subsequent mechanism to carry it out.[25] However embarrassing we may find the thesis that the swerve explains the formation of free impulses, and in some way explains how they are free, that remains the view best supported by the ancient evidence.

As we have seen, however, occasional random swerves cannot produce reliable free actions. The only way that the theory has a hope of working is on the assumption that swerves are extremely frequent, so as to produce a standing physical con-

22. See chapter 6, section a.
23. Fowler (1983).
24. Englert (1988); see part 1, chapter 1, section a.
25. This point is made in the excellent study by Asmis (1990), who gives a useful survey of scholarly options about the role of the swerve.

dition. How, though, do we avoid the obvious objection that trees and stones would also contain frequent swerves, given that it is an important aspect of Epicureanism that human beings are parts of nature, atomic compounds like the others? We can meet this objection by the consideration that swerves are indeed everywhere frequent, but that they produce effects only in human souls, perhaps indeed only in the rational parts of human souls. This is because the human rational soul is a compound of the finest and most tenuous atoms, and only this kind of compound permits swerves to have effects. Thus we are free, and trees are not, because of a physical difference: in our minds atomic swerves produce effects, which somehow enable us to act freely. While the mechanism remains somewhat sketchy, we can see the general idea. Swerves do not operate one per action; rather, because we (and some animals) are the kinds of atomic compound that we are, we are able to act freely, in a way that genuinely chooses between alternatives.

But now we find a striking redundancy, for Epicurus has already postulated the nameless atoms in the soul to account for the complexity of sentient and intelligent behavior. Why do we need swerves as well to account for the same fact? Impressive as the fact may be, we hardly need two such physical differences to account for it. It might be objected that nameless atoms account only for agency, while we need swerves to account for *free* agency. But it is quite unclear from our evidence what this difference would be taken to consist in. This is especially so since Lucretius uses animal behavior as an example of free agency, ruling out the otherwise promising idea that freedom might be a matter of informed choice between alternatives, or something similar which is plausibly found only in humans.

It is very hard not to feel pressured here toward a developmental hypothesis, namely, that Epicurus had both these ideas, but not at the same time. It has been suspected on other grounds that the swerve was a late idea of Epicurus', one developed after he had written his major works, possibly in response to objections.[26] It is also possible that Epicurus himself had no very definite theory of how the swerve underpins free agency, and that later Epicureans filled in the story, possibly in divergent ways, just as modern scholars do. It is hard to conclude, however, that the swerve was a good idea, and the disproportionate emphasis which it has received in discussion of Epicurus' ideas about the mind has been unfortunate.[27]

26. See Asmis (1990) for a discussion of this hypothesis (which she rejects).
27. There are also problems with its cosmological role. The assumption that the atoms have been colliding for all time is far more reasonable than the assumption of the swerve.

9

Emotions and Feelings

The Stoic theory of the *pathē* is a theory of the emotions,[1] but Epicurus' theory of the *pathē* is, in keeping with his stress on basic experience, a theory of the feelings, and emotions turn out to be complex kinds of feelings.

The criteria of truth are the perceptions, the preconceptions (*prolēpseis*), and the feelings.[2] "The feelings, they say, are two, pleasure and pain, which come about in every animal, the former appropriate to us (*oikeion*), the latter alien (*allotrion*); through these are judged choices and avoidances."[3] Lucretius gives us a physical account: "There is pain, where the bodies of matter are disturbed by some force throughout the living flesh and limbs and tremble in their own positions within; and when they settle back into their places, soothing pleasure comes about."[4]

The feelings of pleasure and pain, then, are our practical criterion: pleasure is what we start from in every choice and avoidance, "and we return to it, using the feeling as a rule by

1. See part 2, chapter 5.
2. D. L. 10. 31.
3. D. L. 10. 34.
4. 2. 963–66.

which to judge every good."⁵ However, *pathos* is used for the basic feeling in perception also, and sometimes Epicurus urges us to test the truth of theory by sticking to our perceptions and feelings, so no sharp distinction seems to be drawn between the theoretical and practical criteria.⁶

When I have a pleasant feeling, what does it reveal to me? Not simply that this is pleasant; Cicero presents the Epicurean Torquatus as saying,

> Every animal, as soon as it is born, seeks pleasure, and enjoys it as the chief good, while it recoils from pain as the chief evil and repels it as much as it can; and this it does while it is not yet perverted, while its nature itself is judging in an uncorrupt and honest way. Hence Epicurus denies that we need any reason or discussion as to why pleasure is to be sought and pain avoided. These things are felt, he thinks, just as that fire heats, snow is white, honey sweet; none of these things need to be established by elaborate argument—it is enough just to draw attention to them. (*Fin.* 1.30)

It seems, then, that we can be said to feel that something is pleasant, and so choice-worthy, and so good. This is a strikingly large amount of content to pack into an allegedly straightforward feeling which has nothing to do with reasoning.⁷

Epicurus has a problem analogous to his problem with perception. He wants there to be an element in experience which is simply "given," which puts us directly in touch with reality, so that what we claim about it is always true as long as we rely on experience and do not contaminate that with our corruptible beliefs. But it is hard to find something which is both sufficiently free of belief to count as the given and also rich enough to do the explanatory work required of it. "Feeling,"

5. Epicurus *Ep. Men.* 129.
6. For *pathos* as the basic feeling in perception see Epicurus *Ep. Herod.* 52, 53; on the testing the truth of the theory see, for example, *Ep. Herod.* 38, 63; Asmis (1984, pt. 2).
7. Cf. Gosling and Taylor (1982, chap. 20).

moreover, is used in a rather elastic way; Diogenes of Oenoanda talks of pleasant and painful feelings guiding all action,
and puts under this heading both emotions felt by a person
experiencing some disaster and those of his sympathetic
friends.[8]

What distinguishes those feelings which are complex enough
to be emotions? It is some kind of involvement of the rational
soul, which is the center of emotions like fear and joy as well
as of thinking. Lucretius indeed illustrates the relation of rational to irrational soul by the effects of fear.[9] Presumably,
some kind of belief is involved, but where the Stoics are explicit Epicurus is somewhat hazy. Some fragments of *On Nature* 25 are relevant, though their exact significance is uncertain.[10] Epicurus is discussing the relation of the soul to its own
pathē and its ability to remember them, or have some relation
to them analogous to memory. Memory, it seems, may involve
beliefs (*doxai*). What seems to be crucial is that the *pathos* be
directed at what is defined (*to hōrismenon*), as opposed to what
is indefinite. This recalls the many times Epicurus associates
false beliefs and defective "empty" desires, with "the indefinite."[11] But the passages are too fragmentary for us to see just
how emotions result from the definite focusing of feeling by
some kind of belief or belieflike process.

Emotions, then, can be contrasted with the basic feelings
of pleasure and pain by the fact that they involve the rational
soul. Indeed, in a fragment of Diogenes of Oenoanda we find
that when, as happens in ethical contexts, the body is being
contrasted with the soul, emotions stand on the soul side.[12]
Diogenes contrasts "bodily" with "soul" *pathē*. The latter, he

8. New frag. 10.
9. 3. 152–60.
10. Arrighetti [34.18–20].
11. Arrighetti (1973, 574) is surely right to reject Diano's (1946)
suggestion that *to horismenon* here = *to telos tes phuseōs;* it is just
any well-defined aim. For the association of indefiniteness with false
beliefs, see *Kuriai doxai* 15, 30; *VS* 59; Porph. *Ad Marc.* 27 (= Usener
202), *Abst.* 1. 53–54 (= Usener 465).
12. Frag. 38.

says, are more important, but it is hard to convince the many
of this, since when in bodily pain we think these feelings worse
than any troubles of our soul, and it seldom happens that we
experience extreme feelings of soul and body at the same time,
so we cannot directly compare them.

Philodemus' work *On Anger* makes it clear that an emotion
involves a belief. For example, anger involves the belief that
I have been wronged, since it involves the desire to retaliate
for the wrong. But there is no Epicurean theory of the structure of the emotions. It is never clear whether the belief is to
be regarded as part of the emotion or simply as its cause; most
of the discussion presupposes nothing stronger than the latter.

The end of *On Anger*, however, suggests that the belief is a
necessary, but not sufficient, condition for having the emotion.[13] You cannot become wise without learning to read, but
learning to read alone will not make you wise; similarly, you
will not be angry without believing that you have been harmed,
but Philodemus criticizes those who think that anger will always follow this belief, "unless he can show that the suppo-
sition of harm is also an effective cause (*drastikon aition*) of
anger." Given that Epicurus does not have much of a theory
of causation, it is interesting to find a concern for the effective
or acting cause, and possibly this is taken over from Stoicism.

Philodemus' own answer seems clearly from his earlier discussion to be that the effective cause of an angry reaction is
the person's whole *diathesis* or disposition. Ordinary angry
behavior, which he considers defective, comes "from a very
bad disposition";[14] the ideal Epicurean will still react angrily
on occasion but will do so from a very different character and
set of beliefs. If Philodemus is typical here, then the Epicurean
way of regarding emotions will be broadly like the Stoics'.
Whether or not, and how, I react emotionally will depend on
two factors. One is my disposition and character as a whole,
and the other is a belief I form as a result of present experi-

13. 47.18–42, 49.28–50.8.
14. 38.1–4.

ence. Thus it is not a temporary state, but my whole disposition, which is the effective cause of my anger.

Emotions thus require beliefs (whether as causes or parts of the emotion), and it is an important part of the ethical theory that many of our desires and emotions are thus dependent on beliefs which are false and, in the case of practical beliefs, "empty," that is, not just false, but, because of their falsity, harmful and dysfunctional to the person. Epicurus stresses that desires are either natural or empty, and that the empty ones are those that depend on an empty belief.[15] Natural desires are either necessary or nonnecessary. Necessary ones, which we have to fulfill one way or other, are most plausibly construed as generic desires: desires for food, for shelter, and so on. If we fulfill them in ways which do not involve any empty beliefs, they are just nonnecessary desires, which are varied ways of fulfilling the generic desires that we necessarily have. But if we fulfill our desires in ways which rest on empty beliefs, then the desires themselves become empty, and thus harmful to us. For Epicurus, the best strategy for achieving pleasure, our final end, is to live one's life in such a way that one satisfies only natural, never empty, desires.

We find in Philodemus an interesting analogue in the case of the emotion of anger. There is, Philodemus holds, such a thing as natural anger, which is unavoidable. That is, it is unavoidable that we will get angry and feel desire to retaliate in some way or other. But it is up to us to do so in ways which do not rest on empty beliefs, for if we do, our anger will be empty anger, something which is highly dysfunctional and disruptive in the agent's life. Our emotions are thus dependent on our beliefs in a very direct way; changing our beliefs will change our emotions from being turbulent and a source of unhappiness (as with empty anger, which Philodemus de-

15. Epicurus' use of "empty" in this connection is a development of a use in ordinary Greek of "empty" to mean "futile, pointless." For a full defense of the following claims about Epicurus on natural and empty desires and Philodemus on natural and empty anger see Annas (1989).

scribes at length in a deliberately shocking way) to being a part of the pleasant and untroubled life. In particular, Philodemus singles out the belief that retaliation is in itself pleasant as an empty belief that makes the agent's anger empty; the Epicurean who gets rid of this belief (perhaps as a result of reading Philodemus on the subject) will be happy, being free of the troubles which empty anger brings. In this Philodemus is following Epicurus, who stresses the role of reasoning, especially philosophical reasoning, in changing or getting rid of emotions.[16]

Since our feelings of pleasure and pain are our practical guides, there is nothing wrong with emotions as long as they are rightly related to the basic feelings by true beliefs. This does not mean that our attitude toward the emotions should be guided by the desire to eliminate pain completely. For some emotions, of which anger is one, are in themselves painful; even natural anger, which the virtuous Epicurean will feel, involves some pain. But anger of some kind is unavoidable; it is part of our nature.[17] Hence the best we can do is to avoid the further pain caused by basing our anger on empty beliefs; it is this which makes the difference between a troubled and an untroubled life.

Epicurus holds in fact that most of our emotions are based on false beliefs: as Diogenes of Oenoanda tells us,

> we are now enquiring how life may be made pleasant for us in both states (*katastēmata*) and actions. Let us speak first about states, noting indeed that when the emotions that disturb the soul are removed things that give it pleasure come in to take their place. Now what are those disturbing emotions? They are fears, of the gods, of death and of pain; and, in addition, desire which far exceeds its natural bounds. These are indeed the root of all evil, and if we cut them off no evil will grow up in their stead to trouble us. (Frag. 29. 6.2–7.12)[18]

16. *Ep. Men.* 132.
17. Philodemus *On Anger* 39.26–38.
18. Trans. Chilton, slightly altered.

With this stress on the troubling emotions goes a tendency to use a therapeutic model of philosophy as curing us of bad emotions by removing false beliefs. "Empty is that philosopher's argument by which no human being's emotion is cured; for just as we have no need of medicine that does not expel the body's diseases, so we have none of philosophy which does not expel the soul's emotion."[19] In later writers like Lucretius and Philodemus this idea becomes quite explicit.[20] Philodemus devotes much attention to frankness (*parrhēsia*) in philosophical discussion, and of all the ancient philosophical schools the Epicureans were most frankly and unashamedly personal and confessional in style. Opponents tended to be disgusted by this sometimes emotional way of doing philosophy,[21] but we can see why it is important for the Epicureans: their main point in life is to achieve the pleasures of "tranquillity," *ataraxia*, an untroubled state which is threatened by emotional upset. It is important to face and understand the sources of emotion; we can see when we read Philodemus' lurid and theatrical account of anger and Lucretius' of love, as well as Diogenes of Oenoanda's interesting, though incomplete, reference to what looks like anxiety, how important it is for Epicureans to bring out the deep, and sometimes hidden and dark, aspects of the emotions.[22]

Unlike the Stoic theory, the Epicurean account of the emotions does not have the consequence that all emotions are faulty, but it is highly revisionary of our ordinary beliefs about our emotions. The Epicurean wise person, after all, can be happy on the rack,[23] and that alone shows how much affective transformation Epicureanism requires. Some emotions depend completely on beliefs which Epicurus claims are false, and will therefore disappear with those beliefs. Lucretius

19. Usener 221.
20. See Gigante (1975); Nussbaum (1985).
21. Consider Plutarch's disgusted reaction to Colotes' emotional obeisance to Epicurus (*Adv. Col.* 1117b–c).
22. Philodemus *On Anger* 7–31; Lucr. 4. 1057–1287; Diogenes of Oenoanda frag. 29, col. 2. See Konstan (1973).
23. Usener 600–601.

stresses that *religio*, superstitious fear of the gods, is like this. Here the most spectacular example is that of love (*erōs*). Epicurus defined it as "an intense desire (*orexis*) for sex, with frenzy and distress," a description which already makes it clear that *erōs* should be eliminated rather than modified.[24] Lucretius' famous picture of the evils of love brings home vividly the false and empty beliefs on which love depends, beliefs which lead people into delusion, self-destructive behavior, and permanent frustration.[25] The moral is clear: the Epicurean will have no passionate attachments to particular people. He or she will have untroubling affectionate relationships, distributing his or her affections among a circle of friends without strong dependence on or attachment to any in particular. This is a transformation of emotional life nearly as drastic as Plato's in the *Republic*.

Some emotions are, like anger, accepted rather than eliminated, but even so there are considerable changes. Philodemus in *On Anger* is concerned to show that his view is a middle way, with a more complex view of anger than that of either the Stoics, who think it should be removed, or the Peripatetics, who think that there is much to be said for it.[26] But in fact he does not try to incorporate opponents' positive points; he simply relies on Epicurean theory and asks what the Epicurean wise person would be like in this regard. He recognizes that this is revisionary, at one point revealingly wondering whether in view of the difference we should even use the same word.[27]

24. Usener 483, giving several sources; it was clearly notorious. Cf. also *VS* 24: "The emotion of love is destroyed when sight and company are removed."

25. 4. 1037–1287; this is clearly a set piece, not an expression of a personal attitude of Lucretius' own. We can see this by comparing it to the dramatic first half of Philodemus' *On Anger*, which parades before us the ugly effects of anger. Philodemus refers to his own similar work on love (7.118–21) and (in 7) clearly states the point of the exercise: we can get a clear idea of the evils involved.

26. 37.17–24.

27. 43.1–14; cf. 37.21–23. Philodemus characterizes the ideal Epicurean as giving the appearance (*phantasia*) of an ordinary angry

The treatise begins with a lurid parade of the unattractive and damaging features of anger as we commonly conceive it, namely, a fierce desire for revenge. People angry in this way get distorted features; anger is like a disease; angry people make no progress in philosophy or in any common pursuit; nobody can stand them; they lash out against others, blind their slaves, often kill themselves; and so on for thirty columns. By contrast, the ideal Epicurean is "un-angry" (*aorgētos*). This does not mean, however, that he does not get angry or that he does so seldom or that he is especially hard to provoke. Rather, what differentiates this person's "natural" anger from most people's "empty" anger is, as we have seen, that it is based on different beliefs. The wise person does not believe that retaliation is enjoyable, or worthwhile for its own sake; he retaliates because he has to, not because he gets anything out of it.[28] Because of this, his anger will be brief and will not go very deep. The wise person lacks the beliefs which lead ordinary people to anger, because to him nothing "external" matters very much. It is interesting that the things which the Epicurean does not care about are represented as being external to him. We do not find this internalization of the "real self" in Epicurus himself, and it may be a later development.[29] In any case, it clearly makes a vast difference to the wise person's attitudes. Not thinking anger a good thing, because he does not take retaliation to be in itself a good thing, he does not enjoy it. Hence he will only be as angry as he needs to be; and this, Philodemus claims, will be brief and will not go deep.

---

person (34.24–35.6). The behavior may appear the same, but its causes are so different that we do not really have the same emotion. Philodemus, however, does not use distinct words; for an Epicurean the revised kind of anger is a true kind, of which the ordinary kind is a distortion or corruption.

28. 42–44.

29. It is quite marked in Philodemus. See *On Anger* 47.39–42, 48.18–24 (twice); *On Gratitude* 2.5–6; *Rhet.* 2.10.5–10. See also Diogenes of Oenoanda frag. 41. 1–3. It may well show the influence of Stoicism.

We may find it attractive to be rid of the destructive side of anger. But the change in beliefs that brings this about has other consequences, which can be less attractive. Philodemus says openly that just because to the wise person nothing external matters much, he will not be very grateful for benefits, as well as not very angry at wrongs. He will repay benefits and make grateful gestures but will think of these things merely as what has to be done; he will not feel grateful in the way that we do. For our feelings of gratitude, just as much as our feelings of anger, are based on empty beliefs: we think that things like retaliation and gratitude matter, and to a good Epicurean they do not.[30] The Epicurean remedies that take the damaging heat out of anger turn out to leave us cold in areas where this is not so clearly a good thing.

And anger is relocated as well as calmed down. Revealingly, the area where Philodemus is most concerned about anger is that of frank philosophical interchange.[31] In the Epicurean Garden anger is the appropriate reaction to pupils who are slow on the uptake or to opponents who get one's ideas wrong. To need the anger that sustains fighting or the martial virtues is already to have put yourself in a position where you need to combat people to get what you want, and that cannot be conducive to Epicurean happiness.

The Epicurean wise person, we are told, "will be more susceptible to emotions [than the rest of us]; this would not hinder him in attaining wisdom."[32] His emotions, however, will not be ours, just because his beliefs, and the way they have developed together to produce his disposition, are so different from ours. The wise person, says Philodemus circumspectly, will be susceptible to certain forms of anger.[33] The affectively transformed Epicurean will, like the ideal Stoic, be free from

30. *On Anger* 46.18–40, 48.3–33.
31. *On Anger* 18–19 and 37, where he refers to his own *On Frankness*.
32. D. L. 10. 117–20.
33. *On Anger* 41.30: *suschethesetai tisin orgais ho sophos*. The verb is the same as the one in the Diogenes passage (10.117), and Bignone's emendation *tisi* to qualify *pathesi* in that passage is attractive.

the disturbances of emotion in our everyday sense, and motivated by emotions which have been transformed by a total restructuring of the beliefs that sustain them. Their behavior will not be quite the same—the Stoics have no room for approved forms of the hostile or negative emotions like anger, and the Epicureans do—but they will be equally far from our everyday state.

It is somewhat ironical that this is the end result of a theory allegedly based on uncomplicated feelings which all share. We start from common sense, but we end very far from it.

Conclusion

This book has concentrated on giving full pictures of the philosophy of mind of the Stoics and Epicureans, as well as the background to them. I have proceeded in this way because these theories seem to me to be the major achievements in philosophy of mind in this period and worthy of serious study in their own right; I shall be glad if this work helps to encourage further detailed study of both theories.

I have not done either of two things which might seem to some readers to be a good idea. Firstly, I have not set either theory in the larger picture of Stoicism as a whole or Epicureanism as a whole. I have brought other aspects of these philosophical theories in where this seemed necessary to make sense of the philosophy of mind; for example, I have briefly discussed *lekta* in order to make sense of Stoic views on perception and action. But I have not attempted to define the place of Stoic philosophy of mind in the whole of Stoic philosophy, nor have I located the Epicurean philosophy of mind in Epicureanism. This is not because I do not think such a study worthwhile; on the contrary, it would be valuable in many respects. But it seems to me that prior to doing this it is important to study these theories of mind in their own right, as providing answers to specific questions which arise for this field, without reference to further concerns. Partly this is because properly to understand the relations of any two things one must first study the two things themselves. Partly, also, it is because in the area of philosophy of mind a reading of the texts reveals that both Stoics and Epicureans worked on these problems in a way that reflects independent interest and is not an application of principles from elsewhere in the theory; the links between the theory of mind and the wider theory are complex. The importance of independent study of this area is sometimes missed, because there is no specific niche in the "official" ancient divisions of philosophy that corresponds exactly to what we call philosophy of mind.[1] But this does not mean that the ancients did not do any; there is no ancient division of philosophy corresponding to our "aesthetics," but we can legitimately find ancient contributions to aesthetics. Thus I have left to others the task of presenting Hellenistic theories of mind as integrated parts of the larger theories.

The other thing I have not done is to make a systematic thematic comparison of the two theories. Although my presentation should make it easy enough to compare Epicureans with Stoics on perception, action, and so on, I have treated each theory as a whole, instead of discussing topics such as perception and action and dealing with the contributions of both theories together. My account thus has a complementary restriction; I have extracted the theories of mind from the whole theories, but I have not extracted themes or topics from the theories of mind themselves. Again, this is not because I reject the idea; rather I think that there is a preliminary task to be accomplished, that of carefully trying to understand what Stoic and Epicurean ideas about perception and so on are, and that to accomplish this it is useful first to bring to bear other parts of the same theory.

Plainly, there is plenty of room for detailed comparisons of the Stoic with the Epicurean treatment of perception, action,

1. The division of philosophy into logic, physics, and ethics, originating from the Academy and becoming current after Aristotle, makes it hard to find a place for philosophy of mind. Aristotle presumably regarded his works on the soul as forming part of his biology, and so, in later terms, of his physics or scientific works. But the increased concern with what we call content and the mental in Hellenistic philosophers make their theories close to some of the concerns of logic.

and so on. I will conclude by bringing together some comparisons which I think can legitimately be made between the theories on a fairly high level of generality, comparisons which illuminate what makes Hellenistic philosophy of mind something distinctive and new.

Stoics and Epicureans have differing attitudes toward the scientific paradigm current in their society. Epicurus is at many points committed to presenting himself as a commonsense philosopher, and so tends to see his task as that of defending common sense against various kinds of self-styled experts. Further, he is committed to atomism as the best available general theory to explain the natural world, and tends to work out answers to problems in various areas in terms of atomism's general principles, rather than turning to the appropriate branch of contemporary science. Finally, he holds that while we can be sure of the very general principles of atomism, the answers to more low-level and particular questions may elude us; evidence underdetermines theory, so that in some cases we must remain satisfied with multiple explanations of a phenomenon, all of which are consistent with the evidence. For all these reasons Epicurus is barred from letting his philosophy of mind depend on any specific theory current in the medicine and science of his day. And, as we have seen, he ignores the development of the concept of *pneuma* in the medical schools, using *pneuma* in his own theory in its original sense of wind or breath. His accounts of agency and of the nature of the soul are marked by the clear desire to do justice to commonsense psychology and what is now sometimes called folk psychology; atomic theory is modified to produce results that are acceptable to common sense, not the other way around.

The Stoics, on the other hand, are clearly influenced, particularly from Chrysippus onward, by the current medical and scientific paradigm of human functioning: they accept that what makes humans function in a characteristically human way is a centralized system using the mechanism of *pneuma*, which is understood as the doctors understand it: warm breath which, in a human being, can account, in different varieties,

204   Conclusion

for a wide variety of life functions. While the Stoics rejected the most up-to-date picture of the workings of the nervous system, reverting to the simpler picture, which centralized the *pneuma* system in the heart rather than the brain, they were aware of the need to argue for this. Behind their picture of human functioning lies a vague, ill-understood conception of the nervous system. Indeed, it is not surprising that the Stoic view should seem odd to us, when we reflect on the degree of confusion to be found even in the discoverers of the nervous system themselves as to its mode of operating. The Stoics are also, of course, influenced by the fact that *pneuma* is their principle of explanation for the world as a whole, and not just for humans. However, they think of the world itself as being an organism. So, although they officially hold that we must understand the nature of the world as a whole in order to understand the nature of humans, it is clear that their conception of the nature of humans and of human functioning has played a large role in their theory of the world as a whole.

But, despite their differing attitudes toward contemporary science and medicine, Stoics and Epicureans share some important fundamental assumptions which unite them and distinguish them from their great predecessor, Aristotle. All three theories are physicalist in terms of the initial introduction of that term, namely, that they take the soul to fall under *phusikē*, natural science. And none are reductive; neither atomic theory nor *pneuma* theory explains away what we believe about ourselves. But there is a clear sense in which Stoics and Epicureans are stricter physicalists than Aristotle is. Aristotle's account of the human soul and human functioning is marked throughout by extensive use of his metaphysical concept of form to explain function. Thus the soul itself is defined as the form of the body, and Aristotle's accounts of nutrition and perception are heavily marked by their attempt to explain the nutritive and perceptive functioning of a human being in terms of the reception of form and the actualization of form. The Hellenistic theories consistently refrain from bringing in any metaphysical principle like Aristotelian form to fulfill these tasks. Instead, they appeal to straightforwardly physical factors. The Stoics appeal to the versatile workings of *pneuma;* Epicurus to the nameless atoms, and possibly atomic swerves, in the soul.

It has already been indicated at various points why these moves are not, as they have been held to be in the past, feeble evasions of the issue. Unlike the pre-Socratics whom Aristotle criticizes, the Hellenistic schools are not unaware of the challenge posed by Aristotle, that function must be explained by form as well as matter, by a principle of organization which is different in kind from the physical items being organized. But the Hellenistic schools reject Aristotle's move. We do not possess their arguments for doing so, unfortunately. They cannot have relied on a rejection of teleological explanation, since the Stoics fully accept teleology, and although Epicurus rejects it, the only Epicurean arguments we possess against it argue merely against appealing to purposes and do not touch the Aristotelian teleology involved in the workings of form.[2] Rather, the Hellenistic schools seem to have had two kinds of ground. They found that principles like Aristotelian form offended against an acceptable view of causality; they thought of a cause as essentially what did, or brought about, something, and, given this view, it becomes mysterious how physical items can interact causally with non-physical items. Hence, it is simpler, and avoids appeal to mysterious items and processes, to explain human functioning entirely in terms of physical items and their causal interactions. Secondly, the Hellenistic schools seem to have felt satisfied that in appealing to the kinds of physical item that they cited they were providing a sufficiently complex explanation for it not to be open to the kinds of objection that Aristotle makes against people like Democritus. To our minds, of course, their own explanations appear simple enough. But they are appealing to theoretical entities—the workings of *pneuma*, atoms, and void—not to simple analogies like mirroring, as Democritus seems to have done. Their pro-

2. For the Epicurean arguments we possess see Lucr. 4. 822–75.

cedures are, from the theoretical viewpoint at least, more complex and sophisticated than his. We have seen that at various points the Stoics' and Epicureans' appeal to the complexity of physical matter and its structure is clearly a move to explain function by physical differentiation of material; and while there is still disagreement as to the adequacy of this move, it is philosophically respectable and in no way an admission of defeat.

One theme which has emerged clearly unites the Stoics and Epicureans in opposition to Aristotle. Both the Stoics and the Epicureans are interested in what has been called the content aspect of phenomena like perceiving and acting. Aristotle concentrates on the biological role of the senses and thinks of seeing the son of Diares as "incidental perception";[3] that is, one does not essentially perceive *the son of Diares*, but only incidentally, because what one essentially perceives is *the white object*. One is affected perceptually "as such" by a color, but not by the son of Diares. What matters here to Aristotle is clearly the point that there is no biological mechanism linking sight essentially with anybody's son, whereas sight is essentially linked with colors. Aristotle in fact leaves us with a vague and unsatisfactory account of just what it is that explains how we can see the son of Diares; but it is certainly clear that whatever it is that explains my being able to say, to another or to myself, that I am seeing the son of Diares is not due to perception.

By contrast, the Stoics and Epicureans both hold that perception itself is a mechanism which conveys information; to account for perception is to account not just for the ways in which we are sensitive to colors, sounds, textures, and so forth, but to account also for the ways in which we categorize these items. Perception involves the reception and interpretation of information. As we have seen, the Stoics have by far the neater and more satisfactory account of this. Their theory of the soul

3. *DA* 2. 6.

as a whole explains how all events in the soul involve thinking and reasoning; there is no stage of pure sensual receptivity, to be contrasted with subsequent ratiocination. And their theory of *lekta* explains how perception can involve content; rational appearances contain content which is asserted in a corresponding *lekton*. The theory's main price is an awkwardness over the status of *lekta*. Epicurus, by contrast, has a much less clear and consistent view of the place of reason and thinking in the soul. The Epicurean rational soul is partially independent of the irrational soul, leading to a number of points where processes which involve both are rendered unclear. Further, Epicurus consistently presents perception in terms of images, rather than in terms of language and of communication of information and content. Still, the divergence here is one of clarity of mechanism rather than of principle. Epicurus does not doubt that perception results in the acquisition of information; the person about to act has a belief leading to action, and perceptions and appearances are insistently said to be true. Content for Epicurus as well as for the Stoics is not incidental to perception.

This point can readily be seen as part of a larger shift, one which is again clearer and more marked in the Stoics, but present also in Epicurus. The Hellenistic theories are theories of mind, whereas Aristotle's theory of the soul is not. The Hellenistic theories achieve this without a word or concept answering exactly to "mind"; they use the same word as Aristotle, the soul (*psuchē*), for what makes humans live and function. But, as we have seen in some detail, it would be unreasonable to deny that the Stoic *hēgemonikon* is the mind. It is what registers perceptions and feelings; pain in the foot is felt in the *hēgemonikon*, and it is the *hēgemonikon* which assents to the content of perception, and to the impulses which form actions when bodily movements result from them. We have a model of the mind which makes language and communication prominent, for it operates in what can only be called a language of thought. Further, the *hēgemonikon* unifies

mental phenomena; it is because it centralizes and unites what
is presented to it in the various appearances that we can see
the Stoics as having a concept of the self. While Epicurus'
rational soul does not perform exactly the functions of the
Stoic *hēgemonikon*, it has some of the same roles. It has the
"finest" structure of the parts of the soul; indeed it seems to
be the fineness of its atomic structure which permits atomic
swerves to take effect, resulting in free action, which in turn
constitutes our development as free human agents. Although
the irrational soul seems to function in a partly independent
way in perception, it is the rational soul which organizes and
coordinates perceptual input, and in some way enables us to
conceptualize it. And it is from the rational soul that the impulse to action originates. And it is the rational soul which
enables the Epicurean to be a self, although, as we have seen,
the unity of the Epicurean soul is looser than that of the Stoic
soul.

Some may be inclined to accept all that has been said in
this book about the Stoic and Epicurean theories and yet still
be reluctant to allow that the Stoics and Epicureans are talking
about the mind, or mental events; for we associate these notions with a range of issues which we do not find in the Hellenistic theories. We often find the mental/physical distinction
associated with the distinctions between private and public,
internal and external. Our bodies are part of the objective,
public world, explainable by science. Our minds do not seem
to be; they seem to be the source of subjective impressions,
private to each. Hence a range of controversies as to whether,
for example, I might internally have experience of a color
range different from yours, though our external behavior remained the same, or whether there could be a wholly private
language, given sense solely by private experience. Many dis-
putes center on questions such as: Is the mental essentially
bound to our notions of the private and internal, so that, whatever science discovers, there will always be a residue which
escapes the external, public perspective? Or is it just an ac-

cident of each person's life that she has an internal perspective on the mental, although the mental is in principle subject to external, public scrutiny by science as much as what we already call the physical is?

In the ancient world the mental/physical distinction is not associated with these other contrasts. Ancient philosophers were, I have argued, after the Hellenistic period, aware of what we would call the contrast between the mental and the physical. And they were, after a certain point in the development of ancient scepticism, aware of the possibility of a contrast between my own viewpoint, the way things appear to me, and the objective, external viewpoint, the way things are. But these contrasts were never fused; it was never taken to be a serious possibility that I might have a viewpoint consisting solely of the contents of my *mind*, a viewpoint from which my body was just part of the objective way that things are.[4] Thus the ancient conceptions of the mind are never associated with the agent's privileged access or the ineliminability of the subjective viewpoint or in general with the private and internal, as opposed to the public and external. Because of this, there is a way in which ancient physicalists like the Stoics and Epicureans may strike us as somewhat bland: they never conceive there to be a problem, still less a deep problem, with regard to the physical nature of the mind. As we have seen, Epicurus goes to some lengths to show that his conception of the soul is adequately complex, in physical terms, to provide a plausible account of human functioning. But this is conceived of as an ordinary case of complex *explanandum* and oversimple-seeming *explanans;* it is not a difficulty of principle such as is often found in modern discussions of the physical and the mental.

We are, then, faced with an interpretative problem. If we think that our notion of the mental is essentially connected with privileged access and the internal, private viewpoint, then

4. For a discussion of this point, see Burnyeat (1982).

the Hellenistic theories will be theories of mind, but of a different conception of the mind from ours. However, this is not the only possible response; there is another, indeed more reasonable, one. It may be that our concern with the private and internal is not essential to our conception of the mind, and in that case the Hellenistic theories will be theories of mind in our sense of mind but will be theories which discuss the mental in a different context.

This seems the more reasonable response for two reasons. One is that often in interpreting ancient texts we are initially tempted to say that the ancients are discussing something different from our concerns—that they are not concerned with knowledge or morality, for example, because what they find to be central to the topic is not what we consider central. But usually on closer examination this turns out to be an inferior strategy, alienating us prematurely from the ancient discussions and missing what there is of continuity between the ancient concerns and ours. The second reason is that a great deal of modern philosophy of mind has recently proceeded on the assumption that physicalism is true and that objections based on the ineliminability of the private, internal viewpoint can be discounted; they are based on misconceptions, or concern epistemology rather than the nature of the mind itself, and so on. If this is a lasting trend, then it may be that the modern context for discussing the mind turns out not to be so very dissimilar from the ancient one. At any rate, it seems more fruitful to assume that the mind need not be essentially linked with the private, internal, subjective view, though historically it often has been in the modern period. If so, then the Hellenistic theories' form of physicalism will not be missing a point essential to the mind in ignoring these concerns.

Of course, whether or not this suggestion is on the right lines depends a great deal on the kind of detailed discussion that can be developed about Hellenistic and modern philosophy of mind. This book has not developed such discussions, but I hope that it has paved part of the way for them. Only when Hellenistic philosophy of mind has been the subject of the same kind of detailed and intense discussion, and comparison with modern perspectives, that has been accorded to Aristotle's philosophy of mind will we feel confident that we understand just what kind of theories of mind we find in these stimulating and difficult philosophers.

Bibliography

This bibliography is selective and mentions only works relevant to the topic of this book. For helpful general bibliographies on Stoics, Epicureans, and ancient scepticism see Long and Sedley (1987, vol. 1, Bibliography). On Epicureanism see further the bibliographies in *SUZETESIS̩: Studi sull'epicureismo greco e latino offerti a Marcello Gigante*, vol. 2 (Naples, 1983). On Stoicism see the bibliography in R. Epp, ed., *Recovering the Stoics*, Proceedings of the Spindel Conference 1984, The Southern Journal of Philosophy, vol. 23, Supplement.

Ancient Sources

Aristotle and Aristotle's School

Balme, D. M. 1972. *Translation and commentary on Aristotle's* De partibus animalium I *and* De generatione animalium I. Oxford.

Bekker, I. 1831. *Aristotelis opera*. Berlin.

Fortenbaugh, W. W. Forthcoming. *The fragments of Theophrastus*.

Gottschalk, H. 1965. *Strato of Lampsacus: Some texts*. Proceedings of the Leeds Philosophical and Literary Society, Literary and Historical Section, vol. 11, pt. 6: 95–182.

Hicks, R. 1907. *Aristotle's* De anima. Cambridge.

Peck, A. L. 1942. *Aristotle's* Generation of Animals. Loeb Classical Library. Cambridge, Mass.

Stratton, G. 1917. *Theophrastus and the Greek physiological psychology before Aristotle.* Berkeley.

Wehrli, F. 1944–59. *Die Schule des Aristoteles.* Basel.

———. 1944. *Dikaiarchos.*

———. 1945. *Aristoxenos.*

———. 1948. *Klearchos.*

———. 1949. *Demetrius von Phaleron.*

———. 1950. *Straton von Lampsakos.*

———. 1952. *Lykon und Ariston von Keos.*

———. 1953. *Herakleides Pontikos.*

———. 1955. *Eudemos von Rhodos.*

———. 1958. *Phainias von Eresos, Chamaileon, Praxiphanes.*

———. 1959. *Hieronymos, Kritolaos, Rückblick.*

Wimmer, F. 1854–62. *Theophrastus.* Leipzig.

The Academy

Isnardi Parente, M. 1980. *Speusippo: Frammenti.* Naples.

———. 1981. *Senocrate, Ermodoro: Frammenti.* Naples.

Tarán, L. 1981. *Speusippus of Athens.* Leiden.

Hellenistic Medicine

Diels, H. ed. 1893. *Anonymous Londiniensis.* Supplementum Aristotelicum 3. 1. Berlin.

Jones, W. H. S. 1947. *The medical writings of Anonymous Londiniensis.* Cambridge.

Kühn, C. G. 1821–33. *Claudii Galeni opera omnia.* Leipzig.

Marx, F. 1915. *Celsus, Corpus medicorum Latinorum.* Leipzig and Berlin.

Steckerl, F. 1958. *The fragments of Praxagoras of Cos and his school.* Leiden.

Von Staden, H. 1989. *Herophilus: The art of medicine in early Alexandria.* Cambridge.

Wellman, M. 1901. *Die Fragmente der sikelischen Ärzte Akron, Philistion und Diokles von Karystos.* Berlin.

Stoicism

Arnim, H. von. 1903–5, vols. 1–3. 1924, vol. 4, index. *Stoicorum veterum fragmenta*. Leipzig. (= *SVF*)

———. 1906. *Hierocles: Ethische Elementarlehre*. Berliner Klassikertexte, vol. 4. Berlin.

Cherniss, H. 1976. *Plutarch, Moralia* 13, pt. 2. Loeb Classical Library. Cambridge, Mass.

Dalfen, J. 1987. *Marci Aurelii Antonini ad se ipsum libri xii*. 2d ed. Leipzig.

De Lacy, P. 1978–85. *Galen, On the doctrines of Hippocrates and Plato*. 3 vols. (*Corpus medicorum Graecorum* 5.4.1.2). Berlin. (= *PHP*)

Edelstein, L., and I. G. Kidd. 1988. *Posidonius*. Vol. 1, *The fragments*. 2d ed. Cambridge. Vols. 2 and 3, *Commentary* by I. G. Kidd.

Reynolds, L. D. 1965. *Seneca, Epistulae morales*. 2 vols. Oxford.

———. 1977. *Seneca, Dialogi*. Oxford.

Theiler, W. 1982. *Poseidonios, Die Fragmente*. 2 vols. Berlin.

Todd, R. 1976. *Alexander of Aphrodisias on Stoic physics*. Leiden.

Van Straaten, M. 1962. *Panaetii Rhodii fragmenta*. 3d ed. Leiden.

Epicureanism: Epicurus

Arrighetti, G. 1973. *Epicuro: Opere*. 2d ed. Turin.

Bailey, C. 1926. *Epicurus: The extant remains*. Oxford.

Diano, C. 1946. *Epicuri ethica*. Florence.

Einarson, B., and P. de Lacy. 1967. *Plutarch, Moralia* 14. Loeb Classical Library. Cambridge, Mass.

Sedley, D. 1973. Epicurus *On Nature* book 28. *Cronache Ercolanesi* 3: 5–83.

Usener, H. 1887. *Epicurea*. Leipzig.

Usener, H., M. Gigante, and W. Schmid. 1977. *Glossarium Epicureum*. Rome.

Epicureanism: Other Epicureans

Bailey, C. 1947. *Titi Lucreti Cari De rerum natura libri sex.* 3 vols. Oxford.

Chilton, C. W. 1967. *Diogenes Oenoandensis.* Leipzig. ("Fragments" are cited from Chilton.)

———. 1971. *Diogenes of Oenoanda: The fragments.* London, New York, and Toronto.

Croenert, W. 1906. *Kolotes und Menedemos.* Leipzig.

De Falco, V. 1923. *L'Epicureo Demetrio Lacone.* Naples.

De Lacy, P., and E. de Lacy. 1978. *Philodemus on methods of inference.* Naples.

Ferguson Smith, M. 1970. Fragments of Diogenes of Oenoanda discovered and rediscovered. *American Journal of Archaeology* 74: 51–62. ("New fragments" 1–4 are cited from this publication.)

———. 1971. New fragments of Diogenes of Oenoanda. *American Journal of Archaeology* 75: 357–89. ("New fragments" 5–16 are cited from this publication.)

———. 1972. New readings in the text of Diogenes of Oenoanda. *Classical Quarterly,* n.s. 22: 159–62. (This includes "new fragments" 1, 2, and 7.)

———. 1974. Thirteen new fragments of Diogenes of Oenoanda. *Denkschrift Akad. Wien* 117. (This includes "new fragments" 19–31.)

———. 1978. Fifty-five new fragments of Diogenes of Oenoanda. *Anatolian Studies* 28: 39–92. (This includes "new fragments" 52–106.)

Note: For a complete bibliography of publications on all of Diogenes of Oenoanda's new fragments, see Long and Sedley (1987, 1: 484–85).

Indelli, G. 1978. *Polistrato sul disprezzo irrazionale delle opinioni popolari.* Naples.

———. 1988. *Filodemo: L'ira.* Naples.

Longo Auricchio, F. 1988. *Ermarco: Frammenti.* Naples.

Sudhaus, S. 1892–96. *Philodemi volumina rhetorica.* Leipzig.

Tepedino Guerra, A. 1977. Filodemo sulla gratitudine. *Cronache Ercolanesi* 7: 96–113.

General Ancient Sources

Bruns, I. 1887. *Alexander Aphrodisiensis, De anima liber cum mantissa.* Supplementum Aristotelicum 2. 1. Berlin.

Burnet, J. 1900–1907. *Platonis opera.* 5 vols. Oxford.

Crouzel, H., and M. Simonetti. 1978–80. *Origène, Traité des principes.* 4 vols. Paris.

Diels, H., and W. Kranz. 1951. *Die Fragmente der Vorsokratiker.* 6th ed. Berlin.

Dougan, T. W., and R. M. Henry. 1934. *Cicero, Tusculan Disputations.* Cambridge.

Long, H. 1964. *Diogenis Laertii opera.* Oxford.

Madvig, J. N. 1876. *Cicero, De finibus.* 3d ed. Copenhagen.

Mutschmann, H., and J. Mau. 1912–54. *Sexti Empirici opera.* Leipzig.

Pease, A. S. 1955–58. *Cicero, De natura deorum.* 2 vols. Cambridge, Mass.

Reid, J. S. 1885. *M. Tulli Ciceronis Academica.* London.

Wachsmuth, C. 1884. *Ioannes Stobaeus, Eclogae physicae et ethicae.* Berlin.

Modern Works

Annas, J. 1978–79. How basic are basic actions? *Proceedings of the Aristotelian Society* 79: 195–213.

———. 1986. Doing without objective values: Ancient and modern strategies. In *The norms of nature,* ed. M. Schofield and G. Striker, 3–29. Cambridge and Paris.

———. 1989. Epicurean emotions. *Greek, Roman, and Byzantine Studies* 30: 145–64.

———. 1990. Stoic epistemology. In *Ancient epistemology,* ed. S. Everson, 184–203. Cambridge.

———. 1991. Epicurean philosophy of mind. In *Ancient philosophy of mind,* ed. S. Everson. Cambridge.

————. Forthcoming. Epicurus on agency. In *Passions and perceptions*, ed. J. Brunschwig and M. Nussbaum. Cambridge and Paris.

Annas, J., and J. Barnes. 1985. *The modes of scepticism: Ancient texts and modern interpretations*. Cambridge.

Arthur, E. P. 1983. The Stoic analysis of the mind's reactions to presentations. *Hermes* 111: 69–78.

Asmis, E. 1981. Lucretius' explanation of moving dream figures at IV. 768–76. *American Journal of Philology* 102: 138–45.

————. 1984. *Epicurus' scientific method*. Ithaca, N.Y.

————. 1990. Free action and the swerve. *Oxford Studies in Ancient Philosophy* 8: 275–91.

Avotins, I. 1979. The question of *mens* in Lucretius II, 289. *Classical Quarterly* 29: 95–100.

————. 1980a. Notes on Lucretius II, 251–293. *Harvard Studies in Classical Philology* 84: 75–79.

————. 1980b. Alexander of Aphrodisias on vision in the atomists. *Classical Quarterly* 74: 429–54.

Bailey, C. 1928. *The Greek atomists and Epicurus*. Oxford.

Barigazzi, A. 1958. Cinetica degli *eidola* nel *peri phuseos* di Epicuro. *La Parola del Passato* 13: 249–76.

Barnes, J., J. Brunschwig, M. Burnyeat, and M. Schofield, eds. 1982. *Science and speculation*. Cambridge and Paris.

Bignone, E. 1936. *L'Aristotele perduto*. Florence.

Bonhoeffer, A. 1890. *Epiktet und die Stoa*. Stuttgart.

Bréhier, E. 1950. *Chrysippe et l'ancien stoicisme*. 2d ed. Paris.

Brunschwig, J. 1977. Epicure et le problème du "langage privé." *Revue des Sciences Humaines* 43: 157–77.

Burnyeat, M. 1976. Protagoras and self-refutation in later Greek philosophy. *Philosophical Review* 75: 44–69.

————. 1980. Can the sceptic live his scepticism? In *Doubt and dogmatism*, ed. M. Schofield et al., 20–53. Oxford.

————. 1982. Idealism and Greek philosophy: What Descartes saw and Berkeley missed. *Philosophical Review* 91: 3–40.

Cancrini, A. 1970. Suneidesis: *Il tema semantica della 'conscientia' nella Grecia antiqua*. Rome.

Clay, D. 1980. An Epicurean interpretation of dreams. *American Journal of Philology* 101: 342–65.

———. 1983. *Lucretius and Epicurus.* Ithaca, N.Y.

Cooper, J. Forthcoming. Stoic theories of the emotions.

Davidson, D. 1980. *Essays on actions and events.* Oxford.

Deuse, W. 1983. *Untersuchungen zur mittelplatonischen und neuplatonischen Seelenlehre.* Akademie der Wissenschaftern und der Literature, Abhandlungen der Geistes- und Sozialwissenschaften Klasse, Einzelveröffentlichung 3. Mainz.

Diano, C. 1974. *Scritti epicurei.* Florence.

———. 1974a. La psicologia d'Epicuro e la teoria delle passioni. In 1974, 129–280.

———. 1974b. Le problème du libre arbitre dans le *peri phuseos.* In 1974, 337–41.

Diels, H. 1893. Über die Excerpta von Menons *Iatrika* in dem Londoner Papyrus 137. *Hermes* 28: 407–34.

Dierauer, U. 1977. *Tier und Mensch im Denken der Antike.* Amsterdam.

Dillon, J. 1983. *Metriopatheia* and *Apatheia:* Some reflections on controversy in later Greek ethics. In *Essays in ancient Greek philosophy,* vol. 2, ed. J. P. Anton and A. Preus, 508–17. Albany.

Edelstein, L. 1967. *Ancient medicine.* Baltimore.

Englert, W. 1988. *Epicurus on the swerve and free action.* American Classical Studies 16. Atlanta.

Everson, S. 1990. Epicurus on the truth of the senses. In *Epistemology,* ed. S. Everson, 161–83. Companions to Ancient Thought 1. Cambridge.

Fillion-Lahille, J. 1984. *Le De ira de Senèque et la philosophie stoicienne des passions.* Paris.

Fowler, D. 1983. Lucretius on the *clinamen* and free will. *SUZETESIS,* 329–52. Naples.

———. 1984. Sceptics and Epicureans. Review of *Scetticismo e epicureismo,* by M. Gigante. *Oxford Studies in Ancient Philosophy* 2: 237–67.

Frede, M. 1974. *Die stoische Logik.* Göttingen.

———. 1980. The original notion of cause. In *Essays in ancient philosophy*, 125–50. Minneapolis, 1987.

———. 1984. Stoics and skeptics on clear and distinct ideas. In *Essays in ancient philosophy*, 151–76. Minneapolis, 1987.

———. 1986. The Stoic theory of the affections of the soul. In *The norms of nature*, ed. M. Schofield and G. Striker, 93–110. Cambridge and Paris.

Furley, D. 1967. *Two studies in the Greek atomists*. Princeton.

———. 1986. Nothing to us? In *The norms of nature*, ed. M. Schofield and G. Striker, 75–92. Cambridge and Paris.

Giannantoni, G., and M. Vegetti, eds. 1984. *La scienza ellenistica*. Elenchos 9. Naples.

Gigante, M. 1969. *Ricerche Filodemee*. Naples.

———. 1969a. La chiusa del "de morte" di Filodemo. In 1969, 63–122.

———. 1975. "Philosophia Medicans" in Filodemo. *Cronache Ercolanesi* 5: 53–61.

———. 1981. *Scetticismo e epicureismo*. Naples.

Gill, C. 1983. Did Chrysippus understand Medea? *Phronesis* 28: 136–49.

Giussani, C. 1896. *Studi lucreziani*. Turin.

Glibert-Thirry, A. 1977. La théorie stoicienne de la passion chez Chrysippe et son évolution chez Posidonius. *Revue Philosophique de Louvain* 75: 393–435.

Glidden, D. 1974. Protagorean relativism and the Cyrenaics. In *Studies in epistemology*, ed. N. Rescher, 112–40. Oxford.

———. 1979. Epicurus on self-perception. *American Philosophical Quarterly* 16: 297–306.

———. 1980. *Sensus* and sense-perception in the *De rerum natura*. *California Studies in Classical Antiquity* 12: 155–82.

———. 1983. Epicurean semantics. *SUZETESIS*, 185–226. Naples.

———. 1985. Epicurean *prolepseis*. *Oxford Studies in Ancient Philosophy* 3: 175–217.

Glucker, J. 1978. *Antiochus and the Late Academy*. Göttingen (= *Hypomnemata* 56).

Gosling, J. 1987. The Stoics and *akrasia*. *Apeiron* 20: 179–202.

Gosling, J., and C. C. W. Taylor. 1982. *The Greeks on pleasure*. Oxford.

Gottschalk, H. 1971. Soul as *harmonia*. *Phronesis* 16: 179–98.

———. 1980. *Heracleides of Pontus*. Oxford.

Hackforth, R. 1955. *Plato's* Phaedo. Cambridge. (See especially the appendix, which features a translation of some of Strato's criticisms of Plato.)

Hahm, D. 1977. *The origins of Stoic cosmology*. Columbus.

———. 1978. Early Hellenistic theories of vision and the perception of color. *In Studies in perception*, ed. P. Machamer and R. Turnbull, 60–95. Columbus.

Harris, C. R. S. 1973. *The heart and the vascular system in ancient Greek medicine*. Oxford.

Hoven, H. 1971. *Stoicisme et stoiciens face au problème de l'au-delà*. Paris.

Huby, P. 1969. The Epicureans, animals, and free will. *Apeiron* 3: 17–19.

Hunt, H. A. K. 1976. *A physical interpretation of the universe: The doctrines of Zeno the Stoic*. Melbourne.

Ingenkamp, H. G. 1971. Zur stoischen Lehre vom Sehen. *Rheinisches Museum* 114: 240–46.

Inwood, B. 1984. Hierocles: Theory and arguments in the second century A.D. *Oxford Studies in Ancient Philosophy* 2: 151–83.

———. 1985. *Ethics and human action in early Stoicism*. Oxford.

Ioppolo, A.-M. 1972. La dottrina della passione in Crisippo. *Rivista Critica di Storia della Filosofia* 3: 251–68.

———. 1980. *Aristone di Chio*. Naples.

Isnardi Parente, M. 1980. Stoici, Epicurei e il "motus sine causa." *Rivista Critica di Storia della Filosofia* 38: 190–200.

Jaeger, W. 1913. Das *pneuma* im Lykeion. *Hermes* 48: 29–74.

———. 1938a. *Diokles von Karystos*. Berlin.

———. 1938b. *Vergessene Fragmente des peripatetikers Diokles von Karystos*. Abhandlungen der preussischen Akademie der Wissenschaften, Phil.-hist. Klasse 3. Berlin.

————. 1940. Diocles of Carystus: A new pupil of Aristotle. *Philosophical Review* 19: 393–414.

Kerferd, G. 1971. Epicurus' doctrine of the soul. *Phronesis* 116: 80–96.

Kidd, I. 1971. Poseidonius on emotions. In *Problems in Stoicism*, ed. A. A. Long, 200–215. London.

Kleve, K. 1963. *Gnosis Theon.* Symbolae Osloenses, Supplement 19. Oslo.

————. 1980. Id facit exiguum clinamen. *Symbolae Osloenses* 15: 27–31.

Kneale, W., and M. Kneale. 1962. *The development of logic.* Oxford.

Konstan, D. 1973. *Some aspects of Epicurean psychology.* Leiden.

Laks, A. 1981. Une légèreté de Democrite (Epicurus *De natura liber incertus* = 34.30, 7–15). *Cronache Ercolanesi* 11: 19–23.

Lapidge, M. 1973. *Archai* and *stoicheia*: A problem in Stoic cosmology. *Phronesis* 18: 240–78.

————. 1978. Stoic cosmology. In *The Stoics,* ed. J. Rist, 161–85. Berkeley, Los Angeles, and London.

Laursen, S. 1987. Epicurus *On Nature* Book XXV. *Cronache Ercolanesi* 17: 77–78.

————. 1988. Epicurus *On Nature* Book XXV: Long-Sedley 20 B, C, and j. *Cronache Ercolanesi* 18: 7–18.

Lee, E. N. 1978. The sense of an object: Epicurus on seeing and hearing. In *Studies in perception*, ed. P. Machamer and R. Turnbull, 27–59. Columbus.

Lloyd, A. C. 1978. Emotion and decision in Stoic psychology. In *The Stoics*, ed. J. Rist, 233–46. Berkeley, Los Angeles, and London.

Lloyd, G. E. R. 1973. *Greek science after Aristotle.* London.

Long, A. A. 1971. *Aisthesis, prolepsis,* and linguistic theory in Epicurus. *Bulletin of the Institute of Classical Studies* 18: 114–33.

————. 1977. Chance and natural law in Epicureanism. *Phronesis* 22: 63–88.

————. 1982. Soul and body in Stoicism. *Phronesis* 27: 34–57.

————. 1991. Representation and the self in Stoicism. In *Ancient philosophy of mind*, ed. S. Everson. Cambridge.

Long, A. A., and D. Sedley. 1987. *The Hellenistic philosophers.* 2 vols. Cambridge.

Lonie, I. M. 1964. Erasistratus, the Erasistrateans, and Aristotle. *Bulletin of the History of Medicine* 38: 426–43.

Lynch, J. 1972. *Aristotle's school.* Berkeley, Los Angeles, and London.

McKirahan, V. Tsouna. Forthcoming. The Cyrenaic theory of knowledge. *Oxford Studies in Ancient Philosophy.*

McPherran, M. 1989. *Ataraxia* and *Eudaimonia:* Is the sceptic really happy? *Proceedings of the Boston Area Colloquium in Ancient Philosophy,* vol. 5, ed. J. J. Cleary and D. Shartin, 135–71.

Manuwald, A. 1972. *Die Prolepsislehre Epikurs.* Bonn.

Mitsis, P. 1988a. *Epicurus' ethical theory.* Ithaca, N.Y.

————. 1988b. Epicurus on death and the duration of life. *Proceedings of the Boston Area Colloquium in Ancient Philosophy,* vol. 4, ed. J. J. Cleary, 295–314.

Modrze, A. 1932. Zur Ethik und Psychologie des Poseidonius. *Philologus* 51: 300–331.

Movia, G. 1968. *Anima e intelletto: Ricerche sulla psicologia peripatetica da Teofrasto a Cratippo.* Padua.

Nagel, T. 1979. *Mortal questions.* Cambridge.

————. 1979a. Death. In 1979, 1–10.

————. 1979b. Panpsychism. In 1979, 181–95.

Nussbaum, M. 1978. *Aristotle's De motu animalium.* Princeton.

————. 1985. Therapeutic arguments. In *The norms of nature,* ed. M. Schofield and G. Striker, 31–74. Cambridge.

————. 1987. The Stoics on the extirpation of the passions. *Apeiron* 20: 129–75.

————. 1989. Beyond obsession and disgust: Lucretius on the genealogy of love. *Apeiron* 22: 1–59.

Nussbaum, M., and A. Rorty, eds. 1991. *Essays on Aristotle's De anima.* Oxford.

Peck, A. L. 1953. The connate *pneuma:* An essential factor in Aristotle's solutions to the problems of reproduction and sensation. In *Science, medicine, and history: Essays on the*

evolution of scientific thought and medical practice, written
in honour of Charles Singer, ed. E. A. Underwood, 1: 111–
21. Oxford.

Philippson, R. 1937. Zur Psychologie der Stoa. *Rheinisches
Museum* 86: 140–79.

Phillips, E. D. 1973. *Greek medicine*. London.

Pohlenz, M. 1965. *Kleine Schriften*. Hildesheim.

———. 1965a. Zenon und Chrysipp. In 1965, 1–38.

———. 1970. *Die Stoa*. 4th ed. Göttingen.

Reesor, M. E. 1989. *The nature of man in early Stoic philosophy*. London.

Rist, J. 1972. *Epicurus*. Cambridge.

———, ed. 1978. *The Stoics*. Berkeley, Los Angeles, and London.

Rosenbaum, S. 1986. How to be dead and not care: A defense
of Epicurus. *American Philosophical Quarterly* 23: 217–25.

———. 1989. Epicurus and annihilation. *The Philosophical
Quarterly* 39: 81–90.

———. 1990. Epicurus on pleasure and the complete life. *The
Monist* 73, no. 1 (January). *Hellenistic ethics*, ed. J. Cooper,
21–41.

Sandbach, F. 1971a. *Ennoia* and *prolepsis* in the Stoic theory
of knowledge. In *Problems in Stoicism*, ed. A. A. Long, 22–
37. London.

———. 1971b. *Phantasia kataleptike*. In *Problems in Stoicism*,
ed. A. A. Long, 9–21. London.

———. 1975. *The Stoics*. London.

———. 1985. *Aristotle and the Stoics*. Cambridge Philological
Society, Supplement 10. Cambridge.

Saunders, T. J. 1984. Free will and the atomic swerve in Lucretius. *Symbolae Osloenses* 59: 37–59.

Schofield, M. 1983. The syllogisms of Zeno of Citium. *Phronesis*
28: 31–58.

Sedley, D. 1974. The structure of Epicurus' *On Nature*. *Cronache Ercolanesi* 4: 89–92.

———. 1983. Epicurus' refutation of determinism. *SUZE-
TESIS*, 11–51. Naples.

———. 1989. Epicurean anti-reductionism. In *Matter and meta-physics*, ed. J. Barnes and M. Mignucci, 295–327. Naples.

Sharples, R. 1980. Lucretius' account of the composition of the soul (III 321ff.). *Liverpool Classical Monthly* 5: 117–20.

Sharvy, R. 1983. Aristotle on mixtures. *The Journal of Philosophy* 80: 441–48.

Solmsen, F. 1968. *Kleine Schriften*. Hildesheim.

———. 1968a. Cleanthes or Posidonius?—The basis of Stoic physics. In 1968, 436–60.

———. 1968b. Tissues and the soul: Philosophical contributions to physiology. In 1968, 502–35.

———. 1968c. Greek philosophy and the discovery of the nerves. In 1968, 536–82.

———. 1968d. The vital heat, the inborn *pneuma*, and the aether. In 1968, 605–11.

———. 1968e. *Aisthesis* in Aristotelian and Epicurean thought. In 1968, 612–33.

Sorabji, R. 1988. *Matter, space, and motion: Theories in antiquity and their sequel*. London.

Striker, G. 1977. Epicurus on the truth of sense-impressions. *Archiv für Geschichte der Philosophie* 59: 125–42.

———. 1988. Commentary on Mitsis. *Proceedings of the Boston Area Colloquium in Ancient Philosophy*, vol. 4, ed. J. J. Cleary, 315–20.

Taylor, C. C. W. 1980. "All perceptions are true." In *Doubt and dogmatism*, ed. M. Schofield et al., 105–24. Oxford.

Todd, R. 1973. The Stoic common notions. *Symbolae Osloenses* 48: 47–75.

———. 1978. Monism and immanence: The foundations of Stoic physics. In *The Stoics*, ed. J. Rist, 137–60. Berkeley, Los Angeles, and London.

Vallance, J. T. 1990. *The lost theory of Asclepiades of Bithynia*. Oxford.

Verbeke, G. 1945. *L'évolution de la doctrine du pneuma du stoicisme à S. Augustin*. Paris and Louvain.

Viano, C. A. 1984. Perche non c'era sangue nelle arterie: La cecita epistemologica degli anatomisti antichi. In *La scienza ellenistica,* ed. G. Giannantoni and M. Vegetti, 297–352. Naples.

Voelke, A.-J. 1965. L'unité de l'âme dans l'ancien stoicisme. *Studia Philosophica* 25: 154–81.

———. 1973. *L'idée de volonté dans le stoicisme.* Paris.

White, M. J. 1986. Can unequal quantities of stuffs be totally blended? *History of Philosophy Quarterly* 3: 379–89.

Zucker, F. 1928. *Suneidesis-Conscientia.* Jena.

General Index

Action, 51–56, 63–64, 71, 89,
91–93, 95–102, 105, 107,
111, 124n.3, 125–26,
126n.11, 127–34, 175,
175n.1, 176–84, 201–2, 206,
208
Aenesidemus, 28n.31, 169n.37
Aëtius, 62n.60, 62n.62, 87n.31,
137n.51, 139, 139n.57,
157n.2, 170n.38
Alexander of Aphrodisias, 12,
26, 38n.4, 39n.7, 40n.9, 41,
45n.24, 46n.27, 47nn.30–31,
66n.67, 80n.19, 159n.10,
160n.12
Alexander the Great, 10
Anaxagoras, 5, 5n.9
Andronicus, 8
Animals
Epicurean attitude toward,
126, 126n.11, 133–34,
134n.37, 135, 135n.41,
135n.43, 136, 136n.44,
136n.46, 137, 146n.76, 187
rational capacities of, 59,
59n.57, 60, 64, 90, 90n.3,
91, 101–2, 107n.11, 135,
135n.41, 135n.43, 136,
136.44, 136n.46, 137,
146n.76

Stoic attitude toward, 59,
59n.57, 60, 90, 91, 91n.5,
102, 107n.11
Annas, J., 75n.15, 82n.23,
85n.28, 100n.25, 102n.32,
130nn.21–22, 193n.15
Annas, J., and J. Barnes,
60n.57, 129n.18, 169n.37
Anonymous Londiniensis,
23n.20, 26n.24
Antipater, 13
Apollodorus, 43, 94
Appearance (*phantasia*), 53,
56n.47, 66, 72–78, 80,
80n.19, 81–83, 85, 87, 91–
93, 96, 98, 106, 109, 117,
162, 162n.21, 168–70,
170n.38, 171, 177, 181, 207
Arcesilaus, 102
Ariston of Ceos, 33
Ariston of Chios, 12, 33n.51
Aristotle, 1–2, 2n.2, 3, 3n.5, 6–
11, 11n.15, 12, 17–18,
18n.2, 19, 19nn.8–9, 20–21,
22, 22n.16, 25–26, 26nn.23–
24, 27–28, 30–33, 38,
40n.11, 42, 42n.15, 45n.25,
48, 48n.33, 48n.34, 50, 52,
54, 55, 57n.48, 62–63,
73n.4, 80, 80n.19, 85–86,

Index Locorum

Diogenes Laertius (*continued*)

7. 151	47n.31,
(= *SVF* 2. 479)	48n.34
7. 156	39n.5
(= *SVF* 2. 774)	
7. 157	45n.23,
(= *SVF* 1. 135,	68n.73,
522, 2. 811, 828,	71n.1
867)	
7. 158	85n.28
(= *SVF* 2. 766)	
9. 81	66n.67
10. 22	151n.86
(= Usener 138)	
10. 31	171n.41,
(= Usener 35, 36)	189n.2
10. 32	162n.21,
	169n.36
10. 33	166–167
10. 34	189n.3
(= Usener 260)	
10. 46	157n.2
10. 48	157n.2
10. 117	198n.33
(= Usener 596)	
10. 117–20	198n.32
10. 137	150n.85
(= Usener 452)	

Diogenes of Oenoanda

Fr. 7	159n.8,
	172n.43
Fr. 24, col. 1. 11–13	177n.3
Fr. 29, col. 2	195n.22
Fr. 29. 6.2–7.12	194
Fr. 32	125n.6,
	182
Fr. 34	156n.95
Fr. 35	156n.95
Fr. 37	160n.25
Fr. 37, col. 1	137n.49,
	144n.65,
	145n.72,
	148n.81

Fr. 37, cols. 2–3	143
Fr. 38	191n.12
Fr. 41. 1–3	197n.29
New fr. 1	159n.8,
	172n.43
New fr. 2	156n.95
New fr. 5	158n.6,
	160n.25
New fr. 5, col. 3	160n.14,
	164n.24
New fr. 6	160n.25,
	172nn.43–44
New fr. 9	160n.13,
	169n.37
New fr. 10	191n.8
New fr. 10,	177n.3
col. 2. 3–4	
New fr. 12	172n.43
New fr. 13	159n.10
New fr. 20	143n.64
New fr. 82	138n.53
New fr. 94	143n.64

Epictetus

Fr. 9 (apud Aul. Gell.	110n.17
Noct. Att. 19. 1.14–	
20)	

Epicurus

Ep. Herod.

38	190n.6
46	159n.7
46–48	158n.3
47	160n.15
48	158nn.4–5,
	159n.9
49	159nn.10–
	11, 161n.18
49–50	158n.6
51	162n.21
52	162n.20,
	190n.6
53	190n.6
61	160n.15

Compositor: Impressions
Text: 10/13 Aster
Display: Helvetica Condensed
Printer: Edwards Brothers, Inc.
Binder: Edwards Brothers, Inc.

3

B
187
.M55
A56
1992

Annas, Julia

Hellenistic Philosophy
of Mind

B
187
.M55
A56
1992

Annas, Julia

Hellenistic Philosophy
of Mind

DATE DUE	BORROWER'S NAME

DEMCO